MODERNIST FICTION AND VAGUENESS

Modernist Fiction and Vagueness marries the artistic and philosophical versions of vagueness, linking the development of literary modernism to changes in philosophy. This book argues that the puzzle of vagueness – language's unavoidable imprecision – led to transformations in both fiction and philosophy in the early twentieth century. Both twentieth-century philosophers and their literary counterparts (including James, Eliot, Woolf, and Joyce) were fascinated by the vagueness of words and the dream of creating a perfectly precise language. Building on the connections among analytic philosophy, pragmatism, and modern literature, *Modernist Fiction and Vagueness* demonstrates that vagueness should be read not as an artistic problem but as a defining quality of modernist fiction.

MEGAN QUIGLEY is Assistant Professor of English at Villanova University. Her work has appeared in *The Cambridge Companion to European Modernism*, the *James Joyce Quarterly*, *The Journal of the T. S. Eliot Society*, *Modernism/modernity*, and *Philosophy and Literature*.

MODERNIST FICTION AND VAGUENESS

Philosophy, Form, and Language

MEGAN QUIGLEY
Villanova University

CAMBRIDGE
UNIVERSITY PRESS

CAMBRIDGE
UNIVERSITY PRESS

32 Avenue of the Americas, New York NY 10013-2473, USA

Cambridge University Press is part of the University of Cambridge.

It furthers the University's mission by disseminating knowledge in the pursuit of education, learning and research at the highest international levels of excellence.

www.cambridge.org
Information on this title: www.cambridge.org/9781107089594

First published 2015

A catalogue record for this publication is available from the British Library

Library of Congress Cataloguing in Publication data
Quigley, Megan.
Modernist fiction and vagueness : philosophy, form, and language / Megan Quigley.
pages cm
Includes index.
ISBN 978-1-107-08959-4 (Hardback)
1. Modernism (Literature) 2. Fiction–20th century–History and criticism.
3. Vagueness (Philosophy) 4. Language and languages in literature. I. Title.
PN56.M54Q54 2014
809′.9112–dc23 2014027293

ISBN 978-1-107-08959-4 Hardback

You will no doubt think that, in the words of the poet:
"Who speaks of vagueness should himself be vague."
–Bertrand Russell, "Vagueness"

Contents

Preface

In true Jamesian style, at a fashionable dinner party in New York City several years ago, the young man next to me told me he was writing a play about a person obsessed with vagueness. During the course of the play, the enraged protagonist begins to shout: "It's all vague! It's all vague!" Needless to say, I did not share with my dinner companion the fact that I was busily writing my own book on vagueness.

Vagueness invites insanity and inanity: It is by its very nature impossible to pin down to a single definition, and historically it has been a term of censure. For literary critics and art historians the term *vague* is related to terms such as blurry, hazy, fuzzy, woolly, impressionistic, ambiguous, and subjective. Vagueness conjures up misty images of cloudy mountaintops, Romantic fog, Gothic encounters, and pre-Raphaelite portraiture.

In contrast, in analytic philosophy today the question of vagueness refers to a very specific problem: the problem of borderline cases associated with the sorites or heap paradox. Put simply, this philosophical vagueness refers to the imprecise boundaries of concepts – for instance, how many grains of sand make a heap? Some philosophers argue that this border problem is purely a matter of language; others, that the sorites paradox undermines philosophical realism, which posits a solid and objective rather than a fuzzy and subjective world. Indeed, the simple paradox has no comparably simple solution; hundreds of articles and books aim to solve it. The growth of analytic philosophy and the logical notations found in works like *Principia Mathematica* (1910–13) mirrored Gottlob Frege's and Bertrand Russell's desire to create new "special languages," free of vagueness. The so-called Linguistic Turn in early twentieth-century philosophy analyzed ordinary language's vagueness, making language the subject rather than merely the tool of philosophy. Early pragmatists such as William James and Charles S. Peirce were also fascinated by the problem of vagueness, James calling out, "let the science be as vague as its subject." Ludwig Wittgenstein ended up praising "the blur," and Richard Rorty, more recently, ushered in "the heyday of the fuzzy." Vagueness continues to this day to challenge philosophers, linguists, and logicians, who range from demanding various alternatives to vague language to endorsing Artificial Intelligence studies that indoctrinate robots in the virtues of vagueness to enable "human" communication.

This book links the aesthetic and philosophical versions of vagueness, asking what a fiction would look like that takes seriously the problems posed by vagueness and the sorites paradox: Might objects themselves be vague? Can vagueness be eliminated? Is vagueness really only a property of language rather than of some nonlinguistic reality? *Modernist Fiction and Vagueness* argues that the novels of Henry James, Virginia Woolf, and James Joyce (among others) interrogate exactly these questions. Whether through, for example, the victory of "the great vagueness" in James's "The Beast in the Jungle," Woolf's declaration that she could only bear "vague" symbols, or Joyce's exploration of "vague speech" in *A Portrait of the Artist as a Young Man*, vagueness was a vital feature in the self-definition of the modernist novel, at the level of both form and reference. Novelistic elements as diverse as the narrator's theory in *The Sacred Fount*, Orlando's gender and age, and *Ulysses'* streams of consciousness are in fact linked insofar as each responds to the puzzle of vagueness. Modernist vagueness may reside in dialogue that is impenetrable, characters that are only shadowy subjects, or even novels that create their own languages in order to evade the vagueness of all natural languages. It might reside in a precise simulacrum of vagueness. I argue that the challenge posed to philosophical realism by vagueness offered the parallel problem for literary realism, opening the door to much of what we now recognize as modernist experimentation.

This project stemmed from two observations, one historical and one stylistic. First, vagueness, while an age-old problem, pops up everywhere at the beginning of the twentieth century in both philosophical and literary texts. For just a few examples: Peirce declared himself the first rigorous theorist of vagueness right before Russell gave a lecture entitled "Vagueness," while, on the literary side, Henry James lamented Flaubert's lack of vagueness and Woolf parodied an anti-vague philosopher. These coincidences point to an overlooked subject, particularly within literary criticism: the fascination with the problem of vagueness for a certain group of influential, largely Anglo-American intellectuals in the modernist period. This book aims to restore vagueness to its prominence in a period before it became, as it is now, a thriving topic in contemporary philosophy. In order to emphasize the blurry boundaries between fiction and philosophy in the early twentieth century, each chapter of the project joins a philosopher and a novelist and uses little known biographical facts, as well as analysis of philosophical and literary texts, to prove its claims.

Second, stylistically, literary modernism has two opposing reputations: on the one hand, characterized as intensely subjective, formally disruptive, and aesthetically self-conscious; on the other, associated with the quest for objectivity, impersonality, precision, and structure. This latter analytic temperament, associated with T. S. Eliot and T. E. Hulme, is examined in a growing group of recent critical texts comparing analytic philosophy to literary modernism. While the desire to create a perfect atomistic or pared-down language certainly inspired some modernists, the flip side of modernism, embodied in long indeterminate clauses, blurry impressions, and Joyce's *Finnegans Wakese* reflects a different philosophy. This book aims to correct the impression that analytic philosophy influenced literary modernist theories of language more than pragmatism's "reinstatement of the vague"; instead, both of these significant developments in the Anglo-American philosophy of language are essential contexts for understanding modernist vagueness. If vagueness could not be stamped out, regardless of rigorous philosophical attempts to do so, what would a vague new world look like? My project pinpoints the ramifications of this philosophical question in early twentieth-century fiction: Novelists played with the idea that what was once believed to be certain was now deemed vague, or that what was once a binary opposition between sense and non-sense had come to seem adaptable to context and angle of vision.

Two caveats. Having asserted the vagueness of all language, this book is nonetheless not written in an intentionally vague style. I acknowledge the irony that while often praising fiction writers who critique positivistic approaches to truth, the book itself sometimes adopts such methods in its attempts to embrace the "fuzziness" of literature. *Pace* one of the manuscript's earliest readers who recommended more vagueness in style! In addition, any book on James, Woolf, Joyce, and Eliot needs to justify why we need another book on these canonical figures. In teaching these works, I have found that rather than using contemporary literary theory to analyze modernist texts, highlighting the philosophical questions with which these novelists might actually have been familiar inspires my students to push through the stylistic and philosophical difficulties. While I am sympathetic to and engage here the issues of queerness, feminism, ecocriticism, and politics, I have nonetheless prioritized early twentieth-century philosophy as a lens to read these works. Woolf and Russell dined together on December 2, 1921; Joyce and C. K. Ogden spent hours in the summer of 1929 making one of the only audio recordings of Joyce reading aloud, although Joyce's growing blindness made the progress slow. I think we are all fundamentally nosy and like to imagine we might actually have stumbled upon these historical conversations between Woolf and Russell, or Joyce and Ogden, where they exchanged important ideas. *Modernist Fiction and Vagueness* aims to represent those possible conversations and their impact on well-loved literary texts.

Acknowledgments

Although William James wrote to Henry that he was happy to have "thrown off the nightmare" of being a professor, my former advisors made it seem an enviable lot, and because this project began at Yale University, my thanks will start there. For their generous feedback, their keen insights into my project, and their friendship, I give my heartfelt thanks to David Bromwich and Pericles Lewis.

I am grateful to many people at Yale, at Villanova University, and beyond, for their sustaining help. I would like especially to thank Peter Brooks for his excellent seminar on Flaubert and James where I discovered the "germ" of this book. David Bradshaw's guidance on my *Athenaeum* project helped me to determine the course of my scholarship – I thank him for that. I would also like to acknowledge in particular the scholars who have encouraged me or read sections of this manuscript (although any errors are my own) and who continue to be a source of inspiration: Charles Altieri, Tobias Boës, Sarah Cole, Kevin Dettmar, Richard Eldridge, Jed Esty, Roberta Frank, Laura Frost, Paul Fry, John Fuller, Albert Gelpi, Lyndall Gordon, Langdon Hammer, Seth Koven, Michael LeMahieu, Eric Lindstrom, Doug Mao, Anna Moreland, Jeffrey Perl, Paul Saint-Amour, Lisi Schoenbach, Ronald and Keith Schuchard, Vincent Sherry, Kees van Deemter, and Karen Zumhagen-Yekplé. At Villanova, I would like to thank my entire department, whose general good cheer and intellectual energy are in no small part due to the leadership of Evan Radcliffe. Heather Hicks, Lauren Shohet, Travis Foster, Brooke Hunter, Joseph Drury, Annika Thiem, and James Wetzel have kindly read and carefully commented on sections of this manuscript. My thanks to my research assistants, especially Edward Howell, Grace Oh, Sara Radtke, and Stephen Purcell.

I am grateful for the generosity of the Mellon Fellowship program at the Yale Center for British Art, the Beinecke Rare Book and Manuscript Library Summer Fellowship program, the International James Joyce

Foundation, and the John F. Enders and Mrs. Giles P. Whiting Foundation. Thanks are due as well for the generous fellowships of the Harry Ransom Center and the Henry Huntington Library, and to Villanova University for both a sabbatical and a Summer Research Fellowship. I would also like to thank the librarians at the Berg Collection and the Houghton Library. For their patience, I promise to the kind folks at Falvey Library (especially Luisa Cywinski and Becky Whidden) that I will hold off on Interlibrary Loan for at least six months.

Thank you to my editor, Ray Ryan, the team at Cambridge University Press, and the two anonymous readers for their feedback. Early drafts of sections of this book have appeared in *Modernism/modernity* and *Philosophy and Literature*, and I am grateful to the editors for permissions to reprint them here. Thank you also to Rick Knief at Table of Content for the basis of the cover design.

My thanks to Cannon Quigley Campbell for her boundless support, to Samara Pfohl Bilden, and to my brothers, Matthew and Daniel Quigley. To Rosemary and Jenny Quigley, thank you for production and editorial insights, and to Allison Wade for versions of artistic vagueness. For Eloise Lawrence, who has uncomplainingly lived with this project for years, and for Kelly Lawrence, who liberated her from it, you both inspire me every day. Special thanks to Liesl Olson, my constant comrade since 65 High Street, and to Rebecca Berne, Kamran Javadizadeh, Jean Lutes, and Nick Salvato, who all know this project almost as well as I do at this point; I could not have completed this book without your help.

My children, Nathan, Sophia, and Rosemary, I thank for their joyful commentary and endless love, and I also thank my mom, Josephine Gill, and Nadine McNeil, who have traveled with babies to archives, bolstered me, and generally helped to create a happy home for small children so that I could work.

My final and most heartfelt thanks are reserved for my husband, Eric Gill, who has weathered this vague storm and helped me in refining my thoughts and in bringing the project to completion more than I can say. I love you.

This project is dedicated to my mother, Lynn Pfohl Quigley, and to the memory of my father, Leonard V. Quigley (1933–2005). My mother's wisdom, strength, and courage help me to keep my head up, and my father's humor, love for John Donne and A. E. Housman, and unshakable faith in me guided every line of this work – you were right, Dad, I was lucky to be born to you.

Introduction: Linguistic Turns and Literary Modernism

> Sunsets were redder and more intense; dawns were whiter and more auroral. Of our crepuscular half-lights and lingering twilights they knew nothing. The rain fell vehemently, or not at all. [. . .] The withered intricacies and ambiguities of our more gradual and doubtful age were unknown to them. Violence was all. The flower bloomed and faded. The sun rose and sank. The lover loved and went.
>
> –Virginia Woolf, *Orlando*.[1]

1. Modern Novels and Vagueness

In "*Ulysses*, Order, and Myth," T. S. Eliot declares that the role of art in modern times is to provide a solid "scaffolding" – the "mythical method" in Joyce's case – for a world that is itself meaningless.[2] Eliot's contemporaries and critical descendants also emphasize the "hard" and firmly delineated quality of modernist writing. It must be "the definite and concrete," "economical and spare," "objective," "*particular*"; it must have "fine precision of expression"; it must seek "to refine, to clarify, to intensify"; it must have "unity of form, culminations, and shapes" – above all, it must not be "vague."[3] But are concrete and precise really the best adjectives to describe works like Joyce's "damned monster-novel"?[4] Virginia Woolf offered a very different view of modern fiction when she recorded her revelation while writing *Jacob's Room*:

> happier today than I was yesterday having this afternoon arrived at some idea of a new form for a new novel . . . For I figure that the approach will be entirely different this time: no scaffolding; scarcely a brick to be seen, all crepuscular, but the heart, the passion, humour, everything as bright as fire in the mist.[5]

Woolf's plan for *Jacob's Room* explicitly challenges Eliot's contention that literature ought to provide an objective "scaffolding." But what exactly is the "new form" for the "new novel"? And what would it mean for a novel to be "crepuscular"?

On November 25, 1922, a few months after the publication of both *Ulysses* and *Jacob's Room*, Bertrand Russell delivered a paper entitled "Vagueness" in front of a small group at Oriel College at Oxford University.[6] In contrast to Eliotic precision, Russell lamented that he "propose[d] to prove that all language is vague and that therefore my language is vague." He stated:

> You all know that I invented a special language with a view to avoiding vagueness, but unfortunately it is unsuited for public occasions. I shall therefore, though regretfully, address you in English, and whatever vagueness is to be found in my words must be attributed to our ancestors for not having been predominantly interested in logic.[7]

Russell claimed (with his characteristic wry humor) to regret addressing his audience in English because of its "vagueness." "We can see an ideal of precision [in English], to which we can approximate indefinitely," he asserted, "but we cannot attain this ideal . . . It is therefore not applicable to this terrestrial life, but only to an imagined celestial existence" (*V* 65). However, aspiring to this "celestial existence" linguistically and logically was a serious necessity, and therefore Russell insisted that language ought to be subjected to rigorous scientific standards:

> Science is perpetually trying to substitute more precise beliefs for vague ones; this makes it harder for a scientific proposition to be true than for the vague beliefs of uneducated persons to be true, but makes scientific truth better worth having if it can be obtained. (*V* 68)

Russell explained that he was giving the talk because "vagueness is very much more important in the theory of knowledge than you would judge it to be from the writings of most people," and he intended to demonstrate that "the process of sound philosophizing . . . consists mainly in passing from those obvious, vague, ambiguous things . . . to something precise, clear, definite."[8]

In "Vagueness," Russell highlighted several philosophical questions that were fermenting in 1922 and that are germane to the treatment of language and form in the "new novel." First, to amend the words of Joyce, "it seems language was to blame" for what appeared to be otherwise irresolvable philosophical paradoxes. Russell called this tendency to treat purely linguistic confusions as actual philosophical questions the "fallacy of verbalism" (*V* 62). Second, Russell asserted that analytical methods and logical formulae were needed to clean up the muddle in which philosophy found itself. Scientific methods were granted a status above previous approaches to philosophy. And finally, Russell claimed that our ordinary language, in this "terrestrial life," is so riddled through with vagueness that a new "special language" is required to approach philosophical questions (*V* 61).

What was this vagueness Russell was so worried about? The concept of vagueness has a long and volatile history.[9] Terms with "vague boundaries" have been an object of philosophical debate since Eubulides of Miletus in the fourth century BCE first asserted his sorites paradox (*soros* is "heap" in Greek):

> I say: tell me, do you think that a single grain of wheat is a heap? Thereupon you say: No. Then I say: What do you say about 2 grains? For it is my purpose to ask you questions in succession, and if you do not admit that 2 grains are a heap then I shall ask you about 3 grains. Then I shall proceed to interrogate you further with respect to 4 grains, then 5 and 6 and 7 and 8, and you will assuredly say that none of these makes a heap.[10]

The boundary between several grains of sand and a heap, or a man with little hair and a bald man, appears unstable. Recent theorists of vagueness continue to wrestle with this problem – to such an extent that M. F. Burnyeat exclaims, "Eubulides himself can hardly have foreseen that his modest heap of grain would grow to menace Olympus and undermine the foundations of logic."[11] The sorites paradox menaces logic because:

> If you remove a single grain of sand from a heap of sand, you surely still have a heap of sand. But if you take a heap and remove grains one by one, you can apply that principle at each stage, which will commit you to counting even the solitary final grain as a heap. This is a sorites paradox.[12]

Logicians emphasize that terms such as "heap" and "tall," or even "child" or "belief," have boundaries that are fuzzy so that when logic is applied to define them, although "the premises are highly plausible, [and] the inference seems valid, . . . the conclusions are absurd."[13] Vague boundaries appear to undermine the principle of bivalence – either something is or is not true – therefore shaking the foundations of classical logic.

Although in classical times paradoxes like the sorites were actually used to test scholars' dialectical skills – and the "heap" was so famous a paradox that the average reader was supposed to note allusions to heaps[14] – it was not until the end of the nineteenth century with the origins of the analytic tradition that vagueness resurfaced as a key concept. From the late nineteenth to the early twentieth century, the problem of vagueness in language became a central subject of debate in pragmatism and the philosophy of language. Ideal language theorists such as Gottlob Frege and Russell devised new formal languages and symbolic systems in order to avoid the "irregular, unperspicuous, and ambiguous" qualities of colloquial language, while pragmatists such as Charles Sanders Peirce and William James believed that the logicians' efforts to avoid vagueness were futile and therefore chose to enlist vagueness as a tool.[15] Both Peirce and William James recommended "'vagueness' as a counteraction to the dogmatizing of existent truths and as the necessary condition for the exploratory search for new truths," but Peirce believed that the new truths would themselves be precise, whereas William James asserted that vagueness itself finally had a "proper place in our mental life."[16] The positive re-evaluation of vagueness culminated in Wittgenstein's praise of the "blur" in *Philosophical Investigations*, where all language is defined as necessarily vague, but unproblematically so, because vagueness does not undermine a language's utility. For Stanley Cavell and the Ordinary Language philosophers in Wittgenstein's wake, the vagueness of language is a given, and it is philosophy's duty to demonstrate how ordinary usage acts pragmatically in order to "explain how the language we traverse every day can contain undiscovered treasure."[17]

Russell's lecture participated in this revolutionary movement in philosophy re-evaluating the vagueness of language. His lecture actually stemmed from questions he encountered when writing two essays: one an introduction for the first English publication of Wittgenstein's *Tractatus*, the second a review of John Dewey's *Essays in Experimental Logic*. Russell's claim that an ideal language based on logic would be free of vagueness was also implicitly an argument against pragmatists who pointed to the concept of vagueness to demonstrate the faults of classical logic. In fact, F. C. S. Schiller, expected to hold the opposing pragmatic view, had been asked by the society to prepare a response to Russell's lecture in advance, so the two camps were in place before the talk began. Ideal language theorists, like Russell, posited language's fallibility and advanced a more scientific approach to philosophy, yet this debate over language's possible precision was initiating a drastic change in philosophy. Richard Rorty later called this change in early twentieth-century philosophy "the linguistic turn" – "the view that philosophical problems are problems which may be solved (or dissolved) either by reforming language, or by understanding more about the language we presently use."[18] Whether through G. E. Moore's definition of "good" in *Principia Ethica*, Russell's desired "celestial" language, or Wittgenstein's propositions in the *Tractatus*, some philosophers were turning to an analysis of language to solve philosophical problems.[19] Pragmatists, in contrast, thought these incipient modes of analytical thought and methods of linguistic analysis missed the point: Schiller, in fact, had already written a scathing critique of formal logic (a book that he had dedicated to William James).[20] The question of language's vagueness was at the core of this debate between analytic and pragmatist philosophers, because it underscored either language's shortcomings or its enormous potential, depending upon one's philosophical view.

In this book I argue that the character of modernist fiction is best understood in light of these transformations in early twentieth-century Anglo-American philosophy. Moreover, while early analytical philosophy set up the problem of vagueness that modernist fiction writers explored, their response (by and large) more closely resembles that of the pragmatic philosophers. Modern novelists, from Henry James to James Joyce, were simultaneously enacting their own kind of linguistic turn in fiction, and, in this linguistic turn, too, vagueness played a major role. Henry James declared his "confidence in the positive saving virtue of vagueness," while Woolf, in "Modern Fiction," made a "confession of vagueness," and Joyce created a "vehicle of a vague speech" in *A Portrait of the Artist as a Young Man*.[21] Ian Watt contends there is a close analogy between the epistemological premises of formal realism and those of "philosophical realism."[22] In this book, I am proposing a close analogy between the modern novel's attempt to revise the conventions of the realist novel and the revolt against positivism in the philosophy of language.[23] My book thus tells the other half of Watt's story, arguing that literary modernism is linked to the challenge posed to both philosophical and literary realisms through the problem of vagueness. Significantly, the embrace of vagueness in fiction and the linguistic turn in philosophy is not just a coincidence. There is a historical explanation for modernism's new fuzzy fictions, which experiment with long indeterminate sentences, blur genres, or create new languages. Novelists, I argue, assimilated contemporary linguistic questions, then seen as philosophical questions, into fiction. Indeed, because language was the fiction writer's domain, the novel, it seemed, could offer answers to philosophical problems that philosophy itself could not resolve.

Ironically, William James, who called for the "re-instatement of the vague" in *The Principles of Psychology* (1890), deplored the parallel movement in fiction.[24] Although he emphasized the shortcomings of scientific precision for psychology, he simultaneously expressed his frustration with the vague style of his brother's novel *The Golden Bowl*:

> I don't enjoy the kind of "problem," . . . and the method of narration by interminable elaboration of suggestive reference (I don't know what else to call it, but you know what I mean) . . . won't you, just to please Brother, sit

> down and write a new book, with no twilight or mustiness in the plot, with great vigor and decisiveness in the action, no fencing in the dialogue, no psychological commentaries, and absolute straightness in style? Publish it in my name, I will acknowledge it, and give you half the proceeds.[25]

The novels of James, Woolf, and Joyce (along with others such as Joseph Conrad, Dorothy Richardson, Gertrude Stein, and Jean Rhys), all resist the qualities William James sought and revel instead in "psychological commentaries," indecisiveness in plot and action, and "absolute" vagueness in style. If the conventions of the realist novel can be summarized by an emphasis on "originality" or "the novel" plot, "the repudiation of figurative eloquence," and "the particularization of character and background, of naming, temporality, causation, and physical environment," the modernist novel's focus on subjectivity, resistance to anything easily definable as plot, and figurative and stylistic eloquence pushed to the brink of solipsism all demonstrate a new set of conventions in fiction.[26] Rather than attempting to eliminate vagueness, modernist fiction may probe vagueness as the best way to examine psychological depth, to depict sexual indeterminacy, or to register disenchantment with the capitalist, bourgeois, and symbolic status quo while still existing within those systems.[27] Even William James grudgingly admitted that his brother achieved a "paradoxical success in this unheard of method."[28]

Modernist Fiction and Vagueness contends that early twentieth-century fiction, along with pragmatism's "reinstatement of the vague," often prioritizes the elusive and the unfixable, even as much modernist poetics, famously through the statements of T. S. Eliot, Hulme, and Pound, praises objectivity, precision, and clarity. Indeed, this book works to revise a current trend in literary criticism (that has its roots in early Eliot) that ties modernist linguistic experimentation predominantly to the (then) new analytic philosophy. While the connections between, for example, the analytic grouping of Hulme, Russell, Ogden, Wittgenstein of the *Tractatus*, and Joyce's *Ulysses* are key to note and will be discussed in Chapter 3, the resistance to this logical reform movement, crystallized in pragmatism and in Wittgenstein's later writings, were equally if not more influential on literary modernism, particularly as it is embodied in the fiction of James, Woolf, and Joyce.[29] This book both explains the debate between analytic and pragmatic philosophers over the question of vagueness, shedding light on what logical reform aimed to reform, and simultaneously demonstrates that modernism derived energy from the debate *itself* about language's possible precision. From Ogden's creation of Basic English to Joyce's re-babelization in *Finnegans Wake*, or from Ezra Pound's Imagist

Manifesto to Woolf's "vague way," literary modernism is less defined by Eliotic structure and coherence than by its investigation of the borders of linguistic precision.

But what would it mean to call a novel "vague"? Why, according to Google's Ngram Viewer, which graphs the appearance of words in English fiction, does the use of the word "Vague" hit an all-time high in the early 1920s?[30] This book seeks to answer these questions by tracing a taxonomy of stylistic vagueness in modernist fiction from Henry James's long indeterminate clauses, to Woolf's dissolution of direct discourse, to Joyce's verbal coinages and puns in *Finnegans Wake*. Thematically, the vagueness stretches from James's ineffable secrets, to Woolf's impressionistic renderings of subjectivity, to the climactic moment when Stephen Dedalus and Leopold Bloom finally meet in *Ulysses* and the reader is ultimately radically uncertain of the ramifications. Being vague carries different weight in each of these cases, but what is consistent is the sense that the precision the modernists attributed to British literary realism was stridently under attack.

Vagueness, unlike ambiguity or multiplicity, fails to provide clear, if multiple, ways to read a text, which explains why William Empson, for one, described vagueness as a bad or failed kind of ambiguity. In *The Sacred Fount*, for example, both James's dialogue and his plot have been repeatedly decried as impossibly vague: This combination means readers are not even sure what exactly they are supposed to be unsure about. In *The Waves*, in contrast, Woolf seems to clearly delineate the natural and the human worlds, and yet then this delineation begins to blur. Vagueness, therefore, brings up a range of issues for fiction, of which two are salient and related: On the one hand, an author who seems to be vague may in fact be writing with precision about an atmosphere or situation that is itself vague; on the other hand, another writer may be vague about a precise situation in order to make the reader think. (The following chapters will tackle which kinds of vagueness James and Woolf may be deploying in these works.) Regardless, modernist fiction's affect is usually one of puzzlement and indecision, rather than the satisfaction derived from the closure of a Victorian novel (like Brontë's *Jane Eyre* or Dickens's *Great Expectations*). If, as Sianne Ngai has argued, twenty-first-century aesthetic categories such as zany, cute, and interesting show us "how aesthetic experience has been transformed by the hypercommodified, information-saturated, performance-driven condition of late capitalism," what does an aesthetic of vagueness reveal about the modernist era?[31] Further, and appropriately given our growing distance from the twentieth century, vagueness puts into question the division between twentieth-century modernist and postmodernist fiction. If postmodernism defines itself by "renounce[ing] closed structure, fixed meaning, and rigid order in favor of play, indeterminacy, incompleteness, uncertainty, ambiguity, contingency and chaos," the vagueness of modernist fiction shows it was always already postmodern.[32]

Modernist Fiction and Vagueness begins examining vagueness by explaining why a little question about how many grains of sand make up a heap has prompted philosophical debate since Classical times. Having established the central disagreements between pragmatists and early analytic philosophers about vagueness, I will turn to those for whom "ordinary language" is often an oxymoron: the novelists. Ever since F. R. Leavis in *The Great Tradition* (1948) regretted the "inveterate indirectness of the later James," scholars have sought to justify the Master's stylistic ambiguities and linguistic extravagances.[33] By placing Henry James's fiction in relation to the debate between William James and Peirce over vague language, I give a new explanation for why Lambert Strether is "grandly vague" and how "the great vagueness" overcomes James's characters and plots.[34] Henry James's exclamation to William that he had been "unconsciously" pragmatic in his writing underscores, I argue, their similar interest in the vagueness of language.[35] Therefore, next I turn to the novels of Woolf, who announced "we want to be rid of realism," and for whom even James's fiction was too structured.[36] In contrast to Russell's assertion that each word ought to be used precisely, Woolf parodies the analytic philosopher in her character of Mr. Ramsay and advocates the "vagueness of the finest prose." The increasing formal experimentation in Woolf's later novels such as *Jacob's Room* and *The Waves* embodies the lessons about realism, objectivity, and gender that she teaches Katharine Hillberry in her early work, *Night and Day*.

Just as Russell Goodman argues that there is a "a classical American presence in analytic philosophy" channeled by James through to Wittgenstein, so also this book contends there is a classic American interest in vagueness in literature channeled by the James brothers through to the "British" modernists, Woolf and Joyce.[37] From James and Woolf, therefore, I turn to Joyce, Wittgenstein, and C. K. Ogden and compare Wittgenstein's language games and the "blur" of *Philosophical Investigations* to Joyce's "vague speech" in *A Portrait of the Artist as a Young Man*, *Ulysses*, and *Finnegans Wake*. Ogden, as the translator of both the *Tractatus* and sections of *Finnegans Wake*, acts as a bridge between these two figures because both were writing him letters about their projects at the same time. Moreover, Ogden's translation of Joyce's "Anna Livia Plurabelle" into Basic English, a new simplified language aimed at eliminating miscommunication that Ogden created in the aftermath of World War I, in many ways puts the *Tractatus*' vision of language to work through the art of translation. Just as the idea of the vague undermines Wittgenstein's early "picture" theory of language, leading to his concept of the "language-game" (*PI* §48), so also for Joyce "vague speech" is an alternative to that taught by "christian minstrelsy" (*FW* 371). One of Joyce's central themes is establishing that language, rather than a gift from God, is in fact a social game, enmeshed in the power relations of nationhood, gender, race, and sexuality. I argue that deconstructive readings find fertile ground in Joyce because he was himself interested in debates about pragmatism and language. The accretive and omnivorous language of *Finnegans Wake* shared in its time's vision of constructing an international language, like Ogden's Basic English, and its fecundity parallels the encyclopedic styles of *Ulysses*.

I conclude by returning to the figure of T. S. Eliot ("In my beginning is my end" as he writes in *Four Quartets*) to examine Eliot's own complicated relationship with language's imprecision in his critical essays and their important, sustained influence upon modernist literary criticism.[38] If poststructuralism, as has been argued, is a "Gargantua grown out of Empsonian ambiguity," Empson's ambiguity, in turn, has roots in Eliot's injunction that modern writing must be *difficult* and allusive and yet somehow form an organic "whole."[39] Eliot, like his professor Russell, sought to stem the tide of increasing vagueness, but he acknowledged that "verbalism," "the verbal disease," and the "dissociation of sensibility" came hand-in-hand with modernity.[40] The conclusion juxtaposes Eliot's "Hamlet" essay and Russell's "Vagueness" lecture, arguing that Eliot's contentions for an "objective" art were largely motivated by his admiration for Russell's style, method, and hatred of language's vagueness. Further, in examining Eliot's early essays on James, Woolf, and Joyce (as well as his unpublished lecture notes on other contemporaries, such as Lawrence and Empson), I put forward the case that he promotes both analytic virtues and analytic methods. And yet I also disagree with those who parody Eliot as the ultimate New Critic; instead, Eliot's own move away from analytic philosophy back to a pragmatic approach to language that he somewhat abhorred in his early Harvard years means that his later poetry, such as *Four Quartets*, had more in common with the vagueness of modernist fiction than his early important critical statements would lead us to believe. Just as Woolf portrays the scholar-philosopher as missing the essential questions in life, so also Eliot portrays Russell (and analytic philosophy in general) as blinded by its devotion to positivism, namely its faith in empiricism and logic. This project concludes by examining the way in which New Critical methods of resolving ambiguity – crystallized in Empson's *Seven Types of Ambiguity* – actually worked against the grain of modernist experimentation, attempting to categorize and delimit a style that embodied vagueness.

Each chapter of the book joins a philosopher with a novelist, not only to recall that Woolf and Eliot attended "Bertie's lectures," or that Henry James and Peirce spent a winter as "intimates," but also to give a sense of the urgency surrounding the questions of linguistic vagueness during the modernist period. Primarily, this book engages with literary vagueness, the history of philosophy, and very specific historical debates about vagueness; I am focused on the ways that the literary modernists perceived and portrayed philosophy and vagueness, and I do not aim to discover the solution(s) to vagueness as a philosopher might. That said, there are also moments when the novelists seem to prefigure twenty-first-century analytic and pragmatic approaches to vagueness, or when I will turn to the current scholarship on artistic vagueness (for terms such as de-differentiation, pre-differentiation, and pre-reification) to discuss the various techniques of literary vagueness.[41] In addition, the relationships among the philosophers and the novelists in each chapter are not always the same. While in the James chapter, the philosophers and novelist knew each other intimately, and I make a case for Henry James's reimagining of Peirce's pragmaticism; in the Woolf chapter Russell represents one of many strong philosopher figures that Woolf knew well, including, of course, her father, Leslie Stephen, and G. E. Moore, so her reaction against Russell's impersonal logic fits into a larger picture. In fact, there is a growing element of mediation across the chapters, so that whereas the James chapter focuses on brothers and childhood friends, the Woolf chapter examines acquaintances, and the final chapter's study of the relationship between Joyce and Wittgenstein is triangulated through Ogden. This growing element of mediation works to solidify my argument that the reaction against positivism in literary circles was not merely personal but part of a general trend.

I chose this particular constellation of fiction writers because of their philosophical ties (through their family, friends, or education) and their novels' investment in language's vagueness. But this is not solely an influence study. That is, I do not think it was always as simple as saying that sudden interest in language's vagueness arose in philosophy and then was imported to fiction. Instead of studying how fiction "applies" philosophy, I argue that modernism yields an exemplary case of discursive evolution, where arguments proposed in very different registers simultaneously considered the same questions about nomination, semiotics, and mimesis. As Raymond Williams in *The Politics of Modernism* crucially demonstrated, the explosion of foreign languages and travel through urbanization and imperialism in the early twentieth century affected the approach to language in texts as diverse as Wittgenstein's *Tractatus* and James's *The American Scene*.[42] Vincent Sherry adds to this fact that England's propaganda machine helped to propel the shift against rational discourse in literary and linguistic circles.[43] As early as 1929 in his introductory remarks to a section of *Finnegans Wake*, Ogden explained that the various cultural forces at work that made both linguistic reform and experimentation movements necessary at the beginning of the twentieth century included the ubiquity of newspapers, the power of English academic institutions, and the drive of capitalism.[44] To these explanations, I add the fact that in both philosophy and literature the drive to make a case for language's vagueness – which may seem an absurd move – negates a more structured earlier movement in both disciplines. This negation is a typically modernist gesture of rejecting the generation before, even if the "generations" are nearly simultaneous. Therefore, embracing a modernist "blur" rebuffs, in a parallel movement, both Russell's philosophical realism and Arnold Bennett's literary realism. Exploring this combination of philosophy and literature aims to fulfill Michel Foucault's injunction that revisionist historical criticism will cross disciplinary boundaries.[45]

At the center of this book is a question about modernism and mimesis. It may be that all language is "vague" or "indeterminate"; however, following James and Wittgenstein, that does not mean that vague language cannot connect to our experience of the world. Building on work such as Charles Altieri's *Act and Quality: A Theory of Literary Meaning and Humanistic Understanding* and Michael North's *Reading 1922*, I offer a way to talk about language's indeterminacy without falling into deconstruction's textualism. The "use" for James or the "context" for Wittgenstein enables intersubjective communication even as it produces a possibility of misconstrual. My project illuminates the consequences of this philosophical insight in early twentieth-century fiction: Novelists played with this notion that what was once considered definite was now declared vague, or they depicted a new world in which what was once a stark opposition between sense and non-sense had come to seem subject to perspective. So vagueness becomes a fraught notion – an attack on the one hand and a mark of strategic victory on the other.

It is important to note both the vagueness of literary Impressionism and the fact that modern novels can engage with language's vagueness without being "impressionistic." Literary Impressionism has a thorny history with regard to modern novelists, most of whom (including Joseph Conrad, Woolf, and Joyce) disdained the actual term "Impressionism" for various reasons, primarily for its association with an earlier movement in French painting. In fact, what connects the novels of James to those of Woolf and Joyce is less an interest in conveying an impression than in investigating the very language used to convey impressions, objects, or dialogue. Watt has summarized the main goal of literary Impressionism as replacing the emphasis on the object viewed with the perceptions of the subjective viewer. Ford Madox Ford's insistence, for example, that "the Impressionist" provides "the fruits of his own observations alone" and Conrad's technique of delayed decoding both accentuate the perceptions of the observer rather than the object or person observed.[46] Subjective perceptions certainly play a large role in modern novels, and I will examine the vagueness of Woolf's literary Impressionism in the chapter on her work. However, a focus on the subjectivity of Impressionism fails adequately to account for Henry James's "almost intolerable ambiguity" in the dialogue of *The Golden Bowl* or Joyce's verbal punning in *Ulysses* or *Finnegans Wake*.[47] Moreover, definitions of literary Impressionism vary so widely that Jesse Matz in *Literary Impressionism and Modernist Aesthetics* has wondered whether the term itself becomes "meaningless" and asks, "But what if Impressionism's tendency towards definitional vagueness is itself definitive?"[48] I would concur, although I focus on modern novelists' "bewitchment" (to adopt Wittgenstein's term) with the *vagueness* itself of the word "Impression."

Understanding modernist fiction in line with transformations in philosophy rather than under the rubric of modernist poetry's manifestos has important implications both in terms of our methods of reading these texts and understanding their political implications. New Modernist Studies has helped to rescue modernist literature from the stigma of political elitism by revisiting the works of canonical figures and by extending the literary canon. My project falls into the former category – aiming to divorce difficulty from what D. H. Lawrence deemed purely mental masturbation. While James, Woolf, and Joyce were never quite grouped with Eliot and Pound as anti-democratic, it might seem that vague fiction would be a prime example of modernist aestheticism: an escape from political or social concerns into a world of obscure art, the "retreat in an elitist disgust from modern civilization" of "the modernist hegemony."[49] Being vague can, of course, offer a way to avoid political concerns, and it is usually not the best style for an effective newspaper editorial. However, the modernist desire to fancy itself *other* than the Victorian realist age that preceded it was linked to the sense that literary realism failed to account for new modern social conditions. When Woolf asks, "Is life like this? Must novels be like this?" she suggests that both life and art are, or ought to be, different from realist depictions. While for a literary critic such as Eliot, the futile "chaos" resulting from the Great War required a structured, objective art, for writers like Woolf and Joyce modernity was not necessarily a social ill, nor need art act as a strict taskmaster providing meaning where in fact there was none. Indeed, this is why Henry James provides such a formative influence on the latter two writers; his fiction of pragmatic vagueness depicts the way decisions could be made even in a world lacking fixed or stable truths. I argue that for writers like James, Woolf, and Joyce, changes in philosophy's approach to language encouraged the novelists' rebellion against literary realism and its (for them) inhibiting definitions of subjectivity, citizenship, and gender. On the level of grammar, choosing vagueness over specificity seems to reject the authoritarian nature of the sentence. In fact, there is a surface parallel between the largely poetic search for objectivity and precision (Hulme, Eliot, and Pound) and the mainly fictional investigation of vagueness (James, Woolf, and Joyce), and the tendency to conservative politics versus liberalism. However, Pound and Eliot only represent one stylistic strain in modernist poetry, in contrast to Wallace Stevens, for example, who declared: "It must be abstract."

Finally, one other important motif resurfaces throughout the following chapters. All three novelists play with the connection between the word "vague" and the French word *vague* or wave. The linguistic family of the word "vague," including "vagrancy," "extravagance," and the French *vague* (a connection that the Francophile Henry James would certainly have registered), is connected to movement and "to superfluity."[50] Woolf's new term "vagulous" similarly taps into this wavy, watery sense of language, while Joyce's "fourworded wavespeech" connects to the "vehicle of vague speech" Stephen imbibes.[51] Vagueness need not be solely a quality of bad Romantic writing – a fear that permeates the rhetoric of modernist critics such as Hulme or Eliot. Instead, in *A Pluralistic Universe* (1909), William James lauds the idea that "the whole universe in its different spans and wave-lengths, exclusions and envelopments, is everywhere alive and conscious," foreshadowing the flowing image of the "stream" of consciousness he will describe in *The Principles of Psychology*.[52] Albert

Einstein, moreover, won the Nobel Prize in 1922 for the wave theory of light, and the apparently paradoxical fact that light could consist both of particles and of waves was a topic of considerable news before and after World War I. That words, too, might best be described as wave-like, lacking a precise beginning or ending but immensely powerful in their movement, is an idea that Henry James, Woolf, and Joyce all tease out in images in their novels.[53] And, as Russell, writing of Einstein's theories in the *Athenaeum* in 1919, noted, "every lover of the beautiful must wish it to be true."[54]

2. "The Impossible Heap"

> But let your communication be, Yea, yea; Nay, nay; for whatsoever is more than these cometh of evil.
>
> –Matt. 5:37[55]

"Vagueness is huge," wrote Richard Rorty in *The London Review of Books* in 2005.[56] Whereas in the field of literature the word "vague" continues to be confined primarily to negative comments on students' arguments, "Vagueness Studies" in the discipline of philosophy have "exploded in the last thirty years."[57] Rorty, initially flabbergasted, explained that vagueness studies should interest the general reader as well as philosophers because "[i]t is an underlying concern with the question of whether and how language gets in touch with the world that has made vagueness a hot topic." "The controversy," he noted, can be boiled down to a fight "between realists, who think the notion of truth as correspondence to reality can be saved, and pragmatists, who regard it as hopeless." The question of vagueness, however, is far from new, although the rise of pragmatism corresponded to an explosion of writings on vagueness, both of which closely corresponded in time to the birth of the modernist novel.

Frege, "the father of modern mathematical logic," and Peirce are usually declared the first modern philosophers to focus on the problem of vagueness. Frege created in his 1879 *Begriffsschrift* (*Concept-notation*) a formal language to avoid ordinary language's ambiguities. He argued:

> If it is a question of the truth of something ... We have to throw aside concepts that do not have a meaning ... These are ... such as have vague boundaries. It must be determinate for every object whether it falls under a concept or not; a concept-word which does not meet this requirement on its meaning is meaningless.[58]

Frege noted that, because "a large part of a philosopher's task consists – or at least should consist – in a struggle with language," a philosopher's language needs to be as precise as possible; therefore, "vagueness, like madness, must be mentioned in order to be excluded."[59] Frege, and Russell in his wake, turned their backs on ordinary language's slipperiness in order to address crucial logical questions. Wittgenstein's *Tractatus* – also published in 1922, the *annus mirabilis* of modernism – with its "picture theory of language" can be seen to contribute to the ideal language tradition, if we concur, with Russell's introduction, that the *Tractatus* sets out "the conditions which would have to be fulfilled by a logically perfect language."[60] (Wittgenstein, famously, denied this interpretation.) Similarly, Ogden's and I. A. Richards's *The Meaning of Meaning* (1923) and Ogden's later work on Basic English can be linked to this "ideal language" tradition.[61] Russell's view that a "vague" concept may be the origin of a philosophical question but that vagueness must be eliminated in the approach and in the fruits of philosophy seems typical of the "ideal language tradition":

> The process of sound philosophizing, to my mind, consists mainly in passing from those obvious, vague, ambiguous things, that we feel quite sure of, to something precise, clear, definite, which by reflection and analysis we find is involved in the vague thing that we started from, and is, so to speak, the real truth of which the vague thing is a sort of shadow.[62]

Russell insists that "vagueness" may exist before a problem is addressed but that the final result must be "precise, clear and definite."

However, the pragmatic countercurrent in philosophy, utilizing rather than trying to stamp out vagueness, was gaining momentum in the first decades of the twentieth century. Peirce, a friend of William and Henry James and the coiner of the term *pragmatism*, is often seen as the first pragmatist theorist of vagueness, although his attitude toward vagueness was ambivalent. Regretting that "logicians have been at fault in giving Vagueness the go-by, so far as not even to analyze it," he had "worked out the logic of vagueness with something like completeness."[63] When called upon to define "Vague" for the 1902 *Dictionary of Philosophy and Psychology*, Peirce wrote:

> A proposition is vague when there are possible states of things concerning which it is intrinsically uncertain whether, had they been contemplated by the speaker, he would have regarded them as excluded or allowed by the proposition. By intrinsically uncertain we mean not uncertain in consequence of any ignorance of the interpreter, but because the speaker's habits

> of language were indeterminate; so that one day he would regard the proposition as excluding, another as admitting, those states of things. Yet this must be understood to have reference to what might be *deduced* from a perfect knowledge of his state of mind; for it is precisely because these questions never did, or did not frequently, present themselves that his habit remained indeterminate.[64]

For Peirce, therefore, vagueness is due to the "indeterminate" habit of language, resulting in intrinsically uncertain categories and cases. Peirce does not assert that the world itself might be vague but rather that indeterminacy stems from a speaker's inconsistent relationship to language. Nonetheless, he simultaneously stresses that vague terms, even in science, can be extremely valuable steps along the way to discovering truth, "so, the practice of science is better served by vague predicates than by precise ones."[65] Peirce called the excessive need for clarity in every step of logical thought the "fallacy of over-precision" and warned against it (*CP* 8:244).

In contrast to Peirce's desire to refine vagueness out of existence, William James believed that both the scientific method and the truths discovered are themselves "vague." "[L]et the science be as vague as its subject," he writes in *The Principles of Psychology*. Just as "the boundary line of the mental is certainly vague," so also consciousness and language reflect that vagueness (*PP* 1:6). James resisted fixed truths and concrete mathematical terms. In addition, he found Russell's desire to read language as a precise science ridiculous. He writes:

> A mathematical term, as *a, b, c, x, y,* sin, log, is self-sufficient, and terms of this sort, once equated, can be substituted for one another in endless series without error. Mr. Russell . . . seem[s] to think that in our mouth also such terms as "meaning," "truth," "belief," "object," "definition," are self-sufficients with no context of varying relation that might be further asked about. What a word means is expressed by its definition, isn't it? The definition claims to be exact and adequate, doesn't it? Then it can be substituted for the word – since the two are identical – can't it? Then two words with the same definition can be substituted for one another, *n'est-ce pas*? Likewise two definitions of the same word, *nicht wahr*, etc., etc., till it will be indeed strange if you can't convict someone of self-contradiction and absurdity.[66]

James emphasizes the importance of "varying relations" to definitions and demonstrates that substituting "same" words ("doesn't it?" "*n'est-ce pas*?" "*nicht wahr*?"), as one would substitute equal mathematical terms, quickly leads to "absurdity." Instead, because topics such as psychology, philosophy, and belief are vague, language, that vague medium, is well suited to investigate their principles.

Ludwig Wittgenstein is the central figure to bridge the competing approaches to vagueness. The *Tractatus* can be seen to sum up Frege, Russell, and G. E. Moore's goal of an "instrumental language," but his *Philosophical Investigations* reverses his earlier views. The *Tractatus* presents a new "picture" theory of language, where language, or at least language functioning meaningfully, would have absolute reference and be free of vagueness.[67] *Philosophical Investigations*, however, demonstrates the influence of the pragmatist re-evaluation of vagueness but pushes the reassessment even further.[68] Wittgenstein comes to disagree with Frege's dismissal of "vague boundaries":

> Frege compares a concept to an area and says that an area with vague boundaries cannot be called an area at all. This presumably means that we cannot do anything with it. – But is it senseless to say: "Stand roughly there"? Suppose that I were standing with someone in a city square and said that. As I say it I do not draw any kind of boundary, but perhaps point with my hand – as if I were indicating a particular *spot*.

"Stand roughly there," according to Wittgenstein, is a meaningful command. Moreover, it is not only as useful as less vague assertions, but also often more so. Wittgenstein's notion of the way language itself works, the language "game," is itself necessarily a blurred concept:

> One might say that the concept "game" is a concept with blurred edges. – "But is a blurred concept a concept at all?" – Is an indistinct photograph a picture of a person at all? Is it even always an advantage to replace an indistinct picture by a sharp one? Isn't the indistinct one often exactly what we need? (*PI* 34e)

For Wittgenstein the "indistinct" photograph or "blurred" concept represents an inescapable property of language. Vagueness, according to Wittgenstein's "functionalist" theory of language, cannot truly be evaded and is indeed "exactly what we need" in order to perform philosophical investigations, to capture meaningful images, and to communicate in daily life. Wittgenstein disagreed with those who claimed a new language was needed:

> It is clear that every sentence in our language "is in order as it is". That is to say, we are not *striving after* an ideal, as if our ordinary vague sentences had not yet got a quite unexceptionable sense, and a perfect language awaited construction by us. – On the other hand it seems clear that where there is sense there must be perfect order. – So there must be perfect order even in the vaguest sentence.[69]

In contrast to Russell's and Frege's "perfect language," Wittgenstein shows that truth can be found even in, and precisely in, the "vaguest sentence."

Wittgenstein's change of opinion about the question of vagueness may indeed circle back to Peirce, through the figure of Frank P. Ramsey.[70] Ramsey, a Cambridge mathematician who died at the age of 26, studied Peirce and knew Russell and Wittgenstein personally. (He may have also inspired Woolf's choice in the profession and name of the semi-fictional portrait of the father, the philosopher Mr. Ramsay, in *To The Lighthouse*.[71]) Ramsey's influence on Wittgenstein's philosophical revisions in *Philosophical Investigations* is undeniable – in the Preface, Wittgenstein notes that "to a degree which I myself am hardly able to estimate," the changes were instigated "by the criticism which my ideas encountered from Frank Ramsey, with whom I discussed them in innumerable conversations during the last two years of his life" (*PI* xe). Similarly, Ramsey himself stressed Peirce's influence on his own later thought; in "Truth and Probability" (1929), he writes, "What follows to the end of the section is almost entirely based on the writings of C. S. Peirce."[72] While the extent of Ramsey's effect on the pragmatic strain of the later Wittgenstein is hotly debated, what is notable is Ramsey's emphasis in his last writings (and therefore perhaps in these conversations recalled by Wittgenstein) on the importance of vagueness.[73] For example, in a late paper entitled "Philosophy," Ramsey writes:

> I could not see how we could understand a word and not be able to recognize whether a proposed definition of it was or was not correct. I did not realize the vagueness of the whole idea of understanding … The chief danger to our philosophy, apart from laziness and woolliness is *scholasticism*, the essence of which is treating what is vague as if it were precise and trying to fit it into an exact logical category.[74]

Ramsey's revised approach to the meaning of words like "understanding" and his refusal to treat "what is vague as if it were precise" foreshadow Wittgenstein's focus on the vagueness (*Vagheit*) of language games.

Contemporary debates about vagueness in philosophy, and particularly sorites paradoxes, raise two main issues pertinent to modernist fiction. First, if, as some vagueness theorists argue, vagueness is *epistemic*, that is, if boundaries of vague terms are not actually blurry but "our failure to detect a sharp transition" is "merely a defect in our knowledge," then vagueness could be (ideally) eliminated, and greater and greater precision should smooth the problems apparent in definition and communication.[75] Certain strains of literary modernism, embodied in Ernest Hemingway or

T. E. Hulme, or, as I will discuss, elements of James Joyce, seem to yearn for this ideal precision. Henry James's assertion that Flaubert's *mot juste* nonetheless misses something "beneath and behind, that belongs to the realm of vagueness and uncertainty," seems to deny this possible cure for vagueness.[76] Second, if vagueness is not epistemic but *semantic*, that is, if it is not just that we do not have enough knowledge about the case at hand to determine whether a borderline heap is a grain or a heap (or whether Orlando is a man or a woman) but that there is no actual answer, then vagueness might demonstrate "some real indeterminacy in the non-linguistic world itself"; hence, the arguments that "vague language undermines [philosophical] realism."[77] Writings by both William James and Wittgenstein appear to contend that vagueness might be semantic, and the philosophic idea that there might be "some real indeterminacy in the non-linguistic world itself" dovetails with early twentieth-century discoveries in quantum physics, which, as Karen Barad has argued, put both objective observation and the "indeterminacy" of the matter to study under intense scrutiny.[78] Engagement with semantic vagueness seems particularly germane to the revision of character, motivation, and consciousness occurring in modern novels.

While Henry James, Woolf, and Joyce all had personal ties to the philosophers and thinkers investigating vagueness, particularly William James, Peirce, Russell, and Ogden, they were also writing in a cultural and intellectual climate that encountered and countered the limitations of precision. Why did literary realism, like a transparent language of logic, prove insufficient at the beginning of the twentieth century for capturing the vagaries of consciousness or modern life? Woolf rephrases this question when she asks, "Is life like this? Must novels be like this?" Woolf herself posed one famous answer to those questions, when she argued that fiction needed to change because "on or about December 1910 human character changed" (*EVW* 3:421–422). Woolf labels this a "very vague" assertion and omits mentioning the possible historical factors behind her choice of that date, such as the death of Edward VII and succession of George V in May or the first Post-Impressionist exhibit in November. In addition to changes in government and art, another important event in that year – specifically in December 1910 – was Russell's and Alfred North Whitehead's publication of the first volume of *Principia Mathematica*, setting out proofs for the logical basis of all mathematics.[79] The imprecision of Woolf's declaration – "on or about" – is very different from the logically sound symbolic language set out in that work. Woolf specifically calls attention to the imprecision of her declaration; she writes that the "change" in human character was not "definite," like a "hen [that] had laid an egg" (*EVW* 3:421–422). Indeed, although Woolf adds that one "may well complain of the vagueness of my language" (*EVW* 3:431), assertions such as "on or about December 1910 human character changed" embrace vagueness for tone and irony while crystallizing the distinction between Woolf's vision of "reality" and that endorsed by philosophers like Russell (*EVW* 3:431). In the following pages, I will examine the simultaneous revolt against positivism in certain strains of philosophy and fiction in the modernist era, as I argue that we should read vagueness – whether it be indefinability, fuzziness, or the reconceptualization of literary realism – not as an aesthetic deficiency but as a defining attribute of much modernist fiction.

Most books on literary modernisms must begin by noting the vagueness of the literary period and style they wish to describe. Modernism, critics claim, is a generally recognizable phenomenon, but when it began (1500? 1865? 1890? 1900?) or when it ended (1930? 1939? 2020?) is impossible to pin down. The exact qualities required for a text to count as "modernist" are also up for debate. So, for example, Peter Nicholls begins *Modernisms* with "[t]he beginnings of modernism, like its endings, are largely indeterminate," and Michael Levenson begins his seminal work, *A Genealogy of Modernism*, with the disclaimer:

> Vague terms still signify. Such is the case with "modernism": it is at once vague and unavoidable. Anything more precise would exclude too much too soon; anything more general would be folly. As with any blunt instrument, the best that can be done is to use it for the rough tasks and to reserve the finer work for finer tools.[80]

Modernist Fiction and Vagueness begins neither by lamenting the vague borders of the period it will study, nor by worrying about the "blunt tool" of vague language. Instead, it opens by declaring that the vagueness of the category of modernism itself nicely mirrors the character of much modernist fiction.

CHAPTER I

"The Re-instatement of the Vague": The James Brothers and Charles S. Peirce

1. The Art of Vagueness

> As I breathe over again at any rate the comparative confidence in which I so moved I feel it as a confidence in the positive saving virtue of vagueness.
>
> –Henry James, *Notes of a Son and Brother*[1]

"Logicians have been at fault in giving Vagueness the go-by," declared Charles Sanders Peirce in 1875, but "I have worked out the logic of vagueness with something like completeness" (*CP* 5:446, 5:506). One of the places where he "worked out" his approach to vagueness was, as he remembered, "in a Metaphysical Club in Cambridge, Massachusetts" (*CP* 6:482). In *The Metaphysical Club*, Louis Menand asserts the "enormous" influence that a group of young men including Charles Peirce and William James (as well as John Dewey and Oliver Wendell Holmes) who formed this club in 1872 had on twentieth-century America: "Their ideas changed the way Americans thought – and continue to think – about education, democracy, liberty, justice, and tolerance."[2] This club was where Peirce first presented his "sort of logical gospel" called *Pragmatism*. Pragmatism's investment in vagueness, I will argue, likewise had an "enormous" influence beyond "The American Scene" in the transnational modern novels of Henry James.[3]

To Henry James, on the spot, these meetings of a metaphysical club seemed more amusing than history-making, because, as he recalls, the group included "my brother, and various other long-headed youths" who "wrangle grimly and stick to the question. It gives me a headache merely to know of it."[4] But many years later Henry James found the fruits of these discussions less risible, when he praised William's pragmatism: "I'm *with* you, all along the line . . . As an artist & a 'creator' I can catch on, hold on, to pragmatism, & can work in the light of it."[5] In the following pages I will demonstrate that Henry James was largely "*with*" his brother, because William James's debunking of idealism for pragmatic vagueness mirrored

Henry James's own revision of literary realism to incorporate the vagueness of experience. When William James contends in *The Principles of Psychology*, "It is, in short, the re-instatement of the vague to its proper place in our mental life which I am so anxious to press on the attention," he emphasizes the vagueness of the "stream of consciousness," language, and perception (*PP* 1:254). Similarly, when Henry James declared himself early in his career "*the* novelist of the future," he foreshadows his "major phase" investment in psychological complexity, abstract dialogue, and indeterminate plot and morality.[6] As opposed to the realism of French novelists like Flaubert, Henry James emphasizes that there is a realm of "vagueness and uncertainty" that any good novelist must capture, because "[t]he only reason for the existence of a novel is that it does attempt to represent life."[7]

In *The Trial of Curiosity*, Ross Posnock offers "a study of the relation of Henry and William James and their response to modernity."[8] Part of their mutual "response to modernity," I contend, was an engagement with the vagueness of language as a fruitful means for both philosophic investigation and narrative inspiration. Indeed, if Henry James's writing can be considered pragmatic – as he himself declared to William after reading *Pragmatism*, "I was lost in the wonder of the extent to which all my life I have (like M. Jourdain) unconsciously pragmatised"[9] – the kind of pragmatism Henry James had "unconsciously" been enacting was, importantly, William's. Although Peirce believed himself to be the first rigorous theorist of vagueness, his pragmatism (later renamed "pragmaticism") aimed ideally to eliminate vagueness, because the truths that he sought were concrete and real. Peirce's pragmaticism came full circle to foster a new kind of idealism – an irony that Henry James, I argue, was to dramatize in the victory of "the great vagueness" in "The Beast in the Jungle" (*Beast* 762). Henry James's narrative style and fictional plots (both unconsciously and at times consciously) resist Peirce's philosophy; his major phase stylistic revolution mirrors William James's promotion of vagueness in philosophy.

Henry James's "notoriously abstract" language, coupled with metaphorical extravagance, has led critics since F. R. Leavis to insist that James "went wrong in his later development."[10] William James's endorsement of ordinary language over technological and mathematical formulae, for which he received some scorn, finds parallels in Henry James's later style, for which he, too, was ridiculed. In part, William embraced ordinary language because it enabled popular audiences to benefit from his philosophy. This motivation, of course, could be viewed in exact opposition to Henry, whose writing has often been deemed too difficult for the ordinary reader. However, Henry, like his brother, longed to reach a popular audience, as his desire to write for the stage demonstrates.[11] William did not eschew math only from a desire to be popular, but also because he believed that the flux of language paralleled the flux of life. Similarly, Henry included in his fiction, as William noted, "many pages, and innumerable sentences" that required reading "twice over to see what the dickens they could possibly mean."[12] Ian Watt explains that this difficulty stems from James's "verbal idiosyncrasies," which include a "preference for non-transitive verbs; many abstract nouns; much use of 'that' . . . and the presence of a great many negatives and near-negatives."[13] As with William's own stream of consciousness, Henry James's language in works such as "The Beast in the Jungle," *The Sacred Fount*, and *The Ambassadors* underscores relation and change rather than fixed meanings. In his plots, too, he embraced vagueness, as he replaced marriage plots in works like *The Ambassadors* with long stretches of dialogue and indeterminate revelations. James's vagueness links his predilection for Gothic storytelling to his modern American philosophy. Friends and early critics chastised him for the "inadequacy of the 'story'" or his novels' culmination, far too often, with merely "another evaporated marriage."[14] Yet he was happy to thwart, as William noted, "every traditional canon of story-telling (especially the fundamental one of *telling* the story, wh. you carefully avoid)."[15] Like William, Henry did not want to follow received traditions if they failed to capture the vagueness of consciousness and experience. Indeed, Henry James's literary style forces readers to experience the same bewilderment and uncertainty that William James often analyzed in contemporary society.

To see Henry James as vague may go contrary to his traditional image as the stately, patrician man of letters who created the solid monument of the New York Edition. The aristocratic James would humorously denounce, for example, "The world, stupid and vulgar as it is, and a large part of which has about as much literary sense as the chair on which I sit (or, rather, much less – for the chair is *mine* and has known the contact of my superior person)."[16] This James felt it his duty to theorize the novel for an English reading public who continued wrong-headedly to believe that "a novel is a novel, as a pudding is a pudding, and that our only business with it could be to swallow it" (*HJLC* 1:44). Whereas James declared himself a realist, who vouched that "the air of reality (solidity of specification) seems to me to be the supreme virtue of a novel" (*HJLC* 1:53), his critics have tended to tar him with the brush of aestheticism. Posnock diagnoses James's critical reputation succinctly:

> James's own reputation illustrates the collision between two prestigious ideologies: modernity, which represses ambiguity, and literary modernism, which valorizes it. Because of political and historical circumstances ... American literary intellectuals have tended to conceive of modernism as an enclave of resistance to modernity. James has often been enlisted as a canonical modernist upholding an idealist dichotomy that opposes art to life. Thus it has been easy to assimilate him to antimodernist modernism and to ignore how, in significant ways, his stance actually belies this tradition.[17]

For the last twenty years James critics have worked, with limited success, to overthrow James's reputation as a Wildean aesthete and an embodiment of what Posnock calls "antimodernist modernism." The difficulty of James's dense style often forces critics to look away from the late fiction to nonfiction works such as *The American Scene* to make their case for his modernity.[18] My project, building on work by Posnock, Richard Poirier, Lisi Schoenbach, and Joan Richardson, seeks to overturn the anti-modern approach to James by focusing on his pragmatic modernism. James's difficult fictional style is not a retreat into aestheticism but instead reflects his own engagement with the ramifications of pragmatism on literary realism. I argue that James's meaning of a "realist" and his injunctions for the novel are importantly influenced by pragmatic vagueness.[19] Furthermore, my examination of James's depiction of the indeterminacy of categories such as gender, sexuality, and nationality expands upon studies that argue for a "queer" or "global" James that ultimately challenge Leon Edel's iconic depiction of "The Master."[20]

For William James, the topic of vagueness highlights the question of boundaries. Where does the stream of consciousness end, and where does it begin? How do we terminologically do justice to something that does not have discrete parts but exists in flux? Here, too, Henry James's fiction finds parallels with William's philosophical vagueness. "Really, universally, relations stop nowhere," Henry James writes in his first Preface to his New York Editions in 1907, "and the exquisite problem of the artist is eternally but to draw, by a geometry of his own, the circle within which they shall happily *appear* to do so."[21] Two years later, summing up his approach in *A Pluralistic Universe*, William James asserts, "No philosophy can ever be anything but a summary sketch, a picture of a world in abridgement, a foreshortened bird's-eye view of the perspective of events."[22] Henry James believed that fiction should be "*discutable*" (although not too theoretical) and that careful attention to the techniques of fiction, to point of view, and to the construction of novels was essential to the literary endeavor (*HJLC* 1:44). How to structure a novel carefully while allowing for the free play of experience constituted Henry James's greatest challenge, and his sense of success, in novels like *The Ambassadors*, led to his declaration that "the Novel remains still, under the right persuasion, the most independent, most elastic, most prodigious of literary forms" (*A* xlvii).

In the opening part of my chapter, I will outline the difference between the pragmatisms of William James and Charles Peirce and demonstrate the parallel between William's criticisms of Peirce and Henry's critical essays on Flaubert. Peirce, a notorious American philosopher during his lifetime, and Flaubert, the great French man of letters, may seem an odd coupling, but they were two significant figures whom Henry James befriended in the winter of 1875 in Paris when he was germinating important thoughts about the novel (published as "The Minor French Novelists"). Moreover, the James brothers' critical responses to Flaubert and Peirce challenge the virtue of specificity and precision. This section will set out a hypothesis about Henry James's growing vagueness over the course of his career, from his first novel *Watch and Ward* to his major phase achievement of *The Ambassadors*.

From the James brothers' "re-instatement of the vague" in philosophy and literary criticism, I will move to demonstrate the ways in which Henry James's interest in vagueness manifests itself in his fiction, specifically in James's resistance to marriage plots, investment in vague secrets, and abstract dialogue. I start with James's first novel, *Watch and Ward*, a text that is under-examined by James critics, perhaps because James himself disowned it. With its happily-ever-married conclusion and virtuous protagonists, *Watch and Ward* crystallizes the novelistic tradition from which James was turning away. However, *Watch and Ward* also acts as a rough draft for James's later works in its focus on an overwhelming secret. "The Beast in the Jungle" and "The Figure in the Carpet" can be seen to revise *Watch and Ward* by making their secrets finally unknowable. I contend that these unresolvable secrets are related to pragmatic vagueness and therefore have no precise meaning. In fact, I argue that Charles Peirce (rather than William James or Henry James as had been claimed) is the most likely source for John Marcher because of Peirce's writings on vagueness. James's irony, in these tales and in *The Sacred Fount*, lies in depicting the dire consequences for characters focused on deciphering a secret's meaning while missing the effects – the meaning in pragmatic terms – of the secret on themselves and their fellow spectators. A central paradox in James's fiction is that while his works often dramatize this irony, his later novels lead his readers to the same experience of uncertainty. Like the Atlantic-crossing Lambert Strether in *The Ambassadors*, readers must learn to decipher the fragments and ambiguities offered by an unmoored transnational modernity.

In the final section of the chapter, I turn to *The Ambassadors* to examine the culmination of vagueness in the novel James called "the best, 'all round' of my productions" (*A* xxxi). Overwhelming secrets again permeate *The Ambassadors*, stretching from the indeterminate object manufactured in Woollett, which finances Chad Newsome's life abroad, to the exact nature of Chad's "virtuous attachment" (*A* 128) to Madame de Vionnet. Strether's appreciation of the effects of Chad's "virtuous attachment" leads to the derailment of Strether's "New England conscience" by the "vague voice of Paris."[23] In *The Ambassadors*, in syntax as vague as the relations in which Strether finds himself embroiled, Henry James dramatizes the difficulty of making moral choices in a vague new world.

2. The Two Pragmatisms and Henry James's Criticism

> Philosophically, in short, I am "with" you, almost completely, & you ought to take account of this & get me over altogether.
>
> –Henry James, letter to William James[24]

> there is a danger in
> over-obscurity what
> happened through my
> training danger might be
> lessened if logical
> analysis is an art
>
> –Susan Howe, *Peirce-Arrow*[25]

Vagueness and pragmatism were intimately united from the start. Although Charles Peirce later recalled that he "used to preach" about "Pragmatism" to the metaphysical club, the actual published papers that William James later called "the birth certificates" of pragmatism, entitled "Illustrations of the Logic of Science," most directly address the topic of vagueness.[26] Similarly, it is in the first significant work William James published after their club (although, lamentably to James himself, nearly twenty years in the making) that he calls for his "re-instatement of the vague" (*PP* 1:254). Vagueness, as it affects both the terminology of philosophy and the final truths this reasoning revealed, was a topic of interest to both William James and Charles Peirce, and, as a way to undermine idealism, it was central to the formation of the pragmatic method. Similarly, when Henry James criticized French realist writing, its intrinsic lack of "vagueness" led him to pronounce it "*dead*" (*HJLC* 2:176).

The centrality of vagueness in the formation of the pragmatic method is evident in Peirce's first two papers in "Illustrations of the Logic of Science": "The Fixation of Belief" and "How to Make Our Ideas Clear." In "The Fixation of Belief," Peirce regrets that "common sense, or thought as it first emerges above the level of the narrowly practical, is deeply imbued with that bad logical quality to which the epithet *metaphysical* is commonly applied," so he asserts, "nothing can clear it up but a severe course of logic."[27] Therefore, in his second paper, "How to Make Our Ideas Clear," he applies such a course and attempts to get to the root of vagueness, because "the very first lesson that we have a right to demand that logic shall teach us is, how to make our ideas clear."[28] Rather than generating fuzzy metaphysical ideals, Peirce argues that "the whole function of thought is to produce habits of action"; hence, "Our idea of anything *is* our idea of its sensible effects."[29] Transcendental truths, such as "Evil – with a very big E," as Fanny Assingham calls it in *The Golden Bowl*, have meaning purely in their effects.[30]

By the time Peirce is called upon to write for the 1902 *Dictionary of Philosophy and Psychology*, he defines pragmatism as:

> The opinion that metaphysics is to be largely cleared up by the application of the following maxim for attaining clearness of apprehension: "Consider what effects, that might conceivably have practical bearings, we conceive the object of our conception to have. Then, our conception of these effects is the whole of our conception of the object."[31]

Pragmatism will allow for "clearness of apprehension" because "the whole of our conception of the object" can be reduced to its effects. The pragmatic method, according to Peirce, will eliminate vagueness, because effects are clear and recognizable. Later in his life, Peirce attempted to distance himself both from this assertion and from William James's pragmatism, because he wanted to clarify that pragmatism "was only a method; the truths which it sought to discover were absolute and eternal."[32] However, even Peirce acknowledged that his earlier work smacked of nominalism, which aims to undermine such "absolute and eternal" truths.[33] From its genesis, the pragmatic method focused on the question of vagueness, but Peirce and William James ended up with antithetical opinions about the vagueness of language and the truths that language could reveal.

Indeed, the differing, evolving attitudes to vagueness of Peirce and William James help to explain the precise difference between their pragmatisms, so important to Peirce that he had to coin a new term, *Pragmaticism*, which he hoped "is ugly enough to be safe from kidnappers" (*CP* 5: 414). "Philosophy cannot become scientifically healthy," Peirce warned, until each term "should be confined to a single meaning which, however broad, must be free from all vagueness" (*CP* 8:169). Peirce hoped to eradicate the vagueness of philosophy and to create "a technical vocabulary, composed of words so unattractive that loose thinkers are not tempted to use them." For Peirce, philosophy ought to aim to become a strict science; he was a logician who favored mathematics, and he noted James's "almost unexampled incapacity for mathematical thought, combined with intense hatred for logic" (*CP* 6:182). Peirce chided James in letters for his preference for word-play and metaphor. "It is downright bad morals so to misuse words," he complained, "for it prevents philosophy from becoming a science."

William James, however, resisted Peirce's move to eliminate vagueness through his scientific approach to philosophy and psychology. "Of course you are right in the logical world, where every term is changeless to eternity, but the real world is incongruent," William responded to Peirce's criticisms, and "logical terms only mark static *positions* in a flux which nowhere is static."[34] Because even "logical terms" merely mark feigned "static positions," James preferred ordinary language whose vagueness mirrored that of the world in "flux." James wrote that our normal idea of "language works against our perception of the truth," if we look for a word to refer to a single thing; instead, "[w]hat each really knows is clearly the thing it is named for, with dimly perhaps a thousand other things" (*PP* 1:241). Indeed, this is the strength of language: "a thousand other things" are captured in merely one word.

For William James, even language's conjunctions and prepositions are useful tools, because they capture the sense of consciousness in flux.[35]

> There is not a conjunction or a preposition, and hardly an adverbial phrase, syntactic form, or inflection of voice, in human speech, that does not express some shading or other of relation which we at some moment actually feel to exist between the larger objects of our thought ... it is the stream of consciousness that matches each of them by an inward coloring of its own. In either case the relations are numberless, and no existing language is capable of doing justice to all their shades. We ought to say a feeling of *and*, a feeling of *if*, a feeling of *but*, and a feeling of *by*, quite as readily as we say a feeling of *blue* or a feeling of *cold*. Yet we do not ... (*PP* 1:245–246)

James proposes that one could attribute feelings to prepositions and conjunctions just as well as to nouns and adjectives because all are tinged by their relationship to the words surrounding them and to the individual's stream of consciousness. In contrast to Peirce's prediction that the future of philosophy involved an entirely new kind of terminology, William James thought it was language's very flexibility – and its dependence on *relation* – that made it the best tool to describe psychological and philosophical truths (*CP* 8:169).

Peirce's and James's differences of opinion about vagueness also apply to the kind of truth the pragmatic method aimed to attain. Peirce hoped that the entire scientific community, applying the pragmatic method, was moving toward a single concrete Truth. He argued, "We all hope that the different scientific inquiries in which we are severally engaged are going ultimately to lead to some definitely established conclusion, which conclusion we endeavor to anticipate in some measure" (*CP* 7:188). "Truth" for Peirce was "the opinion which is fated to be ultimately agreed to by all who investigate" (*CP* 5:407). William James, in contrast, stretched pragmatism to its logical extreme, where truth and expediency were equated. In *Pragmatism*, he wrote a sentence that has now become famous: "'The true,' to put it very briefly, is only the expedient in the way of our thinking, just as 'the right' is only the expedient in the way of our behaving."[36] In William James's writing, even the truths (like his image of consciousness as a stream) remain unfixable, "plastic," and "malleable" (*PMT* 36–7). James's tendency to view material action as the end result of the pragmatic method dismayed Peirce; to view pragmatism as both "a method" and "a genetic theory of what is meant by truth," as James announced in *Pragmatism*, was incorrect, according to Peirce.[37] For William James, one final fixed Truth is meaningless; there are merely multiple truths, a claim that constitutes an essential difference between pragmatism and Peirce's pragmaticism. Henry James also dramatizes the moral questions stemming from this difference, a point to which I will return in my reading of *The Ambassadors*.

In the "Stream of Thought" section of *The Principles of Psychology*, where he argues for the reinstatement of the vague, William James depicts the meaning of vagueness in his psychology. In the same year that Henry James published "The Art of Fiction," William James was writing "On Some Omissions of Introspective Psychology," which became, with revisions, the famous stream-of-consciousness chapter. The metaphor of "a stream of consciousness" is vague: "Consciousness, then, does not appear to itself chopped up in bits . . . It is nothing jointed; it flows . . . In talking of it hereafter, let us call it the stream of thought, of consciousness, or of subjective life."[38] The "stream" in philosophical terms is "vague" because its lacks a precise boundary. James's view of human psychology suggests the sorites paradox applied to consciousness. As James writes, "who should say a river consists of nothing but pailsful, spoonsful, quartsful, barrelsful" (etc.)? It would be impossible to divide a river into such parts, just as consciousness and language are not merely made up of their "substantive" parts but derive meaning from their flow.[39] When James advances the notion of "the re-instatement of the vague," he summarizes his approach to consciousness and demonstrates that the vagueness of a "rapid continuous stream" best catches the psychological process. *The Principles of Psychology* also includes a section entitled "*Our Images Are Usually Vague*" and one section that questions, "*Are Vague Images Abstract Ideas?*" (*PP* 2:44). Indeed, William Joseph Gavin states that James's interest in vagueness spans his entire career; "[o]nce James worked out the importance of 'the vague' in *The Principles*," he argues, "he never abandoned it."[40]

Just as William James criticized Peirce's over-precision, so also Henry James criticized the realism of Gustave Flaubert in early critical essays whose central themes would be reiterated throughout James's career. In fact, the similarity of the James brothers' criticisms may not just be coincidental, because Henry James had himself (according to William's description) "fallen into the arms of C. S. Peirce," when Peirce was formulating his key ideas about vagueness and pragmatism during the winter of 1875 in France.[41] In his letters home to William, the young Henry James merely laments Peirce's lack of social skills, but I believe that his response to Peirce's philosophizing – and particular philosophy – found an alternative outlet in his critical essay on Flaubert of that February, "The Minor French Novelists." James's criticism of the "intellectual conviction" underlying Flaubert's style – resulting in a "laborious monument to a treacherous ideal" – while ostensibly aimed solely at Flaubert, simultaneously smacks of an attack on Peirce and his as yet unnamed philosophy (*HJLC* 2:176).

In Henry James's 1881 journal, the "unspotted blank-book" started during his return visit to Boston, he asserts, "I shall not attempt to write the history of that year" – the year 1875 at 29 Rue de Luxembourg.[42] However, he recalls the most important personages from that winter in Paris, a "time by no means misspent," among them Peirce and Gustave Flaubert. James writes: "I saw a good deal of Charles Peirce that winter – as to whom his being a man of genius reconciled me to much that was intolerable in him."[43] In his letters to William, he explains his friendship with Peirce: "We meet every two or three days to dine together; but tho' we get on very well, our sympathy is economical rather than intellectual."[44] Furthermore, he elaborates upon Peirce's "intolerable" behavior: "He is a very good fellow, and one must appreciate his mental ability, but he has too little social talent, too little art of making himself agreeable."[45] Peirce, although he admitted that Henry "isn't as fond of turning over questions as I am," concluded that the younger James brother was also a "splendid fellow."[46]

In "The Minor French Novelists," James famously censures the "realism" of contemporary French novelists, writers like Flaubert who believe that "[h]uman life . . . is before all things a spectacle, a thing to be looked at, seen, apprehended, enjoyed with the eyes" (*HJLC* 2:170). James called reading *L'Education Sentimentale* "like masticating ashes and sawdust" (*HJLC* 2:176). Even those who praise Flaubert's writing, he asserts, admire it for being "philosophical," because "there is always an idea which holds them up and carries them along" (*HJLC* 2:176). James's response to *The Sentimental Education* was part of a more general attack on the version of clarity and the notation of detail favored by some realists, what he called an "artificial method" (*HJLC* 2:178). Just as Peirce's pragmatism asserts that metaphysics can be cleared up by simply observing the effects, so also Flaubert's realism, according to James, reduces life to an observable phenomenon: "What our eyes show us is all that we are sure of; so with this we will, at any rate, begin . . . it is very possible that with this also we may end" (*HJLC* 2:170). James denies that through observation the novelist can capture the reality of "human life," and he distances himself from a theory like Flaubert's in which "[w]e care only for what *is* – we know nothing about what ought to be" (*HJLC* 2:170).

James allows that writers like Flaubert "admit nevertheless that there is something else, beneath and behind, that belongs to the realm of vagueness and uncertainty, and into this we must occasionally dip . . . On the whole, we will leave it to take care of itself, and let it come off as it may" (*HJLC* 2:170). James's tone in this assertion, particularly given that his article culminates with the highest praise for George Sand, who "has the true, the great imagination – the metaphysical imagination," seems highly ironic (*HJLC* 2:183). For a great artist to squander his gifts on the "outside" of life, only to "admit" *of course* that there may be something greater than the squalid details of value in human life, is for James the tragedy of contemporary French literature. James continually laments that the French novel has lost its "charm"; and just as he believed Peirce fell short, in having "too little art of making himself agreeable," so also his final highest praise for Sand is that "she is easy and universal and – above all – agreeable" (*HJLC* 2:182–183). James suggests that being relentlessly caught up in any kind of theory that espouses exactitude, as are Peirce and the school of Flaubert, denies life both its essential meaning and (not a venial sin for James) its essential charm.

James's choice of the term "the realm of vagueness and uncertainty" – as a description of the ineffable, perhaps metaphysical, quality that "*dead*" novels like *L'Education Sentimentale* lack – is pointed in terms of Peirce's pragmatism (*HJLC* 2:176). In contrast to Peirce's aim to refine vagueness out of existence, Henry James chastises Flaubert for ignoring vagueness, which becomes aligned with the imagination. "The French mind likes better to squeeze things into a formula that mutilates them, if need be," James laments, "than to leave them in the frigid vague" (*HJLC* 2:41). The vague may be finally unknowable, but, as James adds in a letter, fiction must be "bodied forth out of the vague of imagination."[47]

Indeed, in "The Art of Fiction" (1884), perhaps James's most pre-eminent critical pronouncement, published nine years after "The Minor French Novelists" (1876), vagueness again becomes central to James's definition of realism. Although an "air of reality" is necessary in fiction, realism is not limited to the detailed observations of Flaubert (*HJLC* 1:53). Rather, in order to be "one of the people on whom nothing is lost!" (*HJLC* 1:53), James insists it is essential to capture experience, which is as vague in Henry James's portrayal as it is in William James's "stream." Henry James writes:

> Experience is never limited, and it is never complete; it is an immense sensibility, a kind of huge spider-web of the finest silken threads suspended in the chamber of consciousness, and catching every air-born particle in its tissue. (*HJLC* 1:52)

Realism cannot confine itself to detail but must also extend to "truth," the truth of this unlimited spider web of "consciousness." Moreover, the forms of fiction are as varied and fluctuating as experience, because "[h]umanity is immense, and reality has a myriad forms; the most one can affirm is that some of the flowers of fiction have the odour of it, and others have not" (*HJLC* 1:52). James is not willing to commit himself to a single view of the "myriad forms" of "reality," nor of realist fiction.

Therefore, he also pointedly undermines Walter Besant's claim to have a strict definition of the moral purposes of "The Art of Fiction." Rhetorically, James appears to agree with Besant that in discussion of artistic morality there must be absolute precision. "Vagueness, in such a discussion, is fatal," he asserts (*HJLC* 1:62). However, he immediately undercuts Besant's assertions against vagueness by asking, "What is the meaning of your morality and your conscious moral purpose? Will you not define your terms and explain how (a novel being a picture) a picture can be either moral or immoral?" (*HJLC* 1:62). James implies that Besant has painted himself into a corner. There are no precise definitions of "conscious moral purpose," a point that James further emphasizes by putting "conscious moral purpose" in quotation marks to distance himself from Besant's suggestion (*HJLC* 1:51). "Vagueness" is not only not "fatal" to the discussion of fiction, but also part of the definition of "The Art of Fiction," because "the value of these different injunctions – so beautiful and so vague – is wholly in the meaning one attaches to them"; this meaning is, however, impossible "to fix" (*HJLC* 1:51).

In contrast to Besant's precise "conscious moral purpose" (*HJLC* 1:62), Henry James dictates that his only moral injunction is for artistic "freedom," which allows for the maximum variety of forms of fiction (*HJLC* 1:64). Indeed, his similar call for artistic freedom in a letter perhaps comes closest to explicating what T. S. Eliot would later mean by his declaration that James "had a mind so fine that no idea could violate it."[48] James insists:

> But I *have* no view of life and literature, I maintain, other than that our form of the latter in especial is admirable exactly by its range and variety, its plasticity and liberality, its fairly living on the sincere and shifting experience of the individual practitioner.[49]

Henry James's choice of terms for depicting life and literature – "range," "variety," "plasticity," and "shifting" – recall William James's similar characterizations of consciousness and philosophical truths. Both James brothers resist precision and fixity.

Indeed, throughout Henry James's fiction, "vagueness" or the "vague" highlights that characters are entering the imaginative realm, where logical exegesis in the vein of Peirce's "How to Make Our Ideas Clear" or Flaubert's realism will not suffice.[50] When James enters the mode of the ghost story, he evokes impenetrable "vagueness." Spencer Brydon feels closest to the ghost of himself in "The Jolly Corner" at twilight:

> Then he could, as seemed to him, most intimately wander and wait, linger and listen, feel his fine attention, never in his life before so fine, on the pulse of the great vague place: he preferred the lampless hour and only wished he might have prolonged each day the deep crepuscular spell.[51]

Similarly, in *The Portrait of a Lady*, James emphasizes Isabel's supernatural connection to Ralph Touchett by reiterating the word "vague":

> It seemed to her for an instant that he was standing there – a vague, hovering figure in the vagueness of the room.[52]

There is no clear explanation for Isabel's knowledge of Ralph's death; rather, she has an obscure intuition, and they communicate with "utterances too vague for words." The inexplicable evil of Gilbert Osmond is also tied to his vagueness: He is "a vague, unexplained American" with "eyes at once vague and penetrating."[53]

Reiteration of the word "vague" for Henry James is not a mere stop-gap; rather, in his fiction as in his literary criticism, it implies suggestiveness, unspecified and unspecifiable fruitfulness. He describes Isabel's unknown future with Gilbert as "a last vague space," which her imagination could not "yet" cross, and *The Portrait of a Lady* itself leaves Isabel's fate famously vague.[54] James knew this was the "obvious criticism" to level against the novel, "that I have left her *en l'air*," but he insisted, "The *whole* of anything is never told."[55] Similarly, to a journalist who queried his vague endings, James replied, "Ah is not that the trick life plays? Life leaves you with a question – it asks you questions."[56] Throughout James's notebook entries, his germs for stories are always "vague, nebulous – the mere hint of a hint."[57] Even as he chastises himself for his "too frequent vagueness of mind," his stories, he asserts, come from "their vast vague murmur" (*HJLC* 2:1087).

Henry James was often criticized for his growing stylistic vagueness over the course of his career, so that one headline in 1901 read: "Henry James at His Vaguest: *The Sacred Fount*, His Latest Work, Is Also His Most Characteristic."[58] Between *Watch and Ward* and *The Sacred Fount* or *The Portrait of a Lady* and *The Ambassadors*, James's sentences and metaphors expand while his plots thin. James himself acknowledged that "[a]s one grows older one's manner inevitably becomes more complicated – one's reach, or embrace, ampler."[59] His increasing complexity also ties James to the modern novelists who came after him, like Woolf and Joyce, who more stridently experimented with the forms of fiction. Indeed, James explains that his new verbal experiments are tied to the "high modernism" of his times and seems to welcome in the linguistic turn in modern fiction: "It is the high modernism of the conditions now surrounding, on this continent, the practice of our language that makes of this chapter in its history a new thing under the sun."[60] James notes that the tide of modernity has reached American shores, indelibly affecting the American English language.

James's own literary high modernism, dramatizing pragmatic vagueness, similarly indelibly affected the British high modernist novelists in his wake.

3. "Guess My Riddle": *Watch and Ward*

> Conjecture was useless; she was a vague spot of light on a dark background.
>
> –Henry James, *Watch and Ward*[61]

From 1907–1909, when Henry James set about putting together his "literary monument," the New York Edition of twenty-four volumes, he omitted seven of his novels. But "of all of James's novels only *Watch and Ward* was decisively off James's list from the start."[62] James not only excluded this, his first novel, from the final list, but also pretended it did not even exist, writing in the Preface to *Roderick Hudson* that it, instead, was "my first attempt at a novel."[63] Did James ignore this novel because of its melodramatic content and stylized characters? Or was he ashamed of its all too semi-autobiographical protagonist?[64] Both of those arguments have repeatedly been voiced, and both have merit: As a heroine, Nora fails to have the depth of introspection of James's later creations; as the effete 29-year-old American hero, Roger certainly has parallels to the young James (James was 27 when he wrote the novel, nearly 29 when its final installments were published in *The Atlantic Monthly*). As opposed to arguments that suggest that James excluded *Watch and Ward* because of "lack of concreteness and specificity," I propose that the reverse may be true. The secrets of *Watch and Ward* fail to be vague enough; James's parody fails to be quite parodic enough; and his first novel is answerable to too many of the canons of the traditional novel that he later disdained.[65]

In an essay of 1914, James briefly sketches the history of the novel and emphasizes certain rules that literature seems to follow, certain "superstitions" that past novelists seemed to believe:

> What had this lion in the path been . . . what had it been from far back and straight down through all the Victorian time, but the fond superstition that the key of the situation, of each and every situation that could turn up for the novelist, was the sentimental key, which might fit into no door or window opening on closeness or on freshness at all?[66]

Earlier novelists of both genius and "mediocrity," according to James, have depended upon the "sentimental key" or, what he later calls the "romantic" plotline, as the basis of their fiction. James's critical essay is entitled "The New Novel," and he believes the new novel must not follow in this old tradition from "far back." However, throughout his career James was encouraged to include marriages and happy endings by his publishers and friends. For example, he protests in a letter to William Dean Howells that "in my next novel I promise you there shall be much marrying," and he explains to Elizabeth Boott, "I *do* incline to melancholy endings – but it had been a part of the bargain with Howells that *this* termination should be cheerful and that there should be distinct matrimony."[67] *Watch and Ward* concludes with "distinct matrimony," although James's own preference for "melancholy endings" seems indicated by his inclusion of elements of self-conscious parody.

Watch and Ward was written in the summer of 1870, two years before William and his friends began their metaphysical club, and it tells the story of Roger Lawrence who, reeling from unrequited love, is serendipitously faced with a newly orphaned girl, whom he adopts and raises to be his wife. "Pray for me more than ever," he writes to a friend, "I have begun at the beginning; it will be my own fault if I have n't [sic] a perfect wife" (*WW* 27). Writing about creating a perfect wife was a popular plot (in fact, while James was writing *Watch and Ward*, other stories appeared in *The Atlantic Monthly* on the same theme), and James allows Nora to be perfect indeed. Nora, although "by no means a pretty child," grows into a striking "beauty," and her soul's dream is "[t]o serve Roger, to please Roger" (*WW* 12, 32, 108). Nora's extreme innocence and good nature are never in doubt throughout James's novel, and his well-intentioned protagonist gains the wife he so desires. *Watch and Ward* seems, at first glance, to demonstrate that James has caved in to popular opinion and written a straightforward romance.

However, James pushes at the boundaries of the incestuous and even pedophilic themes of his story, undermining its clear-cut romance. It is hard to believe that the young James would not have implied some sexual undertones in a sentence where the narrator is made to intrude and comment:

> I may add also that, in his desire to order all things well, Roger caught himself wondering whether, at the worst, a little precursory love-making would do any harm. The ground might be gently tickled to receive his sowing; the petals of the young girl's nature, playfully forced apart, would leave the golden heart of the flower but the more accessible to his own vertical rays. (*WW* 46)

While Leon Edel notes that "this is a curious passage to come from an inveterate reader of French novels," he also asserts that "a large innocence seems to reside in the imagery of these passages."[68] However, in my reading, James here seems to undermine both the alleged "innocence" of Roger's intentions and, at the same time, the reader's enjoyment of Roger's innocent "secret." The narrator's overt intrusion here seems to stress a similar metaphoric intrusion into Roger's superficially philanthropic scheme, revealing the sexual impetus behind his "desire to order all things well." *Watch and Ward*, in its refusal to keep latent content at a distance, acts as a parody of similar tales even as it diligently narrates the success of Roger's dreams. Ellis Hanson, in "Screwing with Children in Henry James," similarly undermines the "innocence" in James's depiction of children. He argues that James plays upon the reader's "inadmissible" desires "to participate with perverse pleasure rather than paranoid disavowal in the queer erotics of children."[69] I would add that in later tales like "The Turn of the Screw," James carefully distances such erotic play with formal attributes such as the framed narrative and ghost story genre, whereas the "erotics of children" is manifest in *Watch and Ward*. This may have contributed to James's desire to suppress this first novel.

James wrote to Charles Eliot Norton that he thought that the subject of *Watch and Ward* was "slight"; however, he added, "I have tried to make a work of art, and if you are good enough to read it I trust you will detect my intention. A certain form will be its chief merit."[70] The "certain form" he refers to may be parody, a Jamesian revision of popular women's fiction.[71] The scene that most discomforts those who promote the innocence of *Watch and Ward* reinforces this reading. Nora has lost the key to her watch and interrupts Roger and the dashing scoundrel Hubert, to ask to borrow a key:

> Roger's key proved a complete misfit, so that she had recourse to Hubert's. It hung on the watch-chain which depended from his waistcoat, and some rather intimate fumbling was needed to adjust it to Nora's diminutive timepiece. It worked admirably, and she stood looking at him with a little smile of caution as it creaked on the pivot. (*WW* 67)

"How conscious James was of the [sexual imagery] is a moot point," Edel argues, but it is not moot if it emphasizes the parody intended by James, which he trusts his readers will "detect." James underscores the sexual inappropriateness of Roger's attraction to Nora – "She's only a child," Hubert warns (*WW* 67) – when Roger's "key" is a "complete misfit." Earlier in the novel, when Roger has figured his heart as locked, it is Nora's "childishness" that opens it – "a child's fingers were fumbling with the key" to his bachelor heart, he thinks (*WW* 65, 14). Roger's attempt to transform the child he adopts into the woman he desires does not take into account the role Nora has learned to play in his life. The title of the novel, *Watch and Ward*, seems both to emphasize Roger's official duty (as Nora's watch and warden) and to highlight this important later "watch" moment. Nora is meant to be a ward to Roger's watch, but his desire to become her husband does not seem to "fit" either his own ideals of what is right or Nora's burgeoning desire. As if foreshadowing his later scornful comments about the centrality of the sentimental "key" to previous generations of novelists, James's own "key" scene undermines his romantic tale.

James solidifies his ironic attitude to earlier novels in Roger's statement about "silly" novels, and here Roger reveals (to the readers at least) his deep "secret."[72] Nora asserts that "no novel is so silly I can't read it" and admits that she indulges in novels in which "a young clergyman endowed with every grace ... falls in love with a fair Papist" (*WW* 104). The plot of *Watch and Ward* neatly mirrors Nora's book, because Hubert, the clergyman, both vies for her affection and warns her not to become a Catholic in Europe, to which she retorts, "I'll have no Pope but you" (*WW* 76). Roger, our stolid hero, has no such delight in novels, nor their romantic tales, or so he alleges. "The fact is, Nora," he tells her, "all novels seem to me stupid. They are nothing to what *I* can Fancy! I have in my heart a prettier romance than any of them!" The irony in Roger's situation is that, of course, the pretty "romance" that he has "in [his] heart" is exactly the stuff of novels and is in fact the plot of *Watch and Ward*. "My *dénouement* is not yet written," Roger states, writing himself into the book. "Wait till the story is finished," he continues, "then you shall hear the whole" (*WW* 39). But as Roger's audience, the readers need not "wait till the story is finished" to learn his secret.

Tzvetan Todorov, in "The Secret of Narrative," argues compellingly that the theme that ties together many of James's narratives is a "quest for an absolute and absent cause," and in his narratives he "constantly postpones, protects the revelation – until the story's end, if not beyond."[73] Todorov traces this pattern in a variety of James's tales from "In the Cage" to *The Turn of the Screw*, and it should be added that such a postponed "revelation" is also at work in the major novels, from the treachery of Gilbert Osmond in *The Portrait of a Lady* to the level of intimacy of Prince Amerigo and Charlotte Stant in *The Golden Bowl*. James constructs his very first novel precisely around such a pattern but, unlike in later works, the "revelation" is shared – with the reader, if not with Nora – from very early in the story. In fact, in many scenes the novel seems both a parody of an earlier genre and a rough draft for James's later tale, "The Beast in the Jungle." In contrast to John Marcher's unknown beast, however, in *Watch and Ward* the "secret," "the riddle," the "pretty romance" is written plain from the start.

Watch and Ward and "The Beast in the Jungle" both share a hero who constructs his life around a "great secret": Roger Lawrence's "great riddle" about his relationship with Nora and John Marcher's feeling that "something rare and strange, possibly prodigious and terrible . . . was sooner or later to happen." Although the narrator of *Watch and Ward* states, "I undertake to tell no secrets" (*WW* 22), in fact the narrative suggests Roger's secret in telling details from the moment Roger meets Nora as a child and explicitly names the secret only twenty-seven pages into the novel. Roger's vision of Nora as a "potential woman" with "tender feminine promise" whom he might carefully "caress," reveals his intentions, and his epistle to Mrs. Keith acts as concrete proof (almost damning proof to Nora) of his deliberate plan (*WW* 13). Unlike the characters in "The Beast in the Jungle," Roger feels that he is master of his own "riddle":

> A dozen times over he was on the verge of making his point, of saying, "Nora, Nora, these are not vulgar alms; I expect a return. One of these days you must pay your debt. Guess my riddle! I love you less than you think – and more! A word to the wise." (*WW* 33)

Both Roger's mastery of his secret plan and his desire to withhold the secret mark his intentions as indeed "vulgar," and even Roger notes that such a revelation of "debt" might seem to smack of "brutality" (*WW* 33). Significantly, however, the fact that Roger can spell out his "riddle" reduces his "secret" to merely the conventional "petty romance" he claims to disdain.

Although *Watch and Ward* and "The Beast in the Jungle" contain many similar scenes in which characters attempt to guess and to verbalize the overwhelming secret, in *Watch and Ward* the reader and Roger can "spell" out what the "secret" is: Nora's fate is to marry Roger. Moreover, the response to this secret seems inevitable: Nora must accept Roger because the other men with whom she has had contact (Hubert and her American Wild-West cousin George) are set up as villains. Nora and Roger are the only characters whose consciousnesses are fully fleshed out. Nora's final acceptance of Roger is figured as an acceptance of Roger's great secret: "Yes, she was in the secret of the universe," Nora realizes, "and the secret of the universe was, that Roger was the only man in it who had a heart" (*WW* 160). Although James puts pressure on the motivations of Roger's agenda (noting its "cunning machinations"), the happy conclusion to the novel seems to valorize Nora's acquiescence to Roger's "secret," which is both revealed and accepted.

Part of the nature of James's "certain form" accounts for the sense of superabundance in *Watch and Ward*: There are too many suitors, too many confessions, and a plot that trickles until the last ten pages, where more occurs than in the previous 100. But even still, the neat ending of the book seems to sit unevenly. Roger's desires for Nora throughout remain strangely unnamable – "He mused ever and anon on the nature of his affection for Nora, and wondered what earthly name you could call it by" (*WW* 28) – and both Roger and Nora need to undergo large and rapid transformations in order to be situated in their happy ending. The dandy Roger must forgo his beloved "lavender gloves" (*WW* 4) and Nora must suddenly see Roger's "key" as a sure fit (*WW* 67). Although Roger admits he has a "strenuous desire to fathom the depths of matrimony," Nora hardly seems to want this marital bliss, and even Roger's desire seems more concerned with power and control than love (*WW* 7). Overall, the marriage plot feels overshadowed by unconvincing acceptances and revelations. Although James originally (facetiously) bragged that his novel was "one of the greatest works of 'this or any age,'" he soon began to feel it was "very thin and as 'cold' as an icicle."[74]

Watch and Ward, then, seems largely uncharacteristic of James because both the secret and the manner in which it is delivered are straightforward and concrete. Rather than a "beast," a "figure," or an "idea" motivating the telling of the tale, a known marriage plot drives Nora's story; and rather than being made privy to conversations of indirection in which we, like the participants, scramble for knowledge, we know throughout what Roger means, even if Nora does not. The fact that James made hundreds of minor changes to this novel before it was printed in book form and then chose still to reject it for the New York Edition demonstrates that something was grossly unconvincing to James about his first novel.[75] *Watch and Ward* depicts a Jamesian scenario, but in a style and form that lacks vagueness. When Roger describes Nora herself as a "vague spot of light," James foreshadows the kind of character and situation that will motivate his future plots (*WW* 15).

4. The Vengeance of the "Great Vagueness": "The Beast in the Jungle"

> My life is built upon a theory: and if this theory turns out false, my life will turn out a failure.
>
> –Charles S. Peirce[76]

> Something or other lay in wait for him, amid the twists and the turns of the months and the years, like a crouching beast in the jungle.
>
> –Henry James, "The Beast in the Jungle"[77]

In 1878, Charles Sanders Peirce closed the first section of "How to Make Our Ideas Clear" – one of the articles that William James later declared the "birth certificates" of pragmatism – on a strangely anecdotal note.[78] Using what would become known as the pragmatic method to demolish the notion of Grand Ideas ("Our idea of anything *is* our idea of its sensible effects"), Peirce also included a lesson from an "old German story":

> It is terrible to see how a single unclear idea, a single formula without meaning, lurking in a young man's head, will sometimes act like an obstruction of inert matter in an artery, hindering the nutrition of the brain, and condemning its victim to pine away in the fullness of his intellectual vigor and in the midst of intellectual plenty. Many a man has cherished for years . . . some vague shadow of an idea, too meaningless to be positively false; he has, nevertheless, passionately loved it, has made it his companion by day and by night, and has given to it his strength and his life, leaving all other occupations for its sake, and in short has lived with it and for it, until it has become, as it were, flesh of his flesh and bone of his bone; and then he has waked up some bright morning to find it gone, clean vanished away like the beautiful Melusina of the fable, and the essence of his life gone with it. I have myself known such a man.[79]

The story of the fled Melusina (a half-woman, half-serpent who gives birth to monsters) acts ostensibly as a warning against the danger inherent in "vague" ideas. "A vague shadow of an idea" can sap the life-blood out of a young man and, therefore, Peirce asserted, we must strive to be clear. But Peirce's anecdote did more than further his argument; it was an autobiographical aside – so personal, in fact, that he ordered the passage to be deleted from all future printings of his essay.

Melusina was not just an allusion to a mythological figure; it was also a reference to the middle name of his wife, Harriet Melusina Fay. Since his schooldays, Peirce's friend and, later, wife, whom he called "Zina," had been his constant companion and even the scribe for his fervent aspirations. Under the title "Theories of C. S. Peirce, 1854," she had transcribed his ambitious declaration that I cite as my epigraph: "My life is built upon a theory: and if this theory turns out false, my life will turn out a failure."[80] By the mid-1870s, Peirce's theory, "passionately loved, ... his companion by day and by night," was finally being elucidated in his articles; however, Melusina herself had "clean vanished away" after two decades of intimacy, leaving Peirce in Paris to what his friend Henry James described as "a very lonely and dreary existence." Peirce's inclusion of an anecdote about his own loneliness – "I have myself known such a man" – is poignant even as it reveals his anger. Melusina is both a monster and "beautiful," and with her disappearance, Peirce has lost "the essence of his life." The personal allusion also highlights the anxiety in the young Peirce's writing. What if his theories came to nothing, remained merely vague, and he lost his whole life and his wife to a misguided dedication? And how ironic would that be given that the idea itself aimed to explode the fallacy of grand ideas? Such an irony was not lost on his main companion during the winter of 1875, Henry James.

In this section, I aim to demonstrate that Charles S. Peirce's anxiety acted as a germ for the beast of John Marcher in James's late story, "The Beast in the Jungle." If "The Beast" acts as a revision of *Watch and Ward*, the salient difference is the clarity of Roger's plan in contrast to the vagueness of Marcher's secret: a vagueness related to Peirce's writings. "More than any of Henry James's tales," Paul Lindholdt writes, "'The Beast in the Jungle' has prompted source studies and psychoanalytic discussions by critics striving to identify" John Marcher.[81] Eager to diagnose the relationship between Marcher and May Bertram, critics have sought both autobiographical and literary sources for Marcher's character.[82] Strangely, however, no one has noted the connection between Peirce and Marcher, an omission that is especially odd given the critical attention directed at the relationship between the story and pragmatism. Since Richard Hocks's *Henry James and Pragmatistic Thought* highlighted the pragmatic tendencies of James's story and called Marcher the "anti-pragmatist" hero, "an epitome of William's philosophical opponents: a priori, monistic, intellectualist," several studies, particularly Posnock's *The Trial of Curiosity* and Sharon Cameron's *Thinking in Henry James*, have sought to identify James's philosophy in its relation to William's and have often located "The Beast" as a fruitful source.[83] William James himself has been pinpointed as a character source for Marcher, given the theory-driven nature of Henry's anti-hero, but William, after all, had become a successful philosopher and professor, whereas Peirce embodied the "failure" Marcher feared.

Directing attention to Peirce rather than to William as a source for Marcher emphasizes two points. First, the connection between Marcher and Peirce sheds light on Marcher's final epiphany – still a focus of critical debate – undermining Marcher's certitude that he has finally understood the meaning of his "beast in the jungle." In contrast to Roger's secret in *Watch and Ward*, the meaning of John Marcher's riddle may not be so easily answered. Second, in presenting a "great vagueness" that a character is thwarted in articulating, James denies Peirce's early maxim that vagueness is merely an excuse for inarticulacy (*Beast* 762). As I noted earlier, William James reacted against Peirce's declaration that he had "worked out the logic of vagueness with something like completeness" (*CP* 5:506) by arguing for the "re-instatement of the vague" in *The Principles of Psychology* (*PP* 1:254). Henry James, in a parallel gesture, reasserts the strength of "vagueness" through the victory of the beast in "The Beast in the Jungle." Moreover, as in "The Figure in the Carpet," James's irony lies in dramatizing his characters' futile efforts to specify vague ideals, while ignoring the effects – that is the *meaning* – of the secrets on their lives. The critic of James ends up, therefore, in a particularly tricky situation, caught in a jungle of James's own devising and unwillingly mirroring James's characters' futile efforts to verbalize vagueness.

The first germ of "The Beast in the Jungle" makes it clear that Marcher's character stemmed from an image of "disappointed ambition," like that of Charles Peirce. In his notebook in 1894, James ponders "the drama, the tragedy" of "disappointed ambition," and he examines in particular the "tragedy" of the failed man of genius, who, despite "the ambition, the pride, the idea of greatness," loses it all.

> There came to me the fancy of a sacrifice ... A young man who has dreamed that he has the genius of a poet – a young man full of dreams of artistic glory – full of brilliant gifts as well ... He forsakes, for this end, a girl whom he has originally loved ... She has been the confidante of his literary, his poetic dreams; she has listened to his verses, believed in his genius and his future. He breaks with her, in an hour of temptation, and casts his lot the other way.[84]

As in Peirce's anecdote in "How to Make Our Ideas Clear," the germ of Marcher forsakes "the confidante" of his theories and chooses "the ambition, the pride, the passion, the idea of greatness" over a woman like Melusina, his "original" love. Moreover, James did not have to look far to find such a "drama ... of disappointed ambition," because to all but a discerning few, Peirce had become the very figure of failure that he had feared.

For many years William had confided to Henry and his friends his fear that Peirce would fail, even for all his "genius." "The poor cuss sees no chance of getting a professorship anywhere," William sadly noted, calling it "a great pity."[85] William asserted, "Peirce is a tragic personality, but he is a *real* genius, of a discontinuous kind, and with all his arbitrariness, has a very lovable side to his character. I never knew a human being like him."[86] William's choice to dedicate *The Will to Believe* "To My Old Friend, Charles Sanders Peirce," and his continued insistence that it was Peirce who coined "the thing and the word pragmatism," were obvious attempts to emphasize publicly Peirce's importance as a theorist.[87] All of William's efforts must have kept Peirce's situation – and the terrible fruition of his anxiety – in Henry's conscious thoughts.

In "The Beast in the Jungle," written while his brother was valiantly supporting their "old friend," Henry James describes a man who, as in Peirce's lament, lives for "some vague shadow of an idea, too meaningless to be positively false," the idea that "something rare and strange, possibly prodigious and terrible . . . was sooner or later to happen" (*Beast* 744). At the same time that James was formulating "The Beast in the Jungle," he was yet again writing a critical essay on Flaubert, this time for an introduction to *Madame Bovary*.[88] From his correspondence with William, Henry could hear of Peirce's repeated setbacks and illnesses. In fact, when Henry James was writing "The Beast," William's efforts to find Peirce some sort of financial support were reaching their climax.[89] Peirce's terrible self-fulfilling prophecy that he would "sink himself" in tending to the "creature" that is his idea is re-enacted in Marcher's realization that devotion and attention to "the Beast" have made him "*the* man," to whom nothing is to happen.[90] Moreover, in "The Beast in the Jungle," Henry James creates a character who is thwarted in his quest to articulate his vague idea, what Marcher calls "the great vagueness" (*Beast* 762). In contrast to a popular interpretation, wherein Marcher is "an ass" and the "palatable moral" of the story is that if "only the hero had been less self-preoccupied, he would have responded to the love of this warm and selfless woman," James's story presents a vaguer lesson if we keep Peirce in mind.[91] Marcher's epiphany may be merely wishful thinking: "[T]he great vagueness," in contrast to Peirce's definition, is not merely the result of unclear thought, but something that cannot be verbalized.

John Marcher and May Bertram's love story, or thwarted love story, starts on a singularly incongruous note: Marcher's absentmindedness. The story begins, "What determined the speech that startled him in the course of their encounter scarcely matters, being probably but some words spoken by himself quite without intention" (*Beast* 737); in other words, James begins

"The Beast" with lost words. If, as with the majority of the tale, this recollection is limited to Marcher's own viewpoint, Marcher acknowledges his own inaccuracy: He cannot really recall "[w]hat" instigated May's startling speech and merely asserts perhaps "some words" were dropped "without intention." These forgotten words underscore not only Marcher's errors about where he had met May before – "it hadn't been at Rome – it had been at Naples; and it hadn't been seven years before – it had been more nearly ten" (*Beast* 739) – but also, and more significantly, the "odd accident of his loss of memory" (*Beast* 748). Marcher admits, "It had never entered into his plan that any one should 'know,' [his secret] and mainly for the reason that it was not in him to tell any one. That would have been impossible . . ." (*Beast* 748). Marcher (and with him the reader) needs to accept that merely his fate had somehow opened his mouth and allowed for his previous confidence, an answer that is strangely unsatisfying. If, as Marcher and May agree, this is really the secret that had isolated Marcher all his life, and if he had truly never told another soul, it seems highly unusual that Marcher would have forgotten confiding in May. However, such an unlikely error emphasizes that from the first sentence the story circles around information that is "impossible" to "fix . . . and hold" (*Beast* 783). Through Marcher's confusion James both sets up a pattern of Marcher's inaccuracy and emphasizes that his tale is based on an "impossible" confession, a confession that, like the exact meaning of the beast, is impossible "to tell any one."

Marcher's culminating realization is that love for May Bertram would have allowed him "to baffle his doom" (*Beast* 782). "The escape would have been to love her; then, *then* he would have lived" (*Beast* 782), James writes, and yet this understanding seems, in Marcher's own words, "an abject anticlimax" (*Beast* 761). From their first interaction, May has posited to Marcher that this may be the lurking beast: "Isn't what you describe perhaps but the expectation – or, at any rate the sense of danger, familiar to so many people – of falling in love?" However, they both resist such a trite solution, as May is willing to verbalize: "You want something all to yourself – something that nobody else knows or *has* known?" (*Beast* 745). Instead, as Marcher and May "wait," what they do together is attempt to describe the lurking beast, "the catastrophe," the "long riddle," "the superstition," a "mysterious fate," "the secret," although they fail to come up with a single definition. May's offer of herself when she approaches him "all expectant," assuring him that "[i]t's never too late," may be her attempt to bridge "the unspoken." However, Marcher's response – "Well, you don't say – ?" – misses her overture (*Beast* 768–9). Physical human contact does not fulfill the need Marcher has "to say" what the beast may be.

In "The Imagination of Metaphor," Ruth Yeazell emphasizes that Marcher is "a man obsessed with a metaphor" and notes this tendency of May and Marcher to make metaphor together, like Strether and Miss Barrace in *The Ambassadors*.[92] However, in her suggestion that "speaking in metaphors, like thinking in metaphors, is a way at once of confronting and of avoiding unpleasant facts," there is an assumption that the "unpleasant fact" of Marcher's "fortune" awaits him, if only he would recognize it.[93] In my opinion, Marcher's "odd obsession" seems to resist even reification into an "unpleasant fact." Rather than avoid the unpleasant topic, Marcher wants to do little other than to try to verbalize his theory. What frustrates Marcher is that he cannot speak his doom: "[D]oesn't the man of courage know what he's afraid of – or *not* afraid of? I don't know *that*, you see. I don't focus it. I can't name it" (*Beast* 756). Merely bantering about the metaphor of the beast does not satisfy him. When May tries to reassure him that his experience has come and that he has survived, he immediately asks if it was a "positive definite occurrence, with a name and a date," but May merely leaves him "too helplessly at sea" by answering: "Positive. Definite. I don't know about the 'name'" (*Beast* 771).

At the end, fearing that his life was "the most grotesque of failures" (*Beast* 761) as he faces his fellow mourner's "deep ravage," Marcher has an epiphany: "He had seen *outside* of his life, not learned it within the way a woman was mourned when she had been loved for herself" (*Beast* 780–1). But is this assessment of a life lived without love really the "measurement of the abyss" or truly the "sounding" of the "depths" (*Beast* 759)? Marcher notes that "[t]he beast had lurked indeed, and the beast at its hour, had sprung; it had sprung in that twilight of the cold April" when he had refused May's love (*Beast* 782). Yet the metaphorical beast, animated in Marcher's hallucination, still rises up "for the leap that was to settle him," at the end of the story (*Beast* 783). Marcher is not able to control his knowledge even at the end of the tale; rather, he still thinks in terms of his metaphor, as if his definition is somehow not satisfactory although he "tried to fix it and hold it" (*Beast* 783). Marcher wants to taste life just as the fellow mourner does, asserting to himself, "This horror of waking – *this* was knowledge ... he kept it there before him so that he might feel the pain" (*Beast* 782–783). Yet by limiting Marcher's realization to his own point of view, James heightens the pathos of Marcher's situation by allowing for the possibility that he is merely deluding himself. Marcher never succeeds in getting to the root of his sensation and the beast still lacks definition even as Marcher flings himself down "on his face, on the tomb" (*Beast* 783). In calling Marcher's story a "great negative adventure" in his Preface, James allows for the possibility that Marcher either has an epiphany of the nothingness of his life or has a negative or meaningless epiphany (*HJLC* 2:1251).

Peter Brooks, in "The Melodrama of Consciousness," notes that "The Beast in the Jungle" mirrors works like Melville's *Moby-Dick*, Conrad's *Heart of Darkness*, and Faulkner's *Absalom, Absalom!*, which are "audacious and desperate attempts to understand and to speak of a central 'darkness' that is finally inexpressible."[94] In "The Beast in the Jungle," Marcher does crave to understand and to verbalize the "inexpressible," the "lost stuff of consciousness," which nonetheless necessarily eludes his grasp (*Beast* 776). James's story presents a parody of Peirce's philosophy that everything meaningful can be expressed: The man obsessed with a theory, seeing that his time is running out for definition, forces an interpretation onto his "great vagueness" and is then overwhelmed by the unsatisfied personification of the metaphor itself. Sadly, Marcher's realization that his life meant nothing was paralleled by Peirce's perception of his own failure. Late in life, having failed to complete his *Magnum Opus*, Peirce lamented that he was a "mere table of contents, so abstract, a very snarl of twine."[95]

In "The Beast in the Closet," Eve Sedgwick agrees that the definition of the beast remains, to the end of the story, "Unspeakable," but she maintains that this signals, in part, Marcher's repressed homosexuality: "the secret of his hidden fate – importantly includes, though it is not necessarily limited to, the possibility of something homosexual."[96] Sedgwick asserts that it is only in the gaze of the fellow male mourner's ravaged face that Marcher realizes the passion that he has missed, but he refuses to accept such knowledge.

> To face the gaze of the Beast would have been, for Marcher, to dissolve it. To face the "kind of hunger in the look" of the grieving man – to explore at all into the sharper lambencies of that encounter – would have been to dissolve the closet. Marcher, instead, to the very end, turns his back – re-creating a double scenario of homosexual compulsion and heterosexual compulsion.[97]

Marcher's "epiphany," therefore, that May's love is what he had missed acts as a kind of forced interpretation, a "denial of the *un*knowability, of the arbitrariness and self-contradictoriness, of homosexual/heterosexual definition."[98] Like Peirce, Marcher refuses to acknowledge an "*un*knowable" drive; rather, he seeks safely to define and to channel his felt desire, even at the cost of his revelation being an error.

Biographically speaking, it is possible that Marcher's attempt to "fix" a kind of heteronormative translation onto desire enacts a further stab at

Peirce – or sexuality like Peirce's – through Marcher's false realization. Part of the public censure of Peirce stemmed from his second marriage to a 16-year-old girl, amid suggestions that he, like at least one of his brothers, may have been involved in a homosexual scandal. Indeed, the winter that Henry James and Peirce were in Paris at the same time even led to William teasing Henry about some "intimacies."[99] William insisted that their mutual friends were agog at the news that Henry was "C. S. Peirce's particular admiration," and chided Henry for having chosen "a rather uncomfortable bedfellow, thorny & spinous."[100] Peirce's marriages publicly defined his sexuality; in contrast, Henry James's indeterminate sexuality itself acts as the "Beast" for Jamesian criticism, with everyone attempting to solve the "long riddle" like May and Marcher.[101]

Acknowledging that "[t]here may come a time when scholars are no longer interested in James's sex life, but that time isn't in sight yet," Hugh Stevens asserts:

> The ambiguity of same-sex meanings in James's fiction might be used to discredit queer readings, whereas the readings themselves show that ambiguity is frequently an inevitable part of literary depictions of same-sex desire and that historical contextualization can help us see how such ambiguities can signal same-sex desires for the "initiated reader."[102]

While part of James's "ambiguity" may indeed signal same-sex desire, Stevens's careful pinpointing also re-enacts the "homosexual compulsion" that vagueness (like that of "The Beast in the Jungle") subtly resists. Marcher's desire to "name" the beast works against James's declared "confidence in the positive saving virtue of vagueness."[103] The linguistic family of the word "vague" connects to movement and to superfluity; likewise, James's vagueness rejects fixed meaning.[104] Perhaps, in fact, a reassertion of vagueness is at root a kind of assertion of libidinal superfluity, a rejection of unilateral desire that Stevens and Marcher both envision. My reading of James's vague stylistics therefore dovetails nicely with Kevin Ohi's argument that "the queerness of James's writing resides less in its representation of marginal sexualities," than "in its elusive and multivalent effects of syntax, figure, voice, and tone." I challenge, however, the notion that this makes James generally an "antimimetic" writer because I believe that James's "effects" aim to depict the vagueness of experience.[105]

James's style, particularly that of the major phase, and even more specifically embodied in the final text that this chapter will examine, *The Ambassadors*, is often criticized for this vagueness. John Marcher's inability to express his sense of doom in any manner but repeated metaphor parallels Henry James's own later style of "interminable elaboration of suggestive reference" that William James laments.[106] A story with "absolute straightness in style" is what Marcher seeks in the explanation of the beast: "a positive definite occurrence, with a name and a date." But for Henry James the "certain indirect and oblique" presentation is perhaps – "any superficial appearance notwithstanding" – the only way to probe "the great vagueness" (*HJLC* 2:1322). James allows his readers to color in the details, such as Osmond's menace, for ourselves: As he states, "Make [the reader] *think* the evil, make him think it for himself, and you are released from weak specifications" (*HJLC* 2:1188). The kind of hallucinated animation of metaphor that John Marcher experiences at the end of "The Beast in the Jungle" parallels James's desire for his ideal reader's active experience, because he wrote his goal was to "reduce one's reader ... to such a state of hallucination by the images one has evoked as does n't [sic] permit him to rest till he has ... set up some semblance of them in his own other medium, by his own other art" (*HJLC* 2:1322).

Richard Poirier asserts that "[p]ragmatism, in [William] James's version of it, is a philosophy that recommends 'vagueness' as a counteraction to the dogmatizing of existent truths and as the necessary condition for the exploratory search for new truths."[107] Ironically, Peirce, who figured as the germ of the disappointed genius for Henry James's "The Beast in the Jungle" and whose apparent nominalism Henry James decried in his criticism of Flaubert's realism, forged the pragmatic theory that fostered William James's reinstatement of the vague. Henry James's praise of William's pragmatism, therefore, applies to Charles Peirce as well. "I was lost in the wonder of the extent to which all my life I have ... unconsciously pragmatized," Henry emphasized, "You are immensely & universally *right*."[108] But in response to Peirce's early desire, in articles like "How to Make Our Ideas Clear," to slay "vagueness" as one would shoot the beast in the jungle, James's insistence upon the fecundity of the inexpressible depths of experience rings out against scientific precision: "No, no, no – I reach beyond the laboratory-brain."[109]

5. The Bad Pragmatist: *The Sacred Fount*'s Narrator

Such a formula is vagueness incarnate.

–William James, Introduction, *The Principles of Psychology*[110]

"I wish so fine a title had not been attached to so ignoble a book," wrote Edith Wharton after having read *The Sacred Fount*, "I could cry over the ruins of such a talent."[111] Wharton was certainly not alone in disdaining what Henry James himself called his "small fantasticality," where the only action involves the "obsessive" narrator nursing his theory about his fellow characters. William James, although he did not comment on this novel in his published letters, would certainly have disliked the lack of story in what Edel describes as a "detective story without a crime – and without a detective." William bemoaned Henry's tendency to write a "story which is not a story at all," and which failed to meet fiction's goals, wherein "the thorough and passionate conception of a story is the highest" priority.[112] Rebecca West's famous comments on the novel, however, while expressing her contempt, also underscore the philosophical tendencies of its protagonist. She believes the novel describes

> [h]ow a week-end visitor spends more intellectual force than Kant can have used on *The Critique of Pure Reason*, in an unsuccessful attempt to discover whether there exists between certain of his fellow-guests a relationship not more interesting among these vacuous people than it is among sparrows.[113]

West correctly notes that there is a philosophical game at play in James's novel. In fact, in *The Sacred Fount*, written in 1901, I propose that Henry James's narrator is a pragmatist, using the pragmatic method William James had propounded in his lectures in 1898. The narrator, however, is a pragmatist gone wrong, entrapped by the beauty of his own theory. This narrator watches for effects, but, like John Marcher, seeks a hard and fast theory that fails to allow for the vagueness of experience.

In "What Pragmatism Means," a lecture delivered in the winter of 1906–1907, collected in *Pragmatism*, William James aims to explain the pragmatic method that he had popularized eight years earlier in a lecture in California. When Henry James read *Pragmatism*, he declared to William that he had been "unconsciously" pragmatic, and William James's pragmatic method was so widespread in 1901 that, he claimed, it "fairly spots the pages of the philosophic journals."[114] Henry James's unnamed narrator in *The Sacred Fount* claims to endorse the "scientific method" and to focus on "effects" and "consequences" just as William James recommends in "What Pragmatism Means" (*SF* 203). The narrator's beloved theory, derived from the observation of effects, is that there is only so much youth and wisdom to be shared in a couple (from a "sacred fount"), and one member of the couple must tap, like a vampire, the life-force of the other. "One of the pair," the narrator hypothesizes, "has to pay for the other" (*SF* 34). However, although the narrator might begin as a good pragmatist, his growing passion for his idea, for what he calls his "priceless pearl of an inquiry" and his desire to protect it make him shun the pragmatic method (*SF* 203).

When Henry James wrote to Mrs. Humphrey Ward about *The Sacred Fount*, he emphasized that it was "hatingly finished" and that it was nothing but a "joke," although "a consistent joke." He added:

> [l]et me say for it, however, that it has, I assure you, and applied quite rigorously and constructively, I believe, its own little law of composition . . . As I give but the phantasmagoric I have, for clearness, to make it *evidential*.[115]

James's emphasis here on the "*evidential*" taps into his narrator's initial, repeated claims for the recorded "evidence" out of which his theory grows. He seeks "a supremely convincing bit of evidence" (*SF* 107) that will prove his "working hypothesis" (*SF* 75). When William James defines "the principle of Peirce, the principle of Pragmatism," he, too, emphasizes the importance of the scientific method for the pragmatist. Moreover, both the narrator and the pragmatist prioritize the evidence of "effects." William James writes:

> To attain perfect clearness in our thought of an object, then we need only consider what conceivable effects of a practical kind the object may involve . . . Our conception of these effects, whether immediate or remote, is then for us the whole of our conception of the object. (*PMT* 29)

For William James the way to achieve "perfect clearness" in thought is to focus on "conceivable effects." Similarly, *The Sacred Fount*'s narrator draws his entire theory about a sacred fount from observed effects; he notes that Mrs. Brissenden "grows younger . . . and prettier" (*SF* 20) while her husband appears aged and haggard. Mrs. Brissenden agrees with the narrator in a pragmatic reverie: "Of course I'm of an astuteness! I see effects!"

Although the narrator's hypothesis seems irrational and unlikely – how can there really be a sacred fount of life into which a couple can tap? – William James also emphasizes that for the pragmatist any hypothesis may prove true, no matter how strange, and that there are "no rigid canons of what shall count as proof" (*PMT* 44). If visual evidence supports the narrator's claims (as it appears to), then perhaps the narrator's "enchanted" theory is true. Pragmatism, William James emphasizes, "will count mystical experiences if they have practical consequences" (*PMT* 44). Importantly, it is initially not only the narrator who recognizes the validity of his theory. Mrs. Brissenden, Ford Obert, May Server, and Gilbert Long are all willing, at one point or another, to entertain the hypothesis of the sacred fount. The narrator's tendency to use the beauty of his theory as proof also connects him to William James, who emphasizes that "[m]any of the so-called metaphysical principles are at bottom only expressions of aesthetic feeling" (*PP* 1:672). The narrator finds his "precious pearl" of an idea so artistic that he uses its symmetry to convince those around him. "That theory will be most generally believed," William James writes, "which, besides offering us objects able to account satisfactorily for our sensible experience, also offers those which are most interesting, those which appeal most urgently to our aesthetic, emotional and active need" (*PP* 2:940). The narrator's theory is both beautiful and based on factual evidence; if "truth happens" to an idea according to pragmatism, this idea is true.

However, from the very first paragraph Henry James alerts readers to the narrator's tendency to see what he wants to see rather than to really observe effects. Sharon Cameron makes the excellent point that one reason that reading *The Sacred Fount* feels so claustrophobic is that we are trapped in our narrator's point of view. She argues that "the novel tyrannizes the reader as well as the characters" because "there is no way to tell the difference between what the narrative mind thinks and whatever objective truth there may be to what the mind thinks."[116] While it is true that the reader cannot obtain some external vantage point, there are, however, clear hints that that narrator's beloved theory is skewed, and not only because of his fellow houseguests' increasingly negative reactions to his idea. The narrator's claim of "premonitions" also sets the reader questioning. When the narrator happily sees Gilbert Long on the train station platform, he even wonders if "the wish [to see Long] was father to the thought" (*SF* 17). Although he dismisses this possibility, that he "longs" to see Gilbert Long seems to underscore that perhaps the vision really might be a product of his fertile imagination, just as the notion that May Server *serves* her husband's needs seems to fit too nicely with her name.[117] James seems to be tipping the reader off that the narrator reads into characters from their names, rather than observing effects and deriving a theory from evidence. Although the narrator contrasts himself, in his initial thoughts, to Long, who "had also, no doubt, his system, which he applied without discernment," the narrator also seems too eager to apply a system to his fellow houseguests, perhaps without discernment. William James warns that for the pragmatist, "[t]heories thus become instruments, not answers to enigmas" (*PMT* 32), but for the narrator the "enigma" begins to determine or "govern" what he observes (*SF* 30).

The narrator's pragmatic method errs in two ways: First, he begins to shield his theory from "the stream of experience" (*PMT* 32); second, he is unwilling to discard his hypothesis when it fails to prove useful. For William James the whole point of employing the pragmatic method is that it "unstiffens" theories and has a "cash-value" – it is useful to believe such a concept is true (*PMT* 43). However, once the narrator has "buil[t] up his house of cards," he is unwilling to account for changes, such as the revitalization of "poor Briss" (*SF* 181). Halfway through the novel the narrator's sleuths present to him information that cannot correspond to his theory. He thinks, "My theory had not at all been framed to embrace the phenomenon thus presented" (*SF* 116). Rather than discarding the theory, however, as the pragmatic method aims to enable an investigator to do, the narrator clings to what he had believed: "I was fairly upset by the need to consider at this late hour whether going in for a new theory or bracing myself for new facts would hold out to me the better refuge" (*SF* 116). Instead, he chooses to hope that "the exception did prove the rule" in order to "minimize, the disconcerting accident" (*SF* 117). The narrator acknowledges his errors, that he should "break off sharp . . . forswearing all returns" to his theory, but he cannot give it up; like William James's "ultra-rationalist," he is now "conditioned" to certain views of truth and is "unable to recognize the concretes from which his own abstraction is taken" (*PMT* 38).

The narrator's theory fails to be useful; it isolates him from others, makes him seem "delusional," and he has strange moral "scruples" about sharing it with the people for whom, theoretically, it could be helpful. He wants to see himself as "the most harmless man in the house" and is therefore unwilling to put his theory to any "objective test" (*SF* 106). His morality allows him to divulge his theory to a few esteemed participants but to wish by and large to avoid a "material clue" (*SF* 57) or any "experience in fact" (*SF* 79). The narrator exclaims that he is "honorable" and that "[w]hat's ignoble is the detective at the keyhole" (*SF* 57). When other characters suggest actually testing whether a couple is having an extramarital affair by asking them direct questions, he is affronted by such a notion of direct action. The problem is that he has begun to view himself as an artist of a theory rather than as an observer – and James makes this connection between the narrator and an artist repeatedly – but he does not want to be confronted by an unruly world that refuses to satisfy his artistic vision of symmetry.

That *The Sacred Fount* is James's only full-length novel in which he employs a first-person narrator easily leads to comparisons between the male protagonist and Henry James himself. The narrator overtly views the characters as part of "my little gallery," "my small collection," and parallels his artistic view to that of the painter, Obert. When Obert becomes uncomfortable with the way the narrator suits actual people to his idea – "How you polish them off!" Obert exclaims (*SF* 34) – the narrator responds, "I only talk . . . as you paint" (*SF* 34.) The ekphrastic moment in which the characters decide what to believe about the painting of "the man with the mask" redoubles the connection between the narrator's theory and art, and he solidifies the connection between his theory and literature when he states, "they were as one; as one, at all events for *my* large reading."[118]

But importantly, the narrator wishes not just to "read" circumstances (what the good pragmatist would do) but to write them. He notes:

> I had an odd sense, till we fell apart again, as of keeping my finger rather stiffly fixed on a passage in a favourite author on which I had not previously lighted. I held the book out of sight and behind me; I spoke of things that were not at all in it – or not at all on that particular page; but my volume, none the less, was only waiting . . . (*SF* 130)

The narrator now disregards the book of experience for his own imagined "volume"; he places an "artificial symmetry" onto what he sees, although he acknowledges that, unlike his vision, "[t]hings in the real had a way of not balancing" (*SF* 130). He revels in the "joy of the intellectual mastery of things unamenable, that joy of determining, almost of creating results" (*SF* 151) and even labels the origins of his idea in James's own terminology, exclaiming "it's all in your germ!" The narrator is not a true pragmatist, after all, but a novelist wanting to write the world around him.

Moreover, he is not even a novelist like Henry James who allows for changes in relations, or whose metaphors are constantly transforming and evolving. If the "sacred fount" is our narrator's version of literary metaphor, it differs from those of Henry James in that it is fixed and static, beautiful in its perfection, but dead. James's metaphors mirror those of John Marcher, which, stemming from the great vagueness, grow and evolve (sometimes seemingly without end).[119] What Thomas Otten notes of the pagoda in *The Golden Bowl* is also characteristic of Marcher's beast and James's late metaphors in general: "[W]hat is conceptually most difficult about images like this one in late James is that they have a lavish material specificity" but they lack "the firm referential moorings that should accompany such a finely specified image."[120] In contrast, the narrator's sacred fount has all too specific a referential mooring. The narrator is, therefore, himself "fixed," a poor reader and writer of the situation, and his desire to "fix" characters in art, uncomfortably recalls – and reveals the sadistic side – of Roger's desire to create his own wife in *Watch and Ward.* Because "[t]heory is sadism for him," this narrator is a nasty character, and "his theory of the sacred fount creates victims, and clearly it is victimization that delights him."[121]

James's failed artist in *The Sacred Fount* may be taken as a critique of James's own desire to find "artistic symmetry" in the vague world. The novel's form, with its sudden ending and its indirect dialogue, further undermines the narrator's longed-for symmetry.

> His question meanwhile, rightly applied by my own thought, brought back to that thought, by way of answer, an immense suggestion, which, moreover, for him too, was temporarily answer enough. "She'll tell me who he *won't* have been!"
>
> He looked vague, "Ah, but *that* –"
>
> "That," I declared, "will be luminous." (SF 164)

The style of this passage, with its labyrinthine syntax and innumerable abstractions ("thought," "suggestion," "answer," "that"), characterizes much of *The Sacred Fount.* Ford Obert's comment to such oblique dialogue seems fully justified to most readers: "How on earth can I tell what you're talking about?" (*SF* 145). But Henry James, by postponing, sometimes indefinitely, the "substantive" parts of language, insists that readers put equal weight on the flow of the language, on emphasis and "transitive" parts of language. His style, in *The Sacred Fount* as well as in other late works like *The Ambassadors*, emphasizes the vagueness of language that William James outlined in *The Principles of Psychology.*

6. "Vague Values": Strether's Dilemma in *The Ambassadors*

Then "all vagueness vanished," Lambert Strether thinks to himself during a key moment in Henry James's *The Ambassadors* (*A* 155). Strether has just imparted to little Bilham his words of wisdom that formed the germ – the "vague little fancy" – of James's entire novel.[122] "Live all you can; it's a mistake not to," Strether, the venerable older American, advises his young compatriot in a pleasant garden in Paris (*A* 153). Through Strether speaks the "vague voice of Paris" (*A* 401); he has been influenced by the atmosphere, the beauty, the "Difference" of Paris from his hometown of Woollett, Massachusetts.[123] However, immediately after Strether's impassioned plea, he sees the object of his ambassadorial visit to Paris, Chad Newsome, accompanied by the young girl Strether believes is Chad's intended. "[A]ll vagueness vanished. It was a click of the spring," James writes, "he saw the truth" (*A* 155). Unfortunately, "Poor Strether" is wrong (*A* 401). He has not seen the truth. Moreover, when he does inadvertently catch Chad with his actual lover, Madame de Vionnet, the vagueness does not vanish. Instead, the "vague values" (*A* 416) of Paris have changed Strether so much that Woollett's values of "perdition on one side, salvation on the other," no longer apply in a culture where one could be counted on "to make deception right."[124] This is a constantly shifting world where Strether must make decisions without faith in the "truth" (*A* 396). In *The Ambassadors*, James conveys Strether's predicament through abstract language that mirrors Strether's newfound vagueness.

Strong parallels exist among "The Beast in the Jungle," *The Sacred Fount*, and *The Ambassadors*.[125] In his extremely detailed, 20,000 word "Project of Novel" of *The Ambassadors*, which James sent to Harper and Brothers publishing house, the similarities among these three major phase texts become even more striking. Strether, in the projected plan, will be "vaguely haunted by the feeling of what he has missed, though this is a quantity, and quality, that he would be rather at a loss to name," James writes.[126] James intends for Strether's initial feeling, like John Marcher's, to be that he is missing something important that, like Marcher's beast, he is unable "to name." Indeed, James notes that Strether will have a "vague sense as of something that looms," and a feeling of "inscrutabilities, mysteries, things shading off into the vague." Strether, in the novel itself, is given to fancies, like Marcher, that "there was something in the great world covertly tigerish . . . as a waft from the jungle," and he begins his journey by intending to get to the heart of the matter: to determine exactly what or who is impeding Chad's return to the bosom of America (*A* 154). In James's plan, Strether believes, as in *The Sacred Fount*, that "some woman, playing a great part in his life" must be "more or less feeding on" Chad in order for Chad to appear so miraculously changed.[127] In the novel itself, however, Strether concludes with the feeling that Chad's new value stems from what he takes from rather than gives to Madame de Vionnet. Most importantly, Strether and Maria Gostrey's tête-à-têtes closely mirror the conversations between Marcher and May, where they try to name the beast. Strether's conscious rather than unconscious rejection of the would-be female partner, however, stems from his absorption of the vagueness that Paris has to offer.[128]

In *The Ambassadors* Henry James highlights the vagueness of language, particularly by tearing Strether away from the terms of his moral absolutes.

Todorov's argument that the theme that ties together many of James's narratives is "a quest for an absolute and absent cause" applies to the language of *The Ambassadors.*[129] The absent cause is the clear moral terminology that Lambert Strether loses upon his arrival in Europe. As James famously notes in the Preface, Strether arrives "at the gate of that boundless menagerie [Paris] primed with a moral scheme of the most approved pattern which was yet framed to break down on any approach to vivid facts" (*A* xxxvii). For Strether, moral categories (good, bad, innocent, guilty), as well as definitions of relationships (friendships, connections, attachments), all of which appear to have strict meanings back in America, seem altered and new when mixed with the "note" of Europe (*A* 95). Unlike his friend Waymarsh, "the good American" (*A* 92), who clings to his American values, Strether gives into "the great hum of Paris coming up in softness, vagueness – for Strether himself indeed already positive sweetness" (*A* 78). As even James's earliest reviewers noted, *The Ambassadors* demonstrates "the way Woollett standards of thought, of conduct, even of abstract right and wrong, are, temporarily at least, infected and impaired by actual agreeable contact with the way things are thought and felt" in Paris.[130] Strether's infection, moreover, is not temporary; rather, James dramatizes how Strether will act with his new "vague values" (*A* 416).

The most celebrated of these new vague definitions concerns, decidedly, the nature of young Chad's relationship with Madame de Vionnet. Little Bilham's assertion to Strether that the relationship is "a virtuous attachment" (*A* 128) satisfies, briefly, both Strether's curiosity and his sense of duty to Chad's mother. But the meaning of a "virtuous attachment" in Europe seems to be constantly shifting before Strether's eyes. James carefully juxtaposes the "vivid facts" of their love affair and Strether's moral terminology. Strether's desire to find Madame de Vionnet a "dreadful woman" is undermined when he meets her and she is a "charming" and "perfect" woman.[131] Indeed, Madame de Vionnet herself, like Paris, brings the virtue of vagueness to Strether. She undermines his belief in language with "her voice itself," which "seemed to make her words mean something that they didn't mean openly" (*A* 211). Strether's attempts to catch this "tone" or "note" of Parisian society reverberate throughout the novel (*A* 119, 95). Strether senses Madame de Vionnet is intentionally vague but appreciates it: "[H]e was struck with the tact, the taste of her vagueness, which simply took for granted in him a sense of beautiful things" (*A* 209). By the time he confronts her relationship with Chad, while the facts of the attachment are clear, the meaning of "virtuous" has nearly disintegrated:

> "Well," said Strether, "it was but a technical lie – he classed the attachment as virtuous. That was a view for which there was much to be said – and the virtue came out for me hugely. There was of course a great deal of it. I got it full in the face, and I haven't, you see, done with it yet." (*A* 419)

Strether still cannot quite shake off the belief that there was something "virtuous" in this "dreadful," according to Woollett's standards, relationship.[132]

In his masterful description of *The Ambassadors*' "notorious" prose in "The First Paragraph of *The Ambassadors*" (1960), Ian Watt explains why "all the idiosyncrasies of diction or syntax" of James's style "are fully justified by the particular emphases they create."[133] Strether's thoughtfulness, his tendency to weigh options carefully as well as to avoid thinking unpleasantries (such as the fact that he is not so excited to see his old friend Waymarsh), and the fact that "the primary location of the narrative [is] in a mental rather than a physical continuum," are mirrored by James's syntax and diction, with its "delayed specification of referents," "preference for non-transitive verbs," "many abstract nouns," "much use of 'that'," and "the presence of a great many negatives and near negatives."[134] James himself proudly argued that he limited the narrative solely to Strether's point of view, while avoiding the confessional first person, by "employing but one centre and keeping it all within my hero's compass"; therefore, the syntax and diction closely align to Strether's mental processes.[135] Strether's fear that he has a tendency to avoid truths, to generate elaborate theories or spin off into generalities, particularly when faced by the facts of Chad's romantic involvement, is mirrored by James's style throughout the novel.

After coming upon Chad and Madame de Vionnet in a boat on their intimate escape from Paris, Strether realizes his affinity for vagueness in prose that reifies his fears:

> It was the quantity of make-believe involved and so vividly exemplified that most disagreed with his spiritual stomach. He moved, however, from the consideration of that quantity – to say nothing of the consciousness of that organ – back to the other feature of the show, the deep, deep truth of the intimacy revealed. That was what, in his vain vigil, he oftenest reverted to: intimacy, at such a point, was *like* that – and what in the world else would one have wished it to be like? It was all very well for him to feel the pity of its being so much like lying; he almost blushed, in the dark, for the way he had dressed the possibility in vagueness, as a little girl might have dressed her doll. He had made them – and by no fault of their own – momentarily

> pull it for him, the possibility, out of this vagueness; and must he not therefore take it now as they had had simply, with whatever thin attenuations, to give it to him? (*A* 396)

Strether continues to rely upon the passive voice, as if his perceptions and emotions are somehow safely distant. His repetition of words like "it," "that," "what," distances the "specifications of his referents," just as Strether would like to be distanced from the intimacy upon which he has intruded. Furthermore, Strether's desire to avoid "the deep, deep truth of the intimacy" is evident in his preponderance of abstract nouns: "quantity," "show," "attenuations," and, most importantly, "vagueness." Indeed, to understand the phrase "the consciousness of that organ," the reader must return to the previous sentence, where Strether laments how much Chad and Madame de Vionnet's lying has upset his "spiritual stomach." His phrase "spiritual stomach" might demonstrate Strether's attempt to be precise, to dictate exactly where their lies have upset him. However, the metaphorical nature of the phrase suggests that Strether is still dressing the truth up in pretty clothes, "as a little girl might have dressed her doll." Strether's dressing image is particularly apt, because it is actually Madame de Vionnet's lack of appropriate attire that forces him to realize that she and Chad must have an overnight lodging nearby where she can change clothes. Nonetheless, Strether continues to dress up the facts in "vagueness" just as she clads herself in beautiful garments. Strether is clearly profoundly upset by his friends' betrayal and particularly by its revelation of his own innocence and loneliness. Yet his verbal, imaginative escapism approaches the "quantity of make-believe" that Chad and Madame de Vionnet's lies have inflicted upon him.

In *Language of Fiction* (1966), David Lodge offers an important and appealingly straightforward reading of James's vagueness and the water imagery in *The Ambassadors*, which nonetheless fails to hold water (pardon the pun) both in terms of the entirety of the novel and in terms of James's general promotion of vagueness. Building on Watt's argument, Lodge contends that for most of *The Ambassadors* Henry James restricts himself to "deliberately *vague* description," to "dissipate the sense of particular time and place and to synthesize the discrete items of local detail into a confused but evocative impression of an historical way of life."[136] Strether's desire (and with this I concur) to see Paris, and the relationships that occur there, through a wash of history and beauty is mirrored in James's "deliberately" vague prose. However, Lodge argues that James crucially interrupts Strether's vagueness in the river scene when he comes face to face with the lovers' betrayal. "For in that scene we find no vagueness at all," Lodge asserts. He contends that James "displays Strether's consciousness violated by facts which, in his absorption in beauty, he has hitherto failed to recognize," a failure that is "conveyed by the partial violation, at the moment of recognition, of the linguistic norms of the novel."[137] Finally, Lodge argues that James's extensive water imagery throughout the book becomes crucial in the river scene, where what was a purely mental phenomenon (Strether's sense that in Paris his values are "at sea") becomes actual when Strether is literally in the wrong boat on the river. Strether's vagueness and metaphorical extravagance is checked, Lodge implies, by James's straightforward brute facts.

This reading is compelling and elegant, and as a "good American" I am tempted by such a clear moral education for Strether, which simultaneously offers an explanation for the occasional stylistic morass of late Jamesian abstraction. However, Strether continues to dress the world in vagueness after his encounter on the river, and the water imagery remains, perhaps indeed floods over, when a sudden thunder shower erupts the next day. "[O]ne would float to it doubtless duly through these caverns of Kubla Khan," Strether thinks of his revelation, demonstrating his tendency to continue to think both metaphorically and in terms of water imagery (*A* 414). Strether persists in painting the scene with what he recognizes as his "historic sense," and Madame de Vionnet appears to him as "Madame Roland must on the scaffold" (*A* 401). As Maria Gostrey notes, he strongly does not give in to "revulsion in favour of the principles of Woollett" (*A* 416), but instead blames himself as well as the lovers for their current situation. Strether admits, "He was mixed up with the typical tale of Paris, and so were they, poor things – how could they altogether help being? They were no worse than he, in short, and he no worse than they – if, queerly enough, no better" (*A* 398). He wonders that there is not some "penal form" for their treatment of him, but instead must accept that he is "as much in the swim as anybody else" (*A* 399). Most importantly, James continues to use his abstract language throughout the novel, with its final culminating and indeterminate assertion by Strether: "Then there we are!" (*A* 438). If, as Lodge argues, Strether needs waking up to the brute facts of his situation, so does James himself – for his continued vague diction and syntax – not only in *The Ambassadors*, but also in his other late novels and his prefaces.

Instead of a tale in which the old American is rudely awakened from his descent into moral relativism, *The Ambassadors* dramatizes Strether's need to make moral decisions without Woollett's absolutes. He sees the "facts" of the situation, but these facts are immersed in what William James calls "the stream" of experience; hence the continued water imagery (*PMT* 32). Strether has become a pragmatist and, as Christopher Butler notes, "All Strether ultimately has to oppose to Woollett judgements and values is a pragmatist's blurring of sharp edges."[138] Strether now declares, "I *have* no ideas, I'm afraid of them" (*A* 437), and yet he still advises Chad not to cast off Madame de Vionnet. He turns Woollett's values on their head because he sees effects – the good influence of Madame de Vionnet on Chad – rather than looking for moral ideals. Indeed, this is why he becomes the "'reconstituted' self of modernity," because he no longer seeks absolutes but "promotes a style of being and inquiry that conceives of subjectivity and social structures as artifacts and thus inherently amenable to revision."[139]

Importantly, Strether still acts as the ambassador because he will not leave without imparting his final advice to Chad. However, his advice is the opposite of what Woollett would expect. He combines an American moral impetus with European moral vagueness.[140] Indeed, Strether represents at the end of the book the true marriage of America and Europe, in a way that James's other texts approach but never fully realize. Strether's rejection of Maria's silent marriage offer is connected to this transformation. Traditionally, Strether's rejection of Maria is read as a weakness on Strether's part, revealing James's tendency toward the "all too familiar ethos of renunciation."[141] Recent readings of Strether's decision, however, emphasize his rejection as contributing to James's portrayal of the power dynamics between the two sexes. As Eric Haralson notes, "*The Ambassadors* simultaneously reflects and confronts the power of the modern gender system, especially in its prescriptions and expectations for masculine performance."[142] Strether's absorption of the vagueness of Europe undergirds his ability to reject the institution of marriage, both with the stolid Mrs. Newsome and with Maria Gostrey.

Symbolically, Strether rejects marriage with Maria Gostrey because he himself already represents the marriage of two cultures. James emphasized that his own writing aimed to mirror such a union:

> I aspire to write in such a way that it would be impossible to an outsider to say whether I am, at a given moment an American writing about England or an Englishman writing about America (dealing as I do with both countries), and so far from being ashamed of such an ambiguity I should be exceedingly proud of it, for it would be highly civilized.[143]

The similarities between James's and Strether's ambiguous citizenship are not incidental; as James noted in a letter, "poor old hero, in whom you will perhaps find a vague resemblance (though not facial!) to yours always, Henry James."[144] Just as James vaguely resembles his "hero," Strether vaguely incarnates Europe and America. His metamorphosis represents James's revised version of the marriage plot.[145] Like Leopold Bloom's parodic self-marriage in *Ulysses*, Strether embraces his own new self. He is the newly transnational citizen who fails to belong fully to any continent but will return to Woolett with his "highly civilized" cosmopolitan values in tow.[146]

Early critics of Henry James often pointed to the way James himself dresses possibilities in vagueness, thus leaving his moral messages as well as his prose unclear to his reader. Arnold Bennett, the writer against whom Virginia Woolf will juxtapose her "Modern Fiction," recollects that *The Ambassadors* made him ask, "'What the dickens is this novel *about*, and where does it think it is going to?' Question unanswerable! I gave up."[147] In "The Ambiguity of Henry James," Edmund Wilson famously bemoans how in James "[a]lmost everything from beginning to end can be read in one of two senses," and Leavis argues, in *The Great Tradition* that, because of the lack of clarity in James's message, "*The Ambassadors* . . . is not only not one of [James'] great books, but a bad one." The reader, according to these critics, is placed in a position akin to Strether's, torn from the certain belief in narrative with which we arrived, but not, so to speak, left in the same boat with Chad and Madame de Vionnet either. Contemporary critics of pragmatism, like Cornell West, similarly argue that a philosophy like that of William James (and therefore Strether) is one "of political impotence."[148] The vagueness of firm beliefs, critics fear, leaves readers and citizens unable to know what firmly to think or believe. However, in *The Ambassadors*, Henry James depicts the pragmatic Lambert Strether's ability to act as a strong ambassador even with vague beliefs. Strether, as Maria Gostrey astutely identifies, is simultaneously "grandly cynical" and "grandly vague" (*A* 419).

CHAPTER 2

When in December 1910?: Virginia Woolf, Bertrand Russell, and the Question of Vagueness

> [I]f one were free and could set down what one chose, there would be no plot, little probability, and a vague general confusion in which the clear-cut features of the tragic, the comic, the passionate, and the lyrical were dissolved beyond the possibility of separate recognition . . .
>
> –Virginia Woolf, "Modern Novels"[1]

1. Mush and the Telescope

It may seem a long jump from the turn-of-the-century American world of the James brothers' conversations about pragmatism to the London neighborhood of Bloomsbury and Virginia Woolf's reaction to Bertrand Russell's new analytic philosophy. Woolf's witty recollection of a meeting with Henry James plays with this idea of a generational gap:

> Henry James fixed me with his staring blank eye – it is like a childs marble – and said "My dear Virginia, they tell me – they tell me – they tell me – that you – as indeed being your fathers daughter nay your grandfathers grandchild – the descendent I may say of a century – of a century – of quill pens and ink – ink – ink pots, yes, yes, yes, they tell me – ahm m m – that you, that you, that you *write* in short." This went on in the public street, while we all waited, as farmers wait for the hen to lay an egg – do they? – nervous, polite, and now on this foot now on that. I felt like a condemned person, who sees the knife drop and stick and drop again. Never did any woman hate "writing" as much as I do. But when I am old and famous I shall discourse like Henry James.[2]

To Woolf, the "condemned" listener, James appears as a remnant of her father's generation, long-windedly reminding her of her obligations to her literary inheritance. Her caricature of James humorously infantilizes and feminizes him, nevertheless conveying her admiration for this hen who takes his time to lay his golden egg. In this chapter I propose to take seriously James's impact on Woolf's literary style – "when I am old and famous I shall discourse like Henry James" – even as the factors of generation and gender (as Woolf highlights in her anecdote) divide the two novelists. Moreover, just as the last chapter aimed to prove that James's vague stylistics, captured in Woolf's anecdote, react against the philosophical precision heralded by Charles Peirce, so also this chapter proposes that Woolf's "'philosophy" challenges the new analytic philosophy embodied in Bertrand Russell. For both James and Woolf the philosophical linguistic turn invited linguistic and stylistic experimentation, even as they resisted its positivism. For Woolf as with James, moreover, this resistance to analytical thought was always linked to gender.

When the Ramsays are finally sailing in *To The Lighthouse*, Mr. Ramsay, the philosopher, looks at his daughter Cam and thinks to himself:

> [W]omen are always like that; the vagueness of their minds is hopeless; it was a thing he had never been able to understand; but so it was. It had been so with her – his wife. They could not keep anything clearly fixed in their minds. But he had been wrong to be angry with her; moreover, did he not rather like this vagueness in women?[3]

Woolf's philosopher, who is "stuck" in his own writing, nonetheless picks apart the minds of women and chooses "vagueness" – an inability to "keep anything clearly fixed in their minds" – as a fault. Although he admits to liking "this vagueness in women," his own work and philosophy of life lie in stark contrast to it – his work is a "definite contribution to philosophy" (*TTL* 39), and his rule to his children is that "life is difficult; facts uncompromising" (*TTL* 11). He thinks of his philosophy in a purely linear fashion; to him, "thought is like the keyboard of a piano, divided into so many notes, or like the alphabet is ranged in twenty-six letters all in order," and "his splendid mind had no sort of difficulty in running over those letters one by one, firmly and accurately, until it had reached, say, the letter Q" (*TTL* 53). The vagueness of his daughter Cam and his deceased wife may be charming, but he does not believe it is the way forward in rigorous intellectual pursuits.[4]

Ramsay is not wrong in believing that the women's minds in *To The Lighthouse* work in opposition to his. When Lily tries to consider Ramsay's work, she feels "vagueness as to what Mr. Ramsay did think about" (*TTL* 232), and she digresses in her thoughts, first about Andrew's sudden death, then about the symbol she has created to imagine Ramsay's philosophy. Her "circular tendency" in thinking is more akin to Woolf's writing in "The Mark on the Wall" or "An Unwritten Novel" than to Mr. Ramsay's orderly keyboard.[5] Both Lily and Mrs. Ramsay also chastise Mr. Ramsay for the impersonal nature of his thought. Mrs. Ramsay admits to herself that "[t]o pursue truth with such astonishing lack of consideration for other people's feelings" seems to her a horrible "outrage of human decency" (*TTL* 51). Lily allows that "[n]aturally, if one's days were passed in this seeing of angular essences, this reducing of lovely evenings, with all their flamingo clouds and blue and silver . . . naturally one could not be judged like an ordinary person" (*TTL* 38). (Her repetition of "naturally" puts into question, however, the notion that "reducing" the world is really natural to her at all.) Woolf later wrote that her depiction of the Ramsays was largely autobiographical and mostly derived from observing her parents. And yet, her portrayal of a philosopher who detests "vagueness," who believes philosophical inquiry must be "impersonal," and who posits that philosophical thought is best rendered in alphabetical letters, also calls to mind her relationship with Bertrand Russell.

At a dinner party in 1921, Woolf's reaction to Russell foreshadowed elements of her creation of Ramsay, composed six years later. Recalling the conversation in her diary, she claimed to have waved her hand about the room and admitted to him that "All this is mush [to me]; & you can put a telescope to your eye & see through it." This comment initiated the following discussion about their different views of life. Woolf writes:

> "If you had my brain you would find the world a very thin, colourless place" he said
>
> But my colours are so foolish I replied.
>
> You want them for your writing, he said. Do you never see things impersonally? [. . .]
>
> But I have a feeling that human affairs are impure.
>
> God does mathematics. That's my feeling. It is the most exalted form of art.
>
> Art? I said. (*DVW* 2:147)

Woolf and Russell parody their own ways of seeing the world ("mush," "colourless"), and yet their characterizations quite succinctly summarize their different approaches. Russell acknowledges the limitations of his method of logical positivism that uses formal logic to explain a strictly scientific world, which is echoed in Woolf's later portrayal of Mr. Ramsay because the "flamingo clouds and blue and silver" do not factor into his colorless world. Similarly, Woolf claims her vision ends in "mush" and is "foolish." Yet Russell's question, "Do you never see things impersonally?" and Woolf's response, that she has a "feeling that human affairs are impure," clearly demonstrate their antagonistic viewpoints. Woolf makes subjective even her statement that human affairs are subjective; Russell sparringly equates mathematics with divinity. Russell grants that Woolf's writing may benefit from feeling and from color, but science and impersonal mathematics direct the brain of the philosopher. Woolf, in contrast, gives herself the last word in her journal, questioning whether mathematics is really an "Art" at all, and implying art is more "exalted" than mathematics.

Less than a year later Russell delivered his "Vagueness" lecture at Oxford and Woolf published *Jacob's Room*. In "Vagueness," Russell advocates moving philosophical inquiry away from traditional questions – What is truth? What is reality? Words are vague, he argues, but the mere fact that words are not precise does not mean that the world itself is not precise; this error stems from the "fallacy of verbalism" (*V* 62). At the same time that Russell advocated new symbolic approaches to philosophy, Woolf's novels take up the philosophical questions Russell has discarded as "vague." Woolf wrote fiction and essays that incarnate an antithetical philosophy to that being ushered in by Russell. In Woolf's view, the world itself and our position within it are necessarily vague, shifting, and blurred. Woolf's famous "semi-transparent envelope" as a description of life is practically the definition of a boundary-less term (*EVW* 3:33). Moreover, the vagueness of language is its strength; it refuses to fix concepts the way Russell's ideal language seeks to do. While Russell aims to move philosophy away from "impure" English, Woolf's novels become "fictionalized epistemology."[6] Her novels explode the realist conventions of the nineteenth-century novel in order to satisfy the question she poses in "Modern Fiction": "Must novels be like this?"[7] Woolf's novels require new complex forms – ironically, themselves precise – in order to render the "vague general confusion" of modern life; rather than a plot that runs from A to Z, she blends genres and includes narrative interruptions, fragmentation, and gaps that necessitate the reader's own associations. Although Woolf often expresses a kind of nostalgia for a time of fact and longs to represent the objective, precise fact, she also insists that modern literature must represent "Life" the way it really is – blurred and distorted – and language is the best tool we have at our disposal.

In the following pages, I will briefly sketch Russell's approach to vagueness and outline Woolf's parody of Russell's dream of a precise language in her radio broadcast, "Craftsmanship" (1937). To underscore Woolf's commitment to vagueness, I will analyze her attitude toward prose's slipperiness in *Night and Day*, a work stylistically different from the rest of her *oeuvre*. Indeed, in *Night and Day*, self-consciously her most "traditional" novel, Woolf introduces her heroine (and by proxy the reader) to a world of emotion and messy interpersonal relationships where a devotion to precise mathematics and straightforward plots must be exchanged for the "vagueness of the finest prose."[8] That modern writers themselves must similarly discard traditional literary realism is made clear both by Woolf's subsequent fragmentary style in novels like *Jacob's Room* and *Mrs. Dalloway* and by Woolf's image of "Modern Fiction" as a "semi-transparent envelope."[9] By tracing this image to its origins in Henry James, I aim to depict a strain of what I am calling the linguistic turn in fiction, which joins James's stylistic ambiguities and linguistic extravagances to Woolf's novels of "vision" (*DVW* 4:151). Finally, I will turn to *The Waves* to argue how Woolf's novel seems to reify categories beloved to Russell, including precision, objectivity, and impersonality. If *The Waves* is Woolf's novel the most emptied of plot, history, and dialogue (a version of *Orlando* inverted), it is also the novel that most fully narrows its focus to the tension between atomized subjects and the external world.[10] Ultimately, through the shared discourse of *The Waves*, Woolf questions philosophical realism and precise boundaries to depict that "in some vague way we are the same person."[11] As Russell makes clear in "Vagueness," such a worldview risked solipsism, and Woolf knew this novel flirted with being "fundamentally unreadable" to an outside audience.[12]

Woolf, of course, was not a philosopher per se.[13] She was a novelist, journalist, and essayist. Although her father, Leslie Stephen (another model for Mr. Ramsay) wrote philosophy and wished to be remembered as a philosopher, Woolf herself exclaimed in her diary, "I dont want a 'philosophy' in the least," and complained that the novels of D. H. Lawrence were tiring because art should be "rid of all preaching" (*DVW* 4:126). In *The Waves*, Bernard, the voice of the novelist, exclaims, "Certain things lie beyond my scope. I shall never understand the harder problems of philosophy."[14] Woolf also professed a rather scathing attitude toward any kind of institutionalized philosophy, as we might expect from the writer shut out of Oxbridge in *A Room of One's Own* – "philosophic words," she wrote there, "if one has not been educated at a university, are apt to play one false."[15] Although she admired the "philosophical novel," she feared the influence that too much knowledge of philosophy might have on a novelist, as well as too much systemization on a philosophy. She wrote in a book review:

> [W]hen philosophy is not consumed in a novel, when we can underline this phrase with a pencil, and cut out that exhortation with a pair of scissors and paste the whole into a system, it is safe to say that there is something wrong with the philosophy or with the novel or with both.[16]

She also minimized her knowledge of philosophy, although she knew both Russell and G. E. Moore personally, attended open lectures, and lived in Bloomsbury society where, as she wrote, "discussing philosophy, art, religion" was in the atmosphere itself.[17]

Still, her essays, such as "Modern Fiction," certainly have a theory (if never a named and explicit one) behind them – what she calls at one point a "philosophy."[18] Recent critics have tried to pin down this philosophy, highlighting Woolf's parallels to, for example, Hume, Heidegger, Benjamin, and poststructuralism more generally.[19] I agree with Mark Hussey's statement in *The Singing of the Real World* that forcing Woolf's fiction into a philosophical school does it a disservice, and with Matz's claim that "Woolf's philosophical affiliations change with the moods of her characters, which is why no philosophical affiliation can define her vague theory of fiction."[20] Nonetheless, juxtaposing her investigations of language and desire to dismantle the "materialist" novel to Russell's disdain for "vagueness" and creation of a new symbolic language demonstrates a clear opposition, one that is also broadly applicable to a reading of Woolf's novels. Further, Woolf's dislike of institutional philosophy is in keeping with her philosophical novels, because she moves epistemological questions out of the academy where they are addressed by only a (usually male) privileged few and into novels, open to the Common Reader.[21]

In her seminal work on Woolf and Russell, *The Phantom Table*, Ann Banfield notes the connection between Ramsay's dislike of vagueness and his "analytic mind" and suggests that Woolf may be positing that vagueness, "the inability to distinguish one thing from another," may in fact be "the way of genius."[22] Banfield's work sets the stage for any further critical discussion of the relationship between Woolf and Russell, highlighting that Woolf was in many ways attracted to Russell's philosophical realism, and that Woolf's experience of philosophy was filtered through the Cambridge apostles, whose group included Russell as well as many Bloomsbury members. My work builds upon Banfield's in seeing Russell's logical atomism and preoccupation with reconciling the relationship between the subject and the object as key to understanding Woolf's fiction. However, my argument diverges from Banfield's significantly in the extent to which we see Woolf as truly committed to a belief in a reality that is mind-independent, a crucial element of both Russell's philosophy and Banfield's reading of Woolf.[23] Woolf's "philosophy" simultaneously yearns for such a reality and questions it, just as her depictions of multiple perspectives are always subordinated to a distinctive style that undermines a decisively objective point of view.

Critics of Woolf's philosophy, as Timothy Mackin notes, can conveniently be divided into those who read Woolf as a realist (as Banfield and other recent critics have argued) or as an idealist (most famously in Eric Auerbach's reading of *To The Lighthouse*).[24] My juxtaposition of Woolf and Russell aims to demonstrate that Woolf's medium, language, allows her to be both. Both Woolf and Russell depict language as unreliable for portraying an objective truth (whether it be realism or idealism), which for Russell is a reason to discard it as a tool. Woolf, in contrast, sees this as an opportunity because, as she argues in "Craftsmanship," language's instability mirrors the multiplicity of "truths." Moreover, Woolf's repeated thematization of subject/object relations and exploration of language's ability to capture this vagueness of our experience anticipates debates in vagueness studies today. Indeed, reading Woolf through the problematic of vagueness is productive for the ways in which it helps us to return her aesthetic concerns to the forefront while still demonstrating that her stylistic and linguistic experimentation underscores her philosophical inquiries.

Ecocritical, phenomenological, and scientific approaches to Woolf have argued that Woolf consistently dissolved the boundaries between self and nature in her fiction.[25] Louise Westling, for example, makes a case for Woolf's "ecological humanism" because she "integrated the radical ontological and epistemological perspectives suggested by quantum physics into her writing, because they accorded so well with her own lifelong awareness of the indeterminacy of consciousness."[26] Patricia Waugh, focused on recuperating Woolf's notion of the "soul," has similarly grouped her among anti-Cartesian thinkers. Noting that William James is the "key source for the current anti-Cartesian turn in psychology, cognitive science, philosophy of mind, and social thought," Waugh writes, "the terms and expression of Woolf's preoccupations resonate so closely with James's, that one wonders why the similarities between their two enterprises have been so conspicuously ignored."[27] My work aims to take up Waugh's challenge in order to resituate Woolf's thinking in the context of William James's influence.

Two disclaimers: First, although throughout his life Russell argued for the notion that "most problems need mathematical logic for their solutions," he also wrote many books on philosophy for a popular audience.[28] Like Woolf's *The Common Reader*, Russell's essays often aimed at a popular audience (leading, for example, Wittgenstein to scoff at some of his less academic works such as *The Conquest of Happiness*).[29] In *Virginia Woolf, the Intellectual and the Public Sphere*, Melba Cuddy-Keane notes an important facet of Bloomsbury thought (a group to which Russell was tangentially related, being a fellow Apostle with Woolf's brother Thoby) was democratizing intellectual pursuits.[30] I therefore wish to emphasize that it was because he valued "Modern analytical empiricism," which is able "to achieve definite answers which have the quality of science rather than of philosophy," that Russell despaired of language's vagueness.[31] Just because Woolf disdains Russell (mostly for his notorious womanizing) does not mean that his philosophy was actually as elitist and patriarchal as Woolf's portrayal implies.[32] Second, mostly due to space, this chapter focuses primarily on Woolf's "novels of vision," rather than focusing on her "novels of fact," essays, or diaries. Woolf once discriminated in her diary between her "novels of fact" (*Night and Day*, *The Years*) and her "novels of vision" (*To The Lighthouse*, *The Waves*), and insisted that in her visionary works she was not being difficult in order to be experimental (as she feared it was perceived) but because her "dissatisfaction was primarily with nature for giving an idea, without providing a house for it to live in."[33] In the original essay sections of *The Years*, Woolf was eager to promote as clearly as possible her social vision. But as her despair over making *The Years*' fictional and essay sections coalesce demonstrates, the boundary between subjective viewpoint and fact was never clear to her.[34] This chapter will examine the instability of boundaries in Woolf's work, between philosophy and fiction, threnody and satire, consciousness and uncompromising fact, and demonstrate that Woolf's most visionary novels find promise in the vagueness of language that Russell abhorred.

2. Vagueness and Vagabonds in "Craftsmanship"

> I think vagueness is very much more important in the theory of knowledge than you would judge it to be from the writings of most people.
>
> –Bertrand Russell, "The Philosophy of Logical Atomism" (1918)[35]

Russell's first foray into "what we may call the problem of 'vagueness'" occurred in 1918, when writing a review of John Dewey's *Essays in Experimental Logic*.[36] Although generally sympathetic to Dewey's book, Russell made it clear that he feared that the Pragmatism or Instrumentalism of writers like John Dewey and William James might chip away at "[t]he common-sense view ... that greater discrimination and more analytic observation yield more knowledge" (*CPBR* 8:138). "The successes of science," he wrote, "whose observation of facts is highly analytic, have confirmed the view that observation of this sort yields the most information." Russell insists that "discrimination" and careful "analysis" are the best means to knowledge.

> But as against this common-sense view we have a sort of artificially archaistic view, which opposes analysis, believes in a faculty of "intuition" possessed by peasant women, dogs, and ichneumon wasps, loves savage religions, and maintains that the progress of intellect has driven wisdom away from almost all men except the few immovable philosophers among whom intellect has not progressed. (*CPBR* 8:138)

Although he quickly notes, "I do not think that Professor Dewey belongs to those who take this view," he does not exempt James from the charge of the "artificially archaistic view." However, it is not only the scientific method (as opposed to the "intuition" of peasant women) that he wishes to preserve in this essay – he also begins to clarify his own view of the "definition of vagueness."

"Common sense" is his primary criterion for defining vagueness (*CPBR* 8:139). He takes as his example "a man walking towards us on a long straight road," who first appears as a "vague dot" but whom eventually we recognize. "In this case," he argues, "it is clear that the more analysed apprehension enables us to know more" (*CPBR* 8:139). In a "vague perception" the man appears as "undifferentiated" or even "the whole man may be absorbed into the smallest discriminated element" until a whole army of soldiers appears "as a speck" (*CPBR* 8:140). He wishes to promote the definition that perceptions that "are less vague are more differentiated; they consist of more parts" (*CPBR* 8:140). Although he accepts that "the vague data of unanalytic attentions are just as 'true' as the more precise data of trained observation, but allow fewer inferences," he emphasizes that any kind of praise of vagueness in philosophy or psychology is a reversion (*CPBR* 8:140). In an essay later that year he asserts:

> The process of sound philosophizing, to my mind, consists mainly in passing from those obvious, vague, ambiguous things, that we feel quite sure of, to something precise, clear, definite, which by reflection and analysis we find is involved in the vague thing that we started from, and is, so to speak, the real truth of which the vague thing is just a shadow.[37]

The vagueness of language, and therefore the vagueness of even his words in discussing his argument do not yet seem to thwart him as he argues that the result of "sound philosophizing" will be to attain the "real truth" behind vagueness. At this point, however, he does assert, "I should like, if time were longer and I knew more than I do, to spend a whole lecture on the conception of vagueness."

His "whole lecture" entitled "Vagueness" in 1922 at Oxford examines three facets of vagueness that are pertinent to the linguistic experimentation of Virginia Woolf: the vagueness of all language, the fallacy of verbalism, and the notion that "scientific truth" is "better worth having if it can be obtained." First of all (to recap my discussion in the introduction to this book), Russell asserts that he proposes "to prove that all language is vague and that therefore my language is vague." He states:

> You all know that I invented a special language with a view to avoiding vagueness, but unfortunately it is unsuited for public occasions. I shall therefore, though regretfully, address you in English, and whatever vagueness is to be found in my words must be attributed to our ancestors for not having been predominately interested in logic.[38]

Russell claims to be apologizing for addressing his audience in English because of its "vagueness." Although his tone is amusing (for its implied accusations of ancestral laziness) his points about vagueness, stemming from his earlier articles, are not. Language is vague because terms such as "red" and "bald" have no definite boundary, are subject to the sorites paradox, and even a proper name of a man is not precise in the way we might imagine because it too has no particular boundary. "If you continue to apply the name to the corpse," he gives as a particularly macabre example, "there must gradually come a stage in decomposition when the name ceases to be attributable, but no one can say precisely when this stage has been reached" (*V* 63). Worse still for Russell, any logical proposition is similarly subject to such vagueness: "Since propositions containing non-logical words are the substructure on which logical propositions are built, it follows that logical propositions also [. . .] become vague through the vagueness of 'truth' and 'falsehood'" (*V* 65).

Russell offers a smudged photograph (a subject to which I will return in my discussion of *Jacob's Room*) as an example of the vagueness inherent in language and in any kind of "representation." "A representation is *vague*," he argues, "when the relation of the representing system to the represented system is not one-to-one but one-many. For example, a photograph which is so smudged that it might equally represent Brown or Jones or Robinson is vague" (*V* 66). Just as in a smudged photograph, language is one-many, because a word does not have one specific bounded meaning: "That is to say, there is not only one object that a word means, and not only one possible fact that will verify a proposition" (*V* 66). The consequence of this vagueness to Russell is catastrophic because it actually undermines the "law of the excluded middle," which depends upon precise symbols, as well as any other linguistic logical principle. "We can see an ideal of precision [in English], to which we can approximate indefinitely," he asserted, "but we cannot attain this ideal . . . It is therefore not applicable to this terrestrial life, but only to an imagined celestial existence" (*V* 65). Russell's "special language" is an attempt to escape the vagueness of language into an "imagined celestial existence." Using the "theory of descriptions," for example, Russell can aim to eliminate the confusion of statements such as "The golden mountain does not exist."[39] But even his logical symbols may be subject to vagueness: "The fact that meaning is a one-many relation is the precise statement of the fact that all language is more or less vague" (*V* 66–67).

For Russell, however, the fact that representations such as language and photographs are vague need not imply that the world itself is vague, a condition defined as ontological or metaphysical vagueness. "[T]hings are what they are and that is an end to it," Russell asserts, returning to his claims for a common sense approach to vagueness (*V* 62). A recent critic suggests that Russell's desire to eschew metaphysical vagueness made him disregard even his own logical principles such as the Law of Indispensability and asserts that "[i]f vagueness is not eliminable from our language and if our best scientific theories are committed to vague objects, it would seem that it is no fallacy to attribute this vagueness to the world."[40] Russell, however, clung to the notion that although the world obeys logical principles, language fails to, and believing otherwise is "muddleheaded" (*V* 62). Any other idea, he concludes, would lead to solipsism, because logical laws or the principles of physics could not apply to vague objects.

Finally, and significantly for Russell's approach to philosophy and science, Russell believed that getting as precise as possible was the goal of philosophy. "It would be a great mistake to suppose that vague knowledge must be false," he notes, "[o]n the contrary, a vague belief has a much better chance of being true than a precise one" (*V* 67). Believing a smudged photograph to be of a man, for example, is a more probable claim than asserting it is Brown or Jones or Robinson. Nonetheless, it is always more worthwhile to have a precise photograph. Russell argues:

> Science is perpetually trying to substitute more precise beliefs for vague ones; this makes it harder for a scientific proposition to be true than for the vague beliefs of uneducated persons to be true, but makes scientific truth better worth having if it can be obtained. (*V* 68)

Russell insists upon a rigorously logical approach to philosophy, an approach his followers in modern analytical philosophy continue to embrace. Philosophy's goal, as he writes in his conclusion to *A History of Western Philosophy*, is "scientific truthfulness" and necessitates "the habit of basing our beliefs upon observations and inferences as impersonal, and as much divested of local and temperamental bias, as is possible for human beings."[41]

In her radio broadcast on "Craftsmanship," Woolf offered a more generous view of language's imprecision than that expressed by Russell in his lecture "Vagueness."[42] The BBC aired the talk on April 29, 1937, near the end of Woolf's life. It was one of only three radio broadcasts that Woolf made – because the first time the whole experience put her into "the devil of a temper" when the station strictly monitored what she was allowed to say.[43] Her broadcast was part of a series entitled, "Words Fail Me," and Woolf's talk acts as a challenge to the series title. In "Craftsmanship," Woolf accepts that she is meant to take "for our starting point the statement that words are not useful" and analyzes the idea that "it is words that are to blame" for the confusion and miscommunication in the world. But, taking advantage of, as she notes, the "crafty" (in the sense of "cajolery" and "cunning") meaning of the word *craftsmanship*, Woolf teasingly plays with philosophies of language like Russell's, undermining the idea of inventing a new language and praising the "democratic," associative, and personal nature of words. Words are "irreclaimable vagabonds," Woolf makes clear, but that is "because the truth they try to catch is many-sided" (*C* 251).

According to the preview of the talk published in the *Radio Times* on April 23rd:

> In Virginia Woolf's opinion, craftsmanship is a word that can be applied to the making of pots and pans, but not to words in the way in which writers use them. There is a distinction to be made between the useful use of words and their literary use. The novelist and the scientist use words very differently.[44]

This is a peculiarly misleading summary of Woolf's talk (perhaps written by the producer). In fact, Woolf makes no distinction between scientific language and literary language, insisting that all words are "not useful." Words always tell the truth, she argues, but that is because "it is the nature of words to mean many things" (*C* 247). The only nod Woolf makes to the scientist's use of words may be in her playful examination of the new "language of signs" that she claims "we are beginning to invent."

Quentin Bell expressed dismay by the tone of the voice in Woolf's (his aunt's) recording: "Her voice is deprived of depth and resonance; it seems altogether too fast and too flat; it is barely recognisable."[45] With more recent critics, however, I would argue that Woolf's tone varies, and that in many moments her quickness marks her attempt to mask her humor and irony.[46] Leila Brosnan, for example, has pointed out a playful political subtext of Woolf's broadcast that may account for some of the rapidity of her tone, and I would like to argue an additional subtext involves an allusion to Russell. Brosnan notes that knowing that Woolf gave the recording right before the coronation of George VI, the story of Edward and Mrs. Simpson "renders many of the phrases and allusions in the essay politically charged puns and satirical jibes."[47] "The less we inquire into the past of our dear Mother English the better it will be for that lady's reputation," Woolf asserts, because "Royal words mate with commoners" (*C* 250). Words, Woolf alleges, "are much less bound by ceremony and convention than we are," perhaps questioning why when Royal people "mate with commoners" (and commoners with a past "reputation"), convention insists that they abdicate.

Similarly wryly, in order to prove that "words are not useful," Woolf chooses as if by hazard "Passing Russell Square" as her first example of three words to repeat "over and over again" as a demonstration of how words "shuffle and change." "Passing Russell Square, Passing Russell Square," she repeats, but in her repetition, she loses the useful meaning of the words and hears instead the resonance of "Passing away saith the world, passing away" (*C* 245). Christina Rossetti's verse makes Woolf forget to exit at Russell Square, the correct tube stop. Woolf concludes that words proved "that they hate being useful" because "it is their nature not to express one simple statement but a thousand possibilities" (*C* 246). Woolf notes:

> At last, happily, we are beginning to face the fact. We are beginning to invent another language – a language perfectly and beautifully adapted to express useful statements, a language of signs. (*C* 246)

This new language of "signs" will be "useful," helping Woolf to exit the train rather than to recite poetry.

Russell Square was a familiar and frequent tube stop for Woolf, so she may have chosen to repeat "Passing Russell Square" by chance as her example for the need to create a new language. However, because the focus of her talk is the multiple meanings of words, she notes that "Russell" suggests "the rustling of skirts and the skirt on a polished floor," as well as "the ducal house of Bedford" (i.e., Bertrand Russell's family) (*C* 247). Moreover, given her knowledge of Bertrand Russell, it seems her new "beautifully adapted" language may be referring to the "special language" Russell invented.[48]

Woolf's praise of "a new language of signs" is heavy with irony. She continues:

> There is one great living master of this language to whom we are all indebted, that anonymous writer – whether man, woman, or disembodied spirit nobody knows – who describes hotels in the Michelin Guide. He wants to tell us that one hotel is moderate, another good, and a third the best in the place. How does he do it? Not with words ... He sticks to signs; one gable; two gables; three gables. That is all he says and all he needs to say. (*C* 246)

Although this method of signs may work very well for Michelin and Baedeker, to address "truth" (and Woolf spells out she means not only "literary truth" but also "God's or gospel truth and home truth"), she returns to words. Words are the "the wildest, freest, most irresponsible, most unteachable of all things" (*C* 249). However, because "the truth they try to catch is many-sided," words are well suited, "being themselves many-sided, flashing this way, then that" (*C* 251). Woolf implies that a new language like Russell's may be satisfactory for certain tasks (like judging hotels) but words, which "lapse and flow into each other like reeds upon the bed of a river," are needed to address truth. In contrast to Russell, who believes that the problem of language is that it is "one-many," Woolf asserts that truth itself is "many-sided," so the many meanings of words are their strength. Moreover, Woolf emphasizes that the kind of truth language can capture is more important than a language of signs – "words are the only things that tell the truth and nothing but the truth," she insists (*C* 245).

Woolf also notes that it is impossible for words to be impersonal, nor can a language remain pure. "But has any writer," she asks, "succeeded in being wholly impersonal? Always, inevitably, we know them as well as their books" (*C* 248). In contrast to Russell's notion (and also that of T. S. Eliot) that "impersonality" is possible or desirable, Woolf insists that language reveals personality; further, "If you start a Society for Pure English, [words] will show their resentment by starting another for impure English" (*C* 250). Just as Woolf commented to Russell over dinner that she feared that "human affairs are impure," so also she insists that language is impure, but its impurity is a strength, because it is "highly democratic, too ... uneducated words are as good as educated words, uncultivated words as cultivated words, there are no ranks or titles in their society" (*C* 250).

Most criticism of Woolf's attitude about language tends to focus on a few stock negative lines from her writings and disregards her important claims that language is "democratic" or that she genders language itself as female.[49] Critics point, for example, to Lily Briscoe's assertion that "in the chambers of the mind and heart of the woman . . . were stood, like the treasures in the tombs of kings, tablets bearing sacred inscriptions, which if one could spell them out, would teach everything," yet the knowledge is "nothing that could be written in any language known to men" (*TTL* 79). Lily longs to understand Mrs. Ramsay in a way freed from language "known to men." Julia Kristeva's view of Woolf is often cited as a truism about Woolf's relationship to the logos:

> In women's writing, language seems to be seen from a foreign land; is it seen from the point of view of an asymbolic, spastic body? Virginia Woolf describes suspended states, subtle sensations, and above all, colors – green, blue – but she does not dissect language as Joyce does. Estranged from language, women are visionaries, dancers who suffer as they speak.[50]

Although my investigation into Woolf's vagueness similarly finds gender and open-endedness essential to Woolf's prose, I hesitate to see Woolf as necessarily more "estranged from language" than male writers like Joyce. I would agree with Kate Flint that it is "misleading" to take Woolf's language as some sort of "prefiguration of new French Feminist thought," which seems essentialist and ahistorical; as Flint argues, "for Woolf, women, language, and consciousness intertwine in a way which is ultimately inseparable from social context."[51]

In fact, one important social context involved access to lectures, such as Russell's, and philosophy departments at Oxbridge. Woolf would not have heard Russell's actual lecture "Vagueness" because it was given at a private club at Oxford. However, Woolf admitted she went to some of his open lectures because "[t]he touchstone of virtue . . . now is whether you attend Bertie's lectures or not" (*DVW* 1:273). Her reaction was none too favorable. She jokes in a letter that "Bertie lectures on Tuesdays, and thinks to issue a new constitution, so we are told, with the help of young Cambridge," but her reaction was to be left "wondering whether all his rant has made a scrap of difference practically."[52] Her thoughts on Russell's lecture and the war lead her to exclaim, "I become steadily more feminist."[53] Russell may have worked for the suffrage campaign, but his philosophy and his new symbolical language voiced from the pulpit of Cambridge irked Woolf. Unlike the ranks and titles of Cambridge – which Woolf deplores in *Three Guineas* – language is open to all. Judith Shakespeare's writing suffered because she lacked education and a room of her own; nonetheless, Woolf suggests language was still her tool: "Anon," she argues, "who wrote so many poems without signing them, was often a woman" (*R* 49).

When Woolf depicts vagueness, it is usually gendered. She recalls, for example, that her father was always "crying down sentiment and vagueness" and "cracking up sense and manliness."[54] When she praises Dorothy Richardson's "psychological sentence of the feminine gender" it is "of a more elastic fibre than the old, capable of . . . enveloping even the vaguest shapes."[55] In Woolf's second novel, *Night and Day,* she contrasts her two heroines as follows:

> Where Katharine was simple, Cassandra was complex; where Katharine was solid and direct, Cassandra was vague and evasive. In short, they represented very well the manly and the womanly sides of the feminine nature. (*ND* 290)

Woolf's narrator here, like Mr. Ramsay and like Leslie Stephen, finds fault with "the feminine nature" for its vagueness. In "Women and Fiction," Woolf wonders if the vote will change women from being "fluctuating and vague" "toward the impersonal" (*CE* 2:147); in *Jacob's Room* young girls and old ladies are "[b]right yet vague"; and Rachel Vinrace in *The Voyage Out* is consistently depicted as vague, although Helen warns, "She seems vague, but she's a will of her own."[56] Rhoda, arguably a stand-in for Woolf herself in *The Waves*, is associated with "vagueness" (*W* 31). When male characters like Terence Hewett in *The Voyage Out* are depicted as vague, their manliness seems at stake. Hirst critically asks Hewett, "I wonder if it's really nice to be as vague as you are?"[57] Solidity and directness are gendered male, whereas vagueness and "dear Mother English" are aligned to "the feminine nature."

Woolf concludes "Craftsmanship" with a conceit comparing writing to moth collecting.

> Perhaps that is [words'] most striking peculiarity – their need of change. It is because the truth they try to catch is many-sided, and they convey it by being themselves many-sided, flashing this way, then that. Thus they mean one thing to one person, another thing to another; they are unintelligible to one generation, plain as a pikestaff to the next. And it is because of this complexity that they survive. Perhaps then one reason why we have no great poet, novelist, or critic writing today is that we refuse words their liberty. We pin them down to one meaning . . . And when words are pinned down they fold their wings and die. (*C* 251)

Woolf asserts that we "have no great poet, novelist, or critic" because writers, like moth collectors, pin words down and kill them in the effort to examine them. "[W]e are trembling on the verge of one of the great ages of English Literature," she proclaims in "Mr. Bennett and Mrs. Brown," and although "Grammar is violated, syntax disintegrated," the language of the moderns will achieve where the Edwardians' flounders.[58] Allowing language its liberty will require freedom from what Woolf calls in her diary, "this appalling narrative business of the realist: getting on from lunch to dinner" (*DVW* 3:209). Woolf calls words "irreclaimable vagabonds" (*C* 251), and just as she discovered craftiness in the root of craftsmanship, we can locate "vague" in the root of the word vagabond. "Wandering, inconstant, uncertain," the vagueness that Woolf praises in language and the new novel is exactly that which Russell would have eliminated in the search for truths.

Indeed, although Woolf generally avoided coining new words, one word that the *Oxford English Dictionary* still cites Woolf as creating is *vagulous.*[59] During the same summer that Woolf commented repeatedly in her diary about Russell's lectures – "They were going to hear Bertie lecture; I preferred the songsters of Trafalgar square" (*DVW* 1:270) – Woolf uses *vagulous* to describe E. M. Forster. "I like Forster very much," Woolf writes, "though I find him whimsical & vagulous to an extent that frightens me with my own clumsiness & definiteness" (*DVW* 1:291). Derived from the Latin *vagulus*, Woolf's word seems both a compliment and also the opposite of "definiteness," the quality praised by Russell, but clearly a fault according to Woolf. Forster's *vagulous* character seems to hold some sort of negative capability that Woolf fears she lacks. This becomes evident when she uses the word in print in *Mrs. Dalloway* in 1925:

> [Old Sir Harry] liked her; respected her, in spite of her damnable, difficult upper-class refinement, which made it impossible to ask Clarissa Dalloway to sit on his knee. And up came that wandering will-o'-the-wisp, that vagulous phosphorescence, old Mrs. Hilberry, stretching her hands to the blaze of his laughter (about the Duke and the Lady), which, as she heard it across the room, seemed to reassure her on a point which sometimes bothered her if she woke early in the morning . . . how it is certain we must die. (*MD* 175)

The "vagulous phosphorescence" of "old Mrs. Hilberry" contrasts with Sir Harry's physicality: his booming laughter and desire to hold Clarissa upon his knee. Yet her indefiniteness is also a kind of knowledge, and, unlike Sir Harry, she emphatically faces the fact that "we must die." Although she may appear inconsequential to the outside observer ("that wandering will-o'-the-wisp,") she shares with other Woolf heroines, particularly Clarissa herself, a self-consciousness about her own mortality that, kept within reason, is the basis of knowledge in Woolf's work. To be *vagulous*, therefore, reflects a kind of wisdom. Woolf's additional use of a variant of *vagulous* in her diary, describing Ottoline Morrell as "undulated & vagulated," connects *vagulous* to the French word *vague* or wave (*DVW* 3:93). Morrell's character appears changeable to Woolf, like the waves, suggesting a relationship between *vagulousness* and waves. Waves, which I will return to in the final section of this chapter, act as important figures of inescapable change in Woolf's writing, and like moths, they also are connected to words themselves in Woolf's texts. Stretching from her recollection of the childhood waves at St. Ives in *Moments of Being* to their depiction in *The Waves*, waves act as an apt metaphor for the ineradicable vagueness of "dear Mother English" (*C* 250) and its openness to new associations and democratic coinages.[60]

3. *Night and Day* and the "Semi-Transparent Envelope"

Night and Day's protagonist, Katharine Hilberry, sounds as if she would gladly help to usher in Russell's new constitution if she had the chance. Katharine thinks to herself:

> [I]n her mind mathematics were directly opposed to literature. She would not have cared to confess how infinitely she preferred the exactitude, the star-like impersonality, of figures to the confusion, agitation, and vagueness of the finest prose. (*ND* 34)

Katherine Mansfield, whose scathing review of *Night and Day* continues to set the standard criticism of Woolf's longest and most neglected novel, comments on the strangeness of this phrase of Woolf's. She emphasizes that the heroine, the granddaughter of one of England's most famous poets, is in "profound protest against the family tradition, against the making of phrases and (what Mrs. Woolf rather curiously calls) 'the confusion, agitation, and vagueness of the finest prose.'"[61] Mansfield's review strives to pigeonhole *Night and Day* as anachronistic, a wartime novel that refuses to acknowledge the war, a traditional English novel, complete with two concluding marriages and Shakespearean laurels, during the "age of experiment." "In the midst of our admiration," she concludes, "it makes us feel old and chill: we had never thought to look upon its like again!" However, this oddity of "Mrs. Woolf's" phrasing, and her heroine's absolute distrust of language – even as the symbolic heir to England's literature – make it both more of a war novel and less a rote exercise in tradition than Mansfield suggests. Woolf's heroine doubts something about language that is actually central to the novel's "love" plot and comic conclusion, and the focus on language's "confusion, agitation, and vagueness" connects Woolf's early novel to her more obviously experimental later works. In fact, in *Night and Day*, Woolf teaches her heroine (ironically named Katharine) in a novel in the realist tradition something about language and the power of vagueness that Woolf embodies in the form of her later experimental novels.

Mansfield not unfairly highlighted the debt of *Night and Day* to an earlier English literary tradition. Woolf wrote in a letter to Roger Fry that *Night and Day* was an attempt at "a large, old fashioned, high minded English novel."[62] A combination of *Bildungsroman*, portraiture, and autobiography, *Night and Day*, in a "leisurely progression," tells the story of Katharine Hilberry's engagements, first to a young suitable man of her same class, next to the clerk whom she comes to "love."[63] As in Jane Austen's novels, the plot focuses on the marriage of a worthy young protagonist, and in the vein of *Pride and Prejudice* and *Sense and Sensibility*, two marriages rather than one bring the novel to its happy conclusion. The omniscient narrative style is strongly reminiscent of the careful control of Austen or Eliot. Woolf chose to set her novel in a literary environment, where Henry James appears in the caricature of "Mr Fortescue, the eminent novelist" (*ND* 4), and Katharine's employment when she is not showing off the literary memorabilia of her ancestor is to read Henry Fielding to her parents (*ND* 84). In fact, contemporary writers, "the moderns," are caricatured as "too clever and cheap and nasty for words."[64]

Rather than admiring her literary ancestors, Katharine strives for a world of impersonal fact beyond the reaches of impure feelings. Just as Rachel, in *The Voyage Out*, states her dislike of literature in contrast to her love of music, Katharine claims to "hate books" and exclaims, "I've never read even Shakespeare" (*ND* 113). To her poetry-loving fiancé she argues, "I do hate books, ... Why do you want to be for ever talking about your feelings? That's what I can't make out. And poetry's all about feelings – novels are all about feelings" (*ND* 120). Katharine muses on her love for "the exactitude, the star-like impersonality, of figures" compared to "the confusion, agitation, and vagueness of the finest prose," when she is working with her mother. She thinks to herself, "Her mother was the last person she wished to resemble" (*ND* 34). But in the world of *Night and Day*, Katharine cannot escape literature, just as she cannot escape being compared to Shakespearean characters. "And why should she read Shakespeare," Rodney states, "since she *is* Shakespeare – Rosalind, you know" (*ND* 146).

Katharine's utter distrust of language makes her impervious to the offers of love she receives. "But I haven't got the sort of feeling – love, I mean –I don't know what to call it," she insists to her mother and fiancé (*ND* 205). She cannot accept that "love" has multiple interpretations, noting that:

> Much depended, as usual, upon the interpretation of the word love; which word came up again and again, whether she considered Rodney, Denham, Mary Datchet, or herself; and in each case it seemed to stand for something not to be passed by. (*ND* 266)

Each time the word "love" means something important, but it fails "to stand for something" static. Language seems insufficient to Katharine so that whereas Mrs. Hilberry argues, "The best of life is built on what we say when we're in love," Katharine merely states, "we talk a lot of nonsense" (*ND* 260). Just as Rosalind in Shakespeare's *As You Like It*, to whom Katharine is three times compared, urges that "men have died from time to time, and worms have eaten them, but not for love," so also Katharine refuses to accept any profundity to the words of love that first Rodney, then Ralph, urge upon her.[65] Instead, Katharine craves "figures, laws, stars, facts" (*ND* 240). Her disbelief in language actually foils the story and stretches Woolf's novel out much longer than one could conceive (and perhaps, honestly, than one would desire), because her heroine repeatedly refuses Woolf's marriage plot.

Yet, through her mother, Katharine learns that language, rather than the precise astronomy she admires, can best suit the "impure" affairs of humanity. Woolf quite self-consciously makes Mrs. Hilberry, modeled after her Aunt Ritchie, the spirit of the Shakespearean fool.[66] Mrs. Hilberry is marked by her Shakespearean obsession throughout the novel: she claims she needs to re-study Shakespeare's sonnets, she promotes a theory that Anne Hathaway had actually written the sonnets (previewing Woolf's own theory of "Shakespeare's sister" to be written in *A Room of One's Own* ten years later), and she wishes she could shout out to "lawyers hurrying to their work, cabmen squabbling for their fares, little boys rolling their hoops," and everyone else who passes her window, "People, read Shakespeare!" (*ND* 259). When thinking of which Shakespearean character she would like to act, she muses, "I'm – well, I'm a bit of them all; I'm quite a large bit of the fool, but the fools in Shakespeare say all the clever things" (*ND* 260). Woolf carefully sets up Mrs. Hilberry's character early in the book as the wise fool, so that the reader is prepared when she suddenly reappears on the stage, with laurels from Shakespeare's grave at the end of the novel, to bring resolution to a stalemate between the four young lovers.

Before Mrs. Hilberry's intervention, Katharine and Ralph are paralyzed, not feeling themselves in the kind of love that the other couple, Cassandra and William, obviously share, although Ralph asks "what other word describes the state we're in?" (*ND* 360). In contrast Katharine thinks:

> Ah, but her romance wasn't *that* romance. It was a desire, an echo, a sound; she could drape it in colour, see it in form, hear it in music, but not in words; no never in words. She sighed, teased by desires so incoherent, so incommunicable. (*ND* 243)

When Ralph tries to make her into something she is not, she fights against his "damned romantic nonsense," stating, "I'm a matter of fact" person (*ND* 323). Their main difficulty is that their love comes and goes, and they often appear to each other as mere illusions. The lovers in *Night and Day* experience a great division between Night and Day, between Dreams and Reality (Woolf's manuscript title for the novel), and they fail to believe language will connect their experiences.

Ann-Marie Priest notes the centrality of linguistic questions to the novel's plot. "[T]he action of the novel," she writes, "hinges on the incapacity of the word love to represent the relationship between Katharine and Ralph, and their struggles to make it do."[67] However, Priest overstates the case when she reads the conclusions, where Katharine accepts marriage, as decisively "ominous."[68] The ending may seem staged and unbelievable, and Katharine's happiness is not at all secure. However, if as readers we see the ending as merely false artifice it is because we, like Katharine, are refusing to accept the evocative power of language and stories that Mrs. Hilberry offers.

Mrs. Hilberry elicits the help of words and stories to beguile the lovers, and upsets Katharine's belief in mathematics by forcing her to speak of her emotions. Unlike the kind of writing that Katharine says she could admire, which "ought to go from point to point" (*ND* 93), Woolf writes that Mrs. Hilberry "veiled purposely by the vagueness of her words." She describes "[t]he night and the stars, the dawn coming up the barges swimming past, the sun setting," all the time staring with "a gaze that was at once very vague and very penetrating" (*ND* 362). Mrs. Hilberry's stories are both "ancient fairy-tale[s] " and fragments of poetry like the natural interludes in Woolf's *The Waves*. Mrs. Hilberry calls Katharine's mathematics (as well as her notion that she and Ralph might just live together rather than get married) "ugly" compared to the mystical tale of love by which Katharine, in listening to her mother's words, similarly feels compelled (*ND* 411). "A plus B minus C equals *xyz*. It's so dreadfully ugly,

Katharine," Mrs. Hilberry retorts to Katharine's mathematics, whereas "a soothing word when uttered by another, a riveting together of the shattered fragments of the world" calms both Ralph and Katharine (*ND* 412). Although "A plus B minus C equals *xyz*" may mirror Russell's approach to philosophy, as a philosophy of life for Woolf's young protagonist it is absolutely stultifying and needs to be replaced by evocative "shattered fragments" of stories to assure growth.[69]

In contrast to a logical formula, the novel concludes with an image of shared imprecision:

> She felt him trying to piece together in a laborious and elementary fashion fragments of belief, unsoldered and separate, lacking the unity of phrases fashioned by the old believers. Together they groped in this difficult region, where the unfinished, the unfulfilled, the unwritten, the unreturned, came together in their ghostly way and wore the semblance of the complete and the satisfactory. (*ND* 431–2)

Although Ralph's image lacks "unity," somehow this new "unfinished" and "unwritten" means of using language holds out hope to the young lovers. The narrator's statement that Katharine "had now to get used to the fact that some one shared her loneliness" suggests that even though Katharine and Ralph fail to understand each other perfectly, their mutual desire to interpret each other's languages, different though they be, alleviates their isolation (*ND* 419).

This element of soul-to-soul connection, furthermore, works against much of the rest of Woolf's novel, which seems to be a long, eventually futile, rant against Romanticism: a Romanticism that is aligned with vagueness.[70] Katharine's famous grandfather, the "great poet, Richard Alardyce," seems a type of late Romantic, and his famous poems include the title, "Ode to Winter" (*ND* 8). Katharine, in contrast, is connected to classics, to the Elgin marbles. "Katharine doesn't like Titian. She doesn't like apricots, she doesn't like peaches . . . She likes the Elgin marbles, and grey days without any sun," Rodney explains (*ND* 143–4). In order to escape her poetic ancestor and her literary parents, Katharine seeks out a pre-Christian Classicism. It could be Katharine, rather than Woolf, who writes in her essay "On Not Knowing Greek": [I]t is to the Greeks that we turn when we are sick of the vagueness, of the confusion, of the Christianity and its consolations, of our own age."[71] Katharine looks to the Greeks when she wants to find "figures, laws, starts, facts," to discern something objective to place against the vagueness and confusion of her environment. In *Jacob's Room* (to which I will return in the following section) the Greeks are again associated with a lofty precision whereas the Christian age is one of vague meanderings: Frazer, "the atheist," "abhorred vagueness – the Christian religion, for example" (*JR* 91). However, in both *Night and Day* and in *Jacob's Room*, the Greeks are discovered to be the name of an illusory precision, another myth created by, and subject to, desire and emotion.[72] "But it is the governesses who start the Greek myth," Jacob thinks to himself in Greece, "[t]he point is, however, that we have been brought up in an illusion" (*JR* 120). Woolf, like Katharine, often seems to want to distance herself from any kind of Romanticism. In a letter about *Night and Day* she writes to Lytton Strachey, "Of course you put your infallible finger upon the spot – romanticism," and asks, "How do I catch it? Not from my father. I think it must have been my Great Aunts."[73] Her novel, however, implies that Classicism like that of Jacob or Katharine (or Hulme or Eliot as well) seems more of an "illusion" than the Romanticism Woolf fears she has caught.[74]

Katharine's affection for the Elgin marbles actually connects her to the other main female character in the book, Mary Datchet, whose role in *Night and Day* is as important as that of Jacques in *As You Like It.* Mary sits and admires the Elgin marbles in the British Museum at the beginning of the book, and, although Ralph might think that "[t]wo women less like each other could scarcely be imagined" than Katharine and Mary, Woolf sets them up in many ways as twins. They both fashion their romantic fantasies around the Elgin marbles by comparing an imagined or real lover to "a young Greek horseman, who reins his horse back so sharply that it half falls on its haunches" (*ND* 190).[75] Their mutual love for Ralph, their need to do something important, and their desire to hide the work they really care about all connect them. Mary is sometimes read as the "real heroine" of the novel because, whereas Katharine is engaged to be married at the end of the book, Mary is engaged to her own writing and socialist work.[76] Woolf writes:

> The whole aspect of the place started another train of thought [for Katharine] and struck her as enviably free; in such a room one could work – one could have a life of one's own.
>
> "I think you're very lucky," she observed. "I envy you, living alone and having your own things" – and engaged in this exalted way, which had no recognition of engagement-ring, she added in her own mind. (*ND* 229)

Night and Day ends with Mary's sitting room light acting as a beacon, like Gatsby's green light, for Katharine and Ralph – "[her light] was a sign of triumph shining there for ever, not to be extinguished this side of the grave" (*ND* 431). Although Mary is prominently excluded, like Jacques, from the happy conclusions at the end of the novel, and although her decision to live purely for work is certainly single-minded, it is hard not to read Mary's "enviable freedom," her writing, and her room of her own as a kind of triumph.[77]

Leonard Woolf, however, found *Night and Day* depressing. "L. finds the philosophy of N&D very melancholy," Woolf noted in her diary, yet, "[t]he process of discarding the old [answers], when one is by no means certain what to put in their place, is a sad one" (*D* I:259). In some ways Woolf's novel's ending is bleak because the heroine must set aside her passion for mathematics to find passion and companionship. Katharine and Mary Datchet, formerly twinned, are exiled from each other at the book's end; Woolf's moral may be that love and work are mutually exclusive. And yet, as a philosophy posited in a novel it is less stark because Woolf argues in favor of the power of literature, noting that mathematics fails to hold the answers that Shakespeare's fool or vague prose can offer. Solid answers, like Katharine's astronomy, and even traditional writing demonstrating "unity of phrase," like that of *Night and Day* itself, must be discarded for a writing that is "unfinished," "unsoldered," and "unwritten." Only the possibilities inherent in this new "unfinished" language, whether in the scribbles of Katharine and Ralph or in Mary's manuscript (bad as it allegedly is) conclude the book with a sense of hope.

Ralph and Katharine agree upon a particular "unfinished" fragment as a significant image at the end of the novel that is importantly vague and relates both to an image from Henry James and to Woolf's essay "Modern Fiction." In an effort to communicate with Katharine, Ralph has drawn with "half-obliterated scratches" a strange symbol for her (*ND* 414). Woolf writes:

> It represented by its circumference of smudges surrounding a central blot all that encircling glow which for him surrounded, inexplicably, so many objects of life, softening their sharp outline, so that he could see certain streets, books, and situations wearing a halo almost perceptible to the physical eye. (*ND* 420)

Woolf's image merits comparison to a passage from Henry James that Woolf liked. Explaining how he viewed his novel *The Awkward Age*, James described:

> The neat figure of a circle consisting of a number of small rounds disposed at equal distances about a central object. The central object was my situation, my subject in itself, to which the thing would owe its title, and the small rounds represented so many distinct lamps, as I liked to call them, the function of each of which would be to light with all due intensity one of its aspects.[78]

In her essay "The Method of Henry James," written for the *Times Literary Supplement* in 1918 while she was writing *Night and Day*, Woolf had quoted this passage admiringly. Woolf notes, "One had almost rather read what [Henry James] meant to do than read what he actually did," and praised James's notion of fiction acting as "so many distinct lamps." If "[w]e want to be rid of realism," as Woolf proclaims, Henry James's theory seems to offer a new method.[79]

However, the image in *Night and Day*, which she would soon reconfigure in "Modern Fiction," is markedly different from James's "neat figure." As in James's image there is a central object of focus and there is a circumference of illumination. Yet in Woolf's novel, James's central object has been blurred, made into a "central blot," and rather than the symmetry of James's lamps at equal distances, Ralph's image is, like Russell's photograph, "smudge[d]." Ralph communicates to Katharine that the world, "streets, books, and situations," is not distinct but blurred and that objects are not precise but they have an "encircling glow."

In his lecture on the vagueness of language Russell emphasizes that words have a similar "penumbra." Russell writes that language cannot maintain precision: "The fact is that all words are attributable without doubt over a certain area," and yet they "become questionable within a penumbra, outside which they are again certainly not attributable" (*V* 63). A word, Russell argues, has an area of certain usage but then a penumbra where usage is vague. And one cannot escape this penumbra:

> Someone might seek to obtain precision in the use of words by saying that no word is to be applied in the penumbra, but unfortunately the penumbra itself is not accurately definable, and all the vaguenesses which apply to the primary use of words apply also when we try to fix a limit to their indubitable applicability. (*V* 63–4)

Ralph's vision of life is like Russell's view of language; a penumbra or halo inexplicably and inescapably smudges certainty.

Having finished *Night and Day*, Woolf writes in "Modern Fiction":

> Life is not a series of gig lamps symmetrically arranged; life is a luminous halo, a semi-transparent envelope surrounding us from the beginning of consciousness to the end. Is it not the task of the novelist to convey this varying, this unknown and uncircumscribed spirit, whatever aberration or complexity it may display, with as little mixture of the alien and external as possible? (*EVW* 4:160–1)

Woolf clearly rejects James's vision of symmetrical lamps, and her earlier depiction of Ralph's picture is now adopted as part of her own belief about "Life."[80] Woolf's essay particularly targets "the materialists," "Mr. Wells, Mr. Bennett and Mr. Galsworthy," whose realist technique "provides scenes of tragedy, comedy, and excitement," and yet fails to capture life. This is where Woolf writes, "if one were free and could set down what one chose, there would be no plot, little probability, and a vague general confusion in which the clear-cut features of the tragic, the comic, the passionate, and the lyrical were dissolved beyond the possibility of separate recognition" (*EVW* 3:33). Woolf's new generation of writers, the moderns or "spiritualists," will embrace the "vague general confusion" of modern existence and will not cling to the conventional distinctions between tragedy and comedy. Her new image of fiction rejects Henry James's "fixed lamps" and symmetry as well as the linear plot and probability of the materialists and seeks to replace their sharp shapes and clear-cut categories. Moreover, the penumbra that Russell attributes to language is for Woolf an actual quality of the world, a necessary function of consciousness; the "semi-transparent envelope" that the novelist must convey may be the ontological vagueness that Russell believes is a fallacy.

After *Night and Day*, even in *The Years* or in *Between the Acts*, Woolf demonstrates she has discarded writing that goes "from point to point to point," in favor of the vision of vagueness that Katherine and Ralph share at the end of *Night and Day* and that she outlines in her essays on modern novels. Woolf's characteristic experimentation of later works like *Mrs. Dalloway*, combining free indirect discourse, multiple perspectives, and interspersed passages of tragedy (Septimus's suicide) and comedy (Clarissa Dalloway's reconnection with Peter Walsh and Sally Seton), embodies the new formal vagueness that *Night and Day* teaches the reader to accept. Clarissa's sense of a penumbra surrounding her, because "she felt herself everywhere," leads to her "transcendental theory" that she has "[o]dd affinities" with strangers and unfamiliar places (*MD* 152–3). Woolf's narrative structure supports Clarissa's sense of her vague connections to the rest of the world by paralleling Clarissa's and Septimus's streams of thought. Indeed, because Clarissa's party is the closest to a metaphor for Woolf's own writing in the novel, Woolf underscores the vagueness of her novel's structure. Fearing Peter Walsh believes she has matured into a mere society hostess, Clarissa asserts that her parties are "an offering; which sounded horribly vague" (*MD* 121). Although the meaning of Clarissa's party, "an offering; to combine, to create," may seem horrible in being "vague" to her, Woolf's narrated monologue mirrors Clarissa's desire to "to combine, to create" in uniting disparate individuals (*MD* 121–2). Clarissa's party is itself a vague symbol of the structure of Woolf's later novels. Indeed,

Woolf asserts that any symbolism in her writing needs to be vague, recalling her distaste for Russell's new symbolic language: "I can't manage Symbolism except in this vague, generalised way," she insisted, "directly I'm told what a thing means, it becomes hateful to me."[81]

In a letter about beginning *Jacob's Room* Woolf noted:

> .. These little pieces [the short stories] . . . were the treats I allowed myself when I had done my exercise in the conventional style. I shall never forget the day I wrote The Mark on the Wall – all in a flash, as if flying, after being kept stone breaking for months. The Unwritten Novel was the great discovery, however . . . How I trembled with excitement; and then Leonard came in, and I drank my milk and concealed my excitement, and wrote I suppose another page of that interminable Night and Day.[82]

Just as Jane Austen had to conceal her writing, Mary has to conceal her excitement about her new work on socialism, and Katharine has to conceal her mathematics, Woolf, during the gestation of *Jacob's Room*, had to conceal her excitement about this "great discovery" in writing. Yet Katharine's decision to share her math, like Mary's decision to join in socialist movements, is a harbinger of Woolf's own experimental style. *Jacob's Room*, stemming from the experimental sketches, extends Katharine's lesson about vagueness in *Night and Day* to challenge the narratives and historical repercussions of "the conventional style."

4. Jacob's Shadow

> A shadow fell across Evelina's window – Jacob's shadow, though it was not Jacob.
>
> –Virginia Woolf, *Jacob's Room*[83]

In one of the asides in *Jacob's Room*, the narrator comments on the impossibility of impersonal judgments. "It seems that a profound, impartial, and absolutely just opinion of our fellow-creatures is utterly unknown," she asserts.[84]

> In any case life is but a procession of shadows, and God knows why it is that we embrace them so eagerly, and see them depart with such anguish, being shadows. And why, if this and much more than this is true, why are we yet surprised in the window corner by a sudden vision that the young man in the chair is of all things in the world the most real, the most solid, the best known to us – why indeed? For the moment after we know nothing about him. (*JR* 60)

Woolf's narrator puzzles over Jacob's reality, how he can suddenly appear "known to us" and a moment after be a stranger. Woolf wrote that in her biography *Roger Fry*, "the central figure remained vague," and this problem of the central character remaining shadowy is also a criticism often leveled at Jacob Flanders.[85] Woolf chooses, however, to depict in *Jacob's Room* this view that "life is but a procession of shadows," which is the exact opposite view from Bertrand Russell's where the "real truth" is "something precise, clear, definite" – "the real truth of which that vague thing is a sort of shadow."[86] Although for a moment Jacob may appear "the most real, the most solid," the next minute he is unknown and also unknowable, because, like Woolf's brother Thoby, he dies when still a young man. What form should an artist use to convey the ironic fact that the "real truth" of life is, finally, that the only knowledge we can acquire is vague? *Jacob's Room* circles around two questions: How do we know someone? And does one brief human life make any difference? Rather than providing "clear, definite" and impartial answers to these questions as *Night and Day* may have done, Woolf's next novel, through its fragmentation, gaps, and narratorial asides, demonstrates the impossibility of ever finding objective answers. Objectivity is in itself challenged, while the disjointed images and "scrap[s] of conversation" provide a kind of smudged photograph of Jacob, which is better than a precise portrait because "[i]t is no use trying to sum people up" (*JR* 111, 135).

Woolf provides two passages that can act as coda for her narrative method in *Jacob's Room*.[87] After Jacob has had an unpleasant dinner with the Plumers at Cambridge, he returns home angered by the stupidity of the conversation. The narrator comments (perhaps vocalizing Jacob's wishes), "there will be no form in the world unless Jacob makes one for himself" (*JR* 28). As Alex Zwerdling writes in *Virginia Woolf and the Real World*, "Unlike the classic *Bildungsroman*, *Jacob's Room* lacks a teleology," because Jacob is "interrupted by death at the stage of experimenting upon himself."[88] Woolf's novel – with multiple line gaps (of different sizes) between sections of chapters, so many names that the reader cannot possibly make sense of them all, and lacunae (what actually happens at the great romantic moment when Sandra Wentworth Williams and Jacob reach the acropolis?) – reveals formally that Jacob's life is ended by the war before he and his story have the chance to choose a conventional design.[89] In contrast to *Night and Day*'s concluding marriages, *Jacob's Room* ends merely with a question.[90]

A "scrap of conversation" could also summarize much of Woolf's narrative method. The narrator comments that, although "Jacob had nothing to hide from his mother," there is much that he leaves out from his letters home (*JR* 114). "Well, not a word of this was ever told to

Mrs. Flanders," the narrator admits, "nor what happened when they paid the bill and left the restaurant, and walked along the Boulevard Raspail" (*JR* 110). Instead the narrator states, "Then here is another scrap of conversation" (*JR* 111). *Jacob's Room* is composed of disjointed, often temporally simultaneous, scraps of conversation, interrupted by a narrator musing on topics, perhaps raised within those conversations.[91] Woolf's narrative jumps apparently at random, including parts that do not seem to add up to any kind of whole. "Nobody sees any one as he is," the narrator notes, "They see a whole – they see all sorts of things – they see themselves ..." (*JR* 23). Woolf asks us to question how Jacob chooses what to relay to his mother and what to leave out, just as we wonder how the narrative chooses which anecdotes to include and which to omit.

Jacob's Room is a novel that seems fixated on the topic of censorship – insisting that even if Jacob had lived, there is much Mrs. Flanders (and any inquiring observer) would never know about him. Some of Jacob's self-censorship is intentional; for example, he does not want to share with Bonamy his feeling that he is in love for fear of his reaction, or he leaves out from his mother's letters (symbolized by her letter waiting outside his closed bedroom door) his sexual encounters with Florinda and Laurette. The text, mirroring Jacob's omissions, enacts its own kind of censorship. Although Jacob himself is writing an angry letter against censorship and calls a version of Wycherly in which "several indecent words and some indecent phrases" are omitted an "outrage ... a breach of faith; sheer prudery; token of a lewd mind and a disgusting nature," the narrative glaringly censors its own content (*JR* 58). Jacob is angry that in the "disembowelled" text the omitted words are "indicated only by asterisks" (*JR* 58–9). And yet a few paragraphs later when Jacob himself tells an "indecent" joke, Woolf places "..." where the "landlady's name" would need to be for the joke to be comprehensible. Woolf seems to highlight that her text too is in some ways disemboweled.[92]

Indeed, much of the omitted information, such as Jacob's philosophical conversations with his friend Timmy, is censored by the text rather than by Jacob. Woolf wittily leaves out the content of Jacob and Timmy's philosophical argument, instead only including, "It follows –" and "It follows –" and Timmy's response, "That is so" (*JR* 40–1). The reader is forced to see the form of the argument and is frustrated (or amused) by being barred from its content. In addition, Woolf suggests that in academic philosophy the content may be irrelevant: It is the form of the argument and formal resolution that matters. The narrator notes, similarly, that we are thwarted by the faces of strangers on the bus: "Each had his past shut in him like the leaves of a book known to him by heart; and his friends could only read the title" (*JR* 53). If we are only reading the title of *Jacob's Room*, we are given Jacob's space but never any definitive access to his character. Like listening to a philosophical argument without content, reading *Jacob's Room* frustrates traditional characterization, highlighting narrative's limitations and refusals.

In a central passage of the novel, Woolf provides a lengthy description of all the objects within Jacob's actual room, his books, slippers, photographs, and other items, but then summarizes: "Listless is the air in an empty room, just swelling the curtain; the flowers in the jar shift. One fibre in the wicker armchair creaks, though no one sits there" (*JR* 31). Scholars have often noted that this passage is Woolf's parody of the "materialist" novel, which would provide exacting details about a person's environment in order to explain his or her character. For Woolf this information is superfluous: "no one sits there." Moreover, this refrain is repeated at the end of the novel when Jacob is dead, suggesting that Jacob's room itself has no intrinsic connection to the live Jacob. Woolf is satisfied, from the perspective of one kind of craftsmanship, that her predecessors can "make a book so well . . . there is not so much as a draught between the frames of the window, or a crack in the boards," but she asks "And yet – if life should refuse to live there?" (*EVW* 4:158–9). We still have Jacob's room at the end of the novel, yet he no longer lives there. Mrs. Flanders and Bonamy are in fact standing in Jacob's room in the final scene – and we still have the novel *Jacob's Room* – but what do we know for certain about Jacob? As the narrator asks of Seabrook, "Had he, then, been nothing?" (*JR* 11).[93]

The questions that Woolf's novel asks about Jacob's meaning are certainly, according to Russell's definition, vague. Like "truth" and "falsehood," which as Russell has demonstrated, fail to have precise values, the narrator's question – "Had he, then, been nothing?" – is not answered within the text; instead, the idiosyncratic form of the novel itself demonstrates the irrelevance of that kind of impersonal question. Woolf has provided, in addition to Jacob's physical space, his impact on those who love him, including Bonamy, Mrs. Flanders, and the narrator. *Jacob's Room* often seems the least possibly impersonal of novels – because the narrator strives but fails to remain omniscient and she admits that she circles around Jacob like one of Jacob's moths around the flame. Sebastian Knowles, in "Narrative, Death and Desire: The Three Senses of Humor in *Jacob's Room*," suggests that the narrator loves Jacob and explains that the shifts in the narrative omniscience and frustrated semiscience involve this love: "Love is blind in this novel, and the narrator is the blindest of all."[94] Indeed, the novel's form itself, in addition to the narrator's perspective, is influenced by the narrator's love for Jacob.

"As for following him back to his rooms, no – that we won't do," the narrator asserts and suggests a kind of distance from Jacob (*JR* 81). However in fact "we" do exactly that; we watch Jacob as "He stretched himself. He went to bed" (*JR* 85). The narrator comments:

> But though all this may very well be true – so Jacob thought and spoke – so he crossed his legs . . . there remains over something which can never be conveyed to a second person save by Jacob himself . . . Then consider the effect of sex – how between man and woman it hangs wavy, tremulous, so that here's a valley, there's a peak, when in truth, perhaps, all's as flat as my hand. Even the exact words get the wrong accent on them. But something is always impelling one to hum vibrating, like the hawk moth, at the mouth of the cavern of mystery, endowing Jacob Flanders with all sorts of qualities he had not at all.[95]

The text itself seems to attempt to demonstrate this "effect of sex," the effect of attraction on narrative, distributing most weight to Jacob's moments with other women, and making unexplained shifts and changes, so it feels "wavy, tremulous." In fact, in the manuscript Woolf writes after, "Then consider the effect of sex," "And here let every~~one~~ body use the pen for himself or herself."[96] The "effect of sex" is connected to the act of writing, and Woolf initially turned to her readers to take upon themselves – specifically every *body* – the act of describing Jacob with this attraction in mind. The narrator's tonal shifts, from bitter irony to longing back to impersonal omniscience, often seem explained by this "effect of sex" – she sounds like a striking mix between a mourning family member and a spurned lover. It is worth comparing Woolf's longing letters to her brother at university when she is left isolated, lacking her intellectual companion, and he has moved on to adult relationships with fellow students and with other women; in both we "feel the want."[97] The novel itself embodies what Mrs. Flanders' letters "can never, never say, whatever it may be . . . come back, come back, come back to me" (*JR* 77). The reader too is party to this longing for Jacob: We have to create him in our minds; we have to compose his story from the gaps in the text. The self-conscious censorship in the narrative insists upon what has been called the "space for the subjectivity of the reader."[98]

Just as in *A Room of One's Own*, the narrator of *Jacob's Room* is frustrated by being excluded from the "great patriarchal machine," both in London and at Cambridge, that has created Jacob.[99] Christine Froula argues in *Virginia Woolf and the Bloomsbury Avant-Garde* that Woolf demonstrates that Jacob's death was the inevitable outcome of his upbringing, and that "Woolf does not tell Jacob's story but unwrites it to expose the social forces that initiate him into masculinity and leave him dead on the battlefield."[100] Jacob's education at Cambridge, including his philosophical training, is one of the social forces at work in his initiation, teaching him the art and tone of academic argumentation: "That is so" (*JR* 41). Woolf's novel connects this learned objectivity, the kind behind scientific advancement, to the causes of the war. Having repeated the gossip of Mr. Bowley and Miss Julia Eliot, the narrator comments that "however long these gossips sit, and however they stuff out their victim's characters till they are swollen and tender . . . they never come to a decision" (*JR* 135). Her disdain for gossip, for "character-mongering," leads her to state: "So we are driven back to see what the other side means – the men in clubs and Cabinets – when they say that character-drawing is a frivolous fireside art, a matter of pins and needles, exquisite outlines enclosing vacancy, flourishes and mere scrawls" (*JR* 136). The narrator appears to concur that "character-drawing" (her goal in telling of Jacob) is an unimportant business. However, immediately following this passage are the lines:

> The battleships ray out over the North Sea, keeping their stations accurately apart. At a given signal all the guns are trained on a target . . . With equal nonchalance a dozen young men in the prime of life descend with composed faces into the depths of the sea; and there impassively (though with perfect mastery of machinery) suffocate uncomplainingly together. (*JR* 136)

If character-mongering is "frivolous" at least it is not lethal, like this nonchalant impassiveness; moreover, insisting that young men are not "machinery" might in fact prevent such violence. "The other side" is clearly implicated in this violence whose "actions, together with the incessant commerce of banks, laboratories, chancellories, and houses of business, are the strokes which oar the world forward, they say" (*JR* 136).[101] If the objective work in "laboratories" is leading to war, Woolf's personal narrative, which, like gossip, relishes interpersonal relations, emotion, and subjective responses, acts as a pacifist gesture.[102]

Woolf's method in *Jacob's Room* is akin to her descriptions of her aunt Julia Cameron's approach to photography: "She used to say that in her photography a hundred negatives were destroyed before she achieved one good result; her object being to overcome realism by diminishing in the least degree the precision of the focus."[103] *Jacob's Room*, too, "overcome[s] realism" in presenting an imprecise picture of Jacob. Russell advocates maps, catalogues, and accurate photographs over language in the search for "precision" (*V* 65). *Jacob's Room* suggests it is this kind of objective and impersonal Oxbridge philosophy that leads to Jacob's demise.

5. "I Begin to Doubt the Fixity of Tables": Solipsism and *The Waves*

> my present feeling is that this vague and dream like world, without love, or heart, or passion, or sex, is the world I really care about, and find interesting. For, though they are dreams to you, and I cant express them at all adequately, these things are perfectly real to me.
>
> –Virginia Woolf, letter to Madge Vaughan[104]

In this final section I would like to turn to the vagueness of *The Waves*, the novel many critics, agreeing with Leonard Woolf, consider Woolf's "masterpiece" (*DVW* 4:36). Waves, themselves, are quintessentially vague, with no real beginning or end. Woolf seems to note this connection, just as she knew that *The Waves*' French translation was called *Les Vagues*. When she admits to her diary the difficulty of crafting *The Waves*, she writes, "never, in my life, did I attack such a vague yet elaborate design":

> whenever I make a mark I have to think of its relation to a dozen others. And though I could go on ahead easily enough, I am always stopping to consider the whole effect ... I am not quite satisfied with this method of picking out things in the room & being reminded by them of other things. (*DVW* 3:259)

The manuscript title was "The Moths," and Woolf's description of her method above recalls her analysis of language in "Craftsmanship."[105] If the "moths" are the words of her book, through her "elaborate design," Woolf tries not to kill them in pinning them down. She strives to allow words their "liberty," relying heavily on metaphors and thinking of a word's "relation to a dozen others." *The Waves*' reduction of narrative to a series of soliloquies juxtaposed to natural interludes investigates what Bernard calls "the world seen without a self" (*W* 230), and finally depicts the vague border between the world and the self.

If in *Orlando* Woolf explodes literary realism through her expansion of time and narrative interruptions by a chatty biographer, in *The Waves*, published right after *Orlando*, Woolf shrinks fiction to its barest parts. As Gillian Beer notes in her comparison of these two novels:

> [T]he characters inhabit a world in which all that is traditionally central to narrative has been peripheralised or obliterated: Percival's adventures in India, Bernard's family, Louis' city career, Jinny's lovers, even the crisis of Rhoda's madness and the love affair between her and Louis are present only as fragmentary allusion.[106]

With a plot like Orlando's "obliterated," *The Waves* gives us in its place the six speakers' soliloquies offset by natural interludes, and Woolf's structure highlights the distinctions among these speakers and between the speakers and what she calls "insensitive nature."[107] "The interludes are very difficult," Woolf wrote in her diary, "yet I think essential; so as to bridge & also give a background – the sea; insensitive nature – I don't know."[108] *The Waves* formally presents us with the same conundrum that *To The Lighthouse* more overtly addresses in Andrew's description of Mr. Ramsay's philosophy: "'Subject and object and the nature of reality'" (*TTL* 26). (Lily, the artist, unable to comprehend, needs Andrew's further description: "'Think of a kitchen table, then' he told her, 'when you're not there.'")[109] Formally *The Waves*' division between the speaking subjects and the natural interludes is very precise: The interludes' italicization both objectifies the natural world and distances the human subjects from this "background."

Indeed, just as the characters in this novel comment on their sense of isolation, *The Waves* formally gives the reader a sense of claustrophobic isolation. "I am alone" acts as a refrain throughout the childhood monologues and a central theme in Bernard's final summation (*W* 7, 9, 22, 231). Structurally the lack of dialogue, strange verb tense in its "declarative discourse," and rigid distinctions between the sections isolates the reader from both the speakers and the natural world.[110] This isolation may indeed stem from Woolf's original sources and plans for what she called this "abstract mystical eyeless book: a playpoem" (*DVW* 3:203). Woolf's novel had multiple sources, including Woolf's crucial vision of a "fin" in 1926 – "how it is not oneself but something in the universe that one's left with. [...] One sees a fin passing far out" (*DVW* 3:113) – as well as Vanessa's letter describing a huge moth "tapping" at a window in 1927.[111] What both the fin and moth image have in common is that they embody an external, natural force jarringly distinct from the perceiving human subject. Woolf's initial plan for the novel reinforces this sense of isolation by reducing even her language down to its most minimalist parts:

> Why not invent a new kind of play – as for instance
> Woman thinks: ...
> He does.
> Organ Plays.
> She writes.
> They say:
> She sings:
> Night speaks:
> They miss (*DVW* 3:128)

This kind of minimalist plan, seeming more in the style of Gertrude Stein than Woolf, boils narrative down to simple noun and verb.[112] Although this fragment is merely a germ of the final version of *The Waves*, Woolf retains in the later versions the contrast between "He does" and "Night speaks." Humanity (distilled to a faceless noun/pronoun) is juxtaposed to the external world (the organ/the night), and both seem impersonally objectified.

Indeed, in *The Waves*, what I believe is Woolf's vaguest and most visionary work, her stated goal was a kind of impersonality described in her essay "The Narrow Bridge of Art" (1927). There, four years after "Modern Fiction," she explains much of the form of *The Waves*, her "playpoem," which she was writing at the same time.[113] In "The Narrow Bridge of Art," she posits that the novel, "[t]hat cannibal" form, is beginning in the modern age to take over the role that poetry used to have.[114] Importantly, these works will no longer be called novels. As early as *The Voyage Out*, Woolf was already dissatisfied with calling her works "novels": "I have an idea that I will invent a new name for my books to supplant 'novel.' A new – by Virginia Woolf. But what? Elegy?"[115] In "The Narrow Bridge of Art," she notes, "we shall be forced to invent new names for the different books which masquerade under this one heading." In the manuscript of *The Waves* she writes a note: "[T]he author would be glad if the following pages were not read as a novel," and having completed *The Waves,* she vows to call her following novels themselves "Waves": "write another 4 novels: Waves, I mean."[116] The role of these "Waves" will be, according to Woolf, to "stand further back from life." "It will give," Woolf writes, "the outline rather than the detail. It will make little use of the marvelous fact-recording power, which is one of the attributes of fiction." In short, Woolf argues, "it will give the relation of the mind to general ideas and its soliloquy in solitude," because "[w]e long for some more impersonal relationship."

This impersonality is exactly what Woolf superficially provides in *The Waves*: "This shall be childhood; but it must not be my childhood," Woolf insists. Each character in *The Waves* is differentiated by having his or her own distinct refrain, whether it is Louis's "My father is a banker in Brisbane" (*W* 13) or Susan's "I love [. . .] and I hate" (*W* 10). The natural portions describe the passage of the sun over the course of an entire day. The voice of the "natural interludes" appears disconnected from those of the six main characters and is "*uncompromising, undeniable.*" Jane Marcus in "Britannia Rules *The Waves*," has pointed out that the "italicized interludes take the form of a set of Hindu prayers to the sun."[117] The continuation of the sun's course, the singing of the birds, and the ceaseless repetition of the waves underscore the indifference of the natural world to the death of Percival, killed by falling off his horse. "The waves massed themselves, curved their backs crashed," Woolf writes, "They swept round the rocks, and the spray, leaping high, spattered the walls of a cave that had been dry before, and left pools inland, where some fish stranded lashed its tail as the wave drew back" (*W* 132). The natural interludes seem as concerned about the suffering of the six characters as the waves are about the stranded fish.

However, it is often very difficult for readers to keep the voices of the six characters separate, because they share a common vocabulary and tone. J. W. Graham, in "Point of View in *The Waves*: Some Services of Style," demonstrates that over the course of revising her manuscript, Woolf gradually eliminated the omniscient voice that originally narrated the soliloquies. Graham explains that initially the characters were filtered through a narrator and that the similarity between their word choices and consistent verb tense (the pure present: "I go") can be explained by this late change. Their voices are like "listening to a running verbatim translation of six different speakers done by a single translator."[118] Woolf's decision to dispose of an omniscient narrator leaves curiously similar-sounding voices and emphasizes the connections between the characters' apparently different experiences. In addition, within the soliloquies the characters finally highlight their unity. When Susan tries to tell Bernard he is separate from her, he insists, "But when we sit together, close ... we melt into each other with phrases. We are edged with mist. We make an unsubstantial territory" (*W* 10). This early sense that they are joined, "edged with mist," sounds like a description of an impressionist painting and foreshadows his realization after Percival's death that he does not know the distinction between himself and his friends: "I am not one person; I am many people; I do not altogether know who I am – Jinny, Susan, Neville, Rhoda, or Louis: or how to distinguish my life from theirs" (*W* 221).

As early as 1903 Woolf had written in her diary: "I think I see for a moment how our minds are all threaded together," and when she was pressed upon to explain whether the voices in *The Waves* were connected she answered:

> But I did mean that in some vague way we are the same person, and not separate people. The six characters were supposed to be one ... I wanted to give the sense of continuity, instead of which most people say, no you've given the sense of flowing and passing away and that nothing matters. Yet I feel things matter quite immensely.[119]

"The six characters are supposed to be one," Woolf argues, but that is because she believes, "in some vague way," that people are not separate. Woolf wishes to portray the "sense of community," which to her does not reduce the significance of each person. Bernard, who recites the final soliloquy of the novel, resists death – "Against you I will fling myself, unvanquished and unyielding, O Death!" (*W* 238). He also sees the world and "everyone with blurred edges" (*W* 39). His voice calling for a resistance to death acts as a communal assertion. Woolf's *The Waves* is a "vague yet elaborate design," depicting a "vague" philosophy.

Even the natural interludes flow into Woolf's "sense of community." Details from the italicized passages, in fact, connect to the characters' refrains. For example, at midday, the time when Percival dies, Woolf writes, "The waves fell; withdrew and fell again, like the thud of a great beast stamping" (*W* 118). Louis repeatedly thinks "I hear tramplings, tremblings, stirrings round me," and hears a "chained beast [which] stamps and stamps on the shore" (*W* 7, 52). The natural interludes, rather than being impersonal, echo the language and images of the characters. The external world and the soliloquies of the six characters are all subsumed into one great visionary monologue. Woolf spells out this notion that "in some vague way we are the same people" and connected to the "whole world" when explaining her philosophy in *Moments of Being*:

> From this I reach what I might call a philosophy; at any rate it is a constant idea of mine; that behind the cotton wool is hidden a pattern; that we – I mean all human beings – are connected with this; that the whole world is a work of art; that we are parts of the work of art . . . we are the words; we are the music; we are the thing itself.[120]

"[A]ll human beings," she explains, are connected by impalpable links; further, as in *The Waves*, they are all elements of "the whole world." The monologues as well as the natural interludes are all part of "a pattern" and that vague pattern forms *The Waves*.[121]

Critics have often argued that in *The Waves* Woolf demonstrates her frustration with language's limitations, and this fact is certainly true for Bernard. Michael Whitworth rightly notes, for example, that "the characters in *The Waves* are highly self-conscious about the attractions and limitations of language. Bernard's facility with 'phrase-making' is seen as both a strength and a limitation."[122] When Bernard tries to "describe the world seen without a self" he laments language's inadequacies: "There are no words. Blue, red – even they distract, even they hide with thickness instead of letting the light through. How describe or say anything in articulate words again?" (*W* 230). Bernard longs for a "little language such as lovers use," which mirrors, in its stripped down depiction, Woolf's minimalist plan for *The Waves* (*W* 236). Bernard's frustration stems from his sense that his phrases are "neat," that they beautify experience and estrange him from reality: "bare things, this coffee-cup, this knife, this fork, things in themselves, myself being myself" (*W* 236). Yet "bare" reality fails him, just as language fails to be precise. "I begin to doubt the fixity of tables, the reality of here and now," he laments, and his final vision is less one of "solid objects" then a visionary parable (*W* 231). Just as he transforms from "being myself" to a horseman galloping against death, so also his language "undergoes a gradual transformation" as each word is followed by "its train of phantom phrases" (*W* 230). Metaphors, personification, and word repetition finally are Bernard's best tools for explaining his sense of "eternal renewal" (*W* 238), just as they are Woolf's tools for describing a world that is both objective – the novel concludes: "The waves broke on the shore" – and also subjective – Bernard concludes: "in me too the wave rises" (*W* 238).

What Woolf's vision in *The Waves* and in her "philosophy" risks is a kind of solipsism. Russell's "Vagueness" lecture concludes by suggesting that the possible end result of ontological vagueness is solipsism: "If you are willing to believe that nothing exists except what you directly experience, no other person can prove that you are wrong, and probably no valid argument exists against your view." He suggests that we slide into solipsism if we refuse to accept the fallacy of verbalism. Woolf's visionary novel illustrating the vagueness of the whole world may be a kind of solipsistic reverie. Both Banfield and S. P. Rosenbaum, two formidable critics of Woolf and philosophy argue that Virginia Woolf is a philosophical realist, following from her reading of either Russell or G. E. Moore (and his "Refutation of Idealism"). Rosenbaum, for example, argues that Woolf consistently criticized "views of reality that ignore or minimize either half of the dualism" of external facts and the perceiving mind.[123] The problem for Woolf, however, as I have argued throughout this chapter, is that the border between external facts and "insensitive nature" is unstable. Woolf seeks to portray the external fact, but insists that facts are not "uncompromising," as Mr. Ramsay (or Russell or Moore) would have us believe. Further, those facts have a penumbra or semitransparent envelope surrounding them. Language may describe this penumbra but cannot provide the kind of impersonality Woolf claims to seek in "The Narrow Bridge of Art."

A significant image for an objective fact – like the fin and the moth that inspired *The Waves* – throughout Woolf's writing is a tree. In *Mrs. Dalloway*, Clarissa's spiritual notion that we are all connected like trees is undermined by the fact that her sister Sylvia has been killed by a falling tree. In *A Room of One's Own*, the narrator asks, "Is that a tree? No, it is a woman" (*R* 99). In *Orlando*, the solidity of the "oak tree" (as tree and as poem) confirms Orlando's identity. In *The Years,* Maggie asks "Would there be trees if we didn't see them?'" Her question makes her wonder: "What's 'I'? ... 'I' ... She stopped. She did not know what she meant. She was talking nonsense." It is nonsense, Woolf seems to posit, that Maggie or Clarissa, or anyone (the examples are numerous) could muddle up a solid tree with subjectivity.

In "The Mark on the Wall," Woolf strives to describe "something definite, something real." Having explored many digressions as to the meaning of the mark on the wall in front of her, Woolf tries to halt her thoughts by thinking of a tree:

> Thus, waking from a midnight dream of horror, one hastily turns on the light and lies quiescent, worshipping the chest of drawers, worshipping solidity [...] worshipping the impersonal world which is proof of some existence other than ours. That is what one wants to be sure of ... Wood is a pleasant thing to think about. It comes from a tree; and trees grow. [...] I like to think of the tree itself. (*CSF* 88)

Woolf seeks to find some escape from the solipsism that, as Russell has highlighted, might result in believing the world to be vague. Fearing that there is no "existence other than ours," Woolf hopes that thinking of a tree – "something definite, something real" – will be a solution. However, even a tree shows itself to be a vague concept. Woolf describes the tree's life, and eventual death, but realizes, "Even so, life isn't done with; there are a million patient, watchful lives still for a tree, all over the world, in bedrooms, in ships, on the pavement, where men and women sit after tea, smoking cigarettes ..." And with that Woolf is off again. The hoped-for security and escape from solipsism offered by a solid tree is in fact just another pathway to describing a boundary-less concept. Indeed, we can recall the moment when Lily Briscoe attempts to imagine what on earth "[s]ubject and object and the nature of reality" means and ends up picturing a kitchen table hanging in a pear tree (*TTL* 26). One could argue that Woolf, like Lily, has moved the characteristic philosophical debate about solid objects as tables and relocated it to trees, making the image organic, and, more importantly, *vague*: the precise border between tree and earth, tree and table, tree and book, is, finally, a matter of debate. The vagueness of language cannot provide an escape from solipsism; however, the "many-sided" nature of "Mother English" may be the perfect, and only, way to render Woolf's vision of this "vague and dream like world."

CHAPTER 3

A Dream of International Precision: James Joyce, Ludwig Wittgenstein, and C. K. Ogden

> Philosophy is a battle against the bewitchment of our intelligence by means of our language. –Ludwig Wittgenstein, *Philosophical Investigations*[1]

> by the light of philophosy, (and may she never folsage us!) things will begin to clear up a bit one way or another within the next quarrel of an hour
> –James Joyce, *Finnegans Wake*[2]

1. "The Study of Languages": Logical versus Natural Languages

"The most important study for the mind is Mathematics," declared a young scholar in a university essay called "The Study of Languages," wherein he sought to prove that "the study of languages is based on a mathematical foundation."[3] Because "Grammar, or Letters, is a science," no "stern demarcation" exists between the sciences of Literature and Arithmetic, and therefore there are "methods of correct expression" that are "ruled and directed by clear regulations." An "innate symmetry" must exist in language, and "both in style and syntax" we can expect "a carefulness, a carefulness bred of the first implantings of precision." Thus far – although perhaps tipping his hat as the future author *of Finnegans Wake* with "implantings" – 17-year-old James Joyce decrees a logical and systematic approach to language that has much in accord with one of the twentieth century's most famous philosophical treatises, Ludwig Wittgenstein's *Tractatus Logico-Philosophicus* (1921). With "innate symmetry," the *Tractatus*, published in English the same year as Joyce's *Ulysses*, sets out "the conditions for a logically perfect language."[4] Believing language to be inherently logical and referential, and seeking to clear up age-old philosophical problems, Wittgenstein shows the "*limits of my language*" through "the *application* of logic" in the *Tractatus* (*T* 5.6, 5.557). But neither Wittgenstein nor Joyce maintained this vision of a logically precise language – and for both, this change was spurred on by the puzzle of language's vagueness.

Indeed, even in "The Study of Languages," the young Joyce's attempt to remain scientifically objective quickly crumbles as he admits to "taking up the cudgels on behalf of Language and Literature" against the arguments of "obnoxious mathematicians."[5] Significantly for his later attitude toward language, when Joyce turns to analyze "the history of words," he cannot help but note language's constant flux. In contrast to "correct expression ruled and directed by clear regulations," the history of language mirrors the "history of men," and "external influences" alter "the very words of a race." "[T]he advent of an overcoming power" gives way to "crippled diction," he notes, and often there is "complete disuse of the original tongue, save in solitary, dear phrases, spontaneous in grief or gladness." (For "complete disuse" one thinks of the Englishman Haines trying to converse with Stephen Dedalus's milkwoman in Irish in *Ulysses.*) Joyce may seek to prove that language is "inviolate," but his essay, in focusing on "the masters of English," repeatedly emphasizes language's imprecision and susceptibility to power. By the conclusion of the essay, Joyce's claim that "the Grammar of a language" can be studied "in the same manner as tables in Arithmetic" has transformed into an argument against British imperialism and an endorsement of language's untranslatable idioms and indefinable "delicate shades." Language is no longer based on precise foundations but instead subject to human history and resistant to mathematical analysis.

Joyce merely implies that language is vague in "The Study of Languages," but by *A Portrait of the Artist as a Young Man*, eighteen years later, vagueness has become a metaphor for the very qualities of language he admits in his early essay. Stephen Dedalus imbibes "vague" language from kissing a prostitute that undermines his already shaken faith in language's connection to the Word of God (*P* 108). So strong is her kiss that "Vague words for a vague emotion" become all that Stephen, who seeks Aristotelian logic, believes he can write by the end of *A Portrait of the Artist as a Young Man* (*P* 274). Stephen's recognition of his two yokes – the "overcoming power" of Rome and England – undermines his youthful certainty in a God-given language, and vagueness replaces Stephen's security that "God's real name was God" (*P* 13). "Vague speech," connected to water imagery, can be seen as a metaphor running throughout Joyce's oeuvre for language's imprecision, where texts revel in language's slipperiness, puns, and portmanteaux (*P* 108). Anthony Burgess famously notes the seemingly inevitable trajectory of Joyce's approach to language – "The roots of *Ulysses* are here [in *A Portrait of the Artist as a Young Man*] ... *Finnegans Wake* must seem, not a wilful aberration from sense, but a logical conclusion."[6] Indeed, vague speech flows from Stephen's disillusionment in *A Portrait of the Artist as a Young Man*, through Molly's puns in the "Penelope" section of *Ulysses*, to the "hitherandthithering waters of" the "Anna Livia Plurabelle" (ALP) section of *Finnegans Wake* (*FW* 216:4–5). *Finnegans Wake*, rather than demonstrating that Joyce "has gone off his head, I am afraid," as Joyce's father put it, is the ultimate divorce of the word from the word of God that Joyce began in *A Portrait of the Artist as a Young Man*.[7]

Joyce's change of heart from the logical dream of "The Study of Languages" to the "vague speech" of ALP bears a striking resemblance to Wittgenstein's reconsideration of language from the *Tractatus* to his later philosophical writings – if we take Wittgenstein's word for it. There are three major ways of reading the *Tractatus*, which, for shorthand and following James Conant, I will call the *positivist*, *ineffability*, and *austere* readings.[8] This chapter will use two of the approaches, acknowledging that they both cannot simultaneously be correct. The first approach, historically, was to see it as an important text for logical positivism. Bertrand Russell's introduction, for example, urges us to take Wittgenstein's "logically perfect language" seriously.[9] Second, another standard account, popularized in literary studies by Marjorie Perloff in *Wittgenstein's Ladder*, argues that Wittgenstein's mystical pronouncements aim to show important points about the ineffable. Finally, more recently, Cora Diamond and James Conant have argued for a more "resolute" or "austere" reading of the *Tractatus*, which rejects the standard idea that sense can be made of the *Tractatus*' nonsensical statements. For Diamond and Conant, Wittgenstein's mystical pronouncements, just like his logical pronouncements that the "proposition is a picture of reality" (*T* 4:021), are all themselves nonsense that must be discarded. My reading combines the first two ways, building on Wittgenstein's own statement that he had made "grave mistakes" in the *Tractatus*, which therefore allows for the logical positivist reading, even as it is clear, from Wittgenstein's famous gesture of kicking away the ladder, that he was unhappy with some of these ideas even as he wrote them.[10]

For Wittgenstein, throughout his career, "philosophical problems" could be resolved "by looking into the workings of our language" (*PI* §109). However, he altered his earlier logical approach to language in the *Tractatus* in his later (posthumously collected and published) works, including *Philosophical Grammar* and *Philosophical Investigations*. "I have been forced to recognize grave mistakes in what I wrote in that first book," Wittgenstein warns in the Preface to the *Investigations*. In the work itself he specifies that it was failing to acknowledge the "multiplicity of kinds of word and sentence" that undermines "what logicians have said about the structure of language. (Including the author of the *Tractatus Logico-Philosophicus.*)"[11] (Joyce similarly readdressed his earlier works in his later works, referring to *A Portrait of the Artist as a Young Man* as "a poor trait of the artless" (*FW* 114:32) and *Ulysses* as the "usylessly unreadable Blue Book of Eccles" (*FW* 179:26–7).) *Philosophical Investigations,* instead, defines words pragmatically by their usage: "[T]he meaning of a word is its use in the language" (*PI* §43); moreover, there are "*countless*" usages for each word (*PI* §23). Language, rather than by strict definitions, now works as a "language-game," and in a language-game words cannot be rigorously analyzed because words' definitions are "vague," "blurred," and "indistinct" (*PI* §71). Philosophy, according to the later Wittgenstein, no longer works as a kind of explanation or solution, but as purely description, a description that shows the variety and power of our ordinary language.

From *A Portrait of the Artist as a Young Man* through to *Finnegans Wake,* Joyce's word play, variety of styles, and rhetorical techniques aim to chart what Ford Madox Ford proclaimed "the verges of the word user's habitable universe," exploring the vagueness that Wittgenstein finds constitutive of language.[12] In the following pages, I will demonstrate that just as the idea of vagueness (*Vagheit*) undermines Wittgenstein's early "picture" theory of language, leading to his concept of the "language-game" (*PI* §48), so also for Joyce "vague speech" is an alternative to that taught by "christian minstrelsy," leading to the verbal play of *Finnegans Wake.*[13] Throughout *A Portrait of the Artist as a Young Man*, Stephen is attracted to various religious and logical approaches to language, and, in particular, to a version of nominalism (the rejection of universals or abstract objects) also manifest in the positivist *Tractatus,* but these systematic approaches never quite stick.[14] Instead, like the changing styles of *Ulysses* itself, each system is only temporary and malleable because words' meanings are vague: They shift according to usage and context. Establishing that languages – rather than God-given or quantifiable – are social games, enmeshed in the power relations of nationhood, gender, race, and sexuality, is one of Joyce's most central and continuous themes. Joyce's comment that *Finnegans Wake* is "a game that I have learned to play in my own way" in no way undermines the seriousness of the project over which he labored for sixteen years.[15] His verbal play, in fact, marks his desire to challenge both the traditional form of the novel and the "general paralysis" of Irish society.[16]

Wittgenstein's concept of the way language works as a game and the inherent "constant befuddled negotiation[s]" among language games is particularly applicable to the "novel" *Ulysses.*[17] Marjorie Perloff notes that

Wittgenstein's philosophy reveals his status as a cultural outsider to England: "Only someone who is not fully at home in the world will talk as much as Wittgenstein does about 'the language-game which is [one's] original home.'"[18] Michael North builds on Perloff's observation to show that Wittgenstein's approach taps into "one of the twentieth century's most influential beliefs, that understanding is bounded by specific social practices, that knowledge is not eternal and fundamental but situated in a context."[19] Through Bloom's culturally "befuddled" state in *Ulysses*, as well as the text's own shifting styles, Joyce similarly demonstrates the difficulty of using the practices that create meaning and allow for communication in different contexts. Joyce's *Ulysses* forces readers to be self-conscious about the language games and the novel game they are playing. Simultaneously, its insistence that readers constantly re-examine their linguistic assumptions through its encyclopedia of styles suggests parallels between the structures of *Ulysses* and the extra-literary world. Through *Ulysses*, Joyce rejects the insularity of any single "eternal" or "fundamental" knowledge, and that rejection allows for the possibility of change: When languages work as games, the rules are malleable. Just as the *Philosophical Investigations* enacts philosophy as a kind of therapy, an activity that helps to rid us of our metaphysical prejudices or logical positivist certainty, so also *Ulysses* acts as therapy for readers, helping us to reimagine our preconceived notion of genre, character, and community.[20]

Of course, one might reasonably think there is nothing "ordinary" about the language of *Finnegans Wake*, therefore contesting my claim that Wittgenstein and Joyce follow a similar trajectory from exploring a conventional picture theory of meaning to embracing vagueness.[21] While Joyce's fictions and Wittgenstein's philosophical works similarly explore, as Joyce put it, the working of words "in their ordinary relations and connections," they significantly diverge on their view of language's limitations.[22] "I can do anything with language I want," Joyce remarked to Samuel Beckett, whereas for Wittgenstein, the fact that language is a human and social practice curtails discussion of transcendental knowledge, such as ethics and religion (*JJ* 702). Joyce's desire to break through any such "inviolate" sphere to demonstrate the dangers of sanctified rhetoric (whether it be religious, ethical, literary, etc.) underscores his vague speech.[23] For Wittgenstein, particularly the early Wittgenstein, such "inviolate" topics are "nonsense" (*Unsinn*).[24] Wittgenstein's definition of "nonsense" indeed provides a useful lens with which to examine the "comedy of letters" that is *Finnegans Wake* (*FW* 425:24). Juxtaposing Wittgenstein's "Lecture on Ethics" to Joyce's "desophisticated language" in *Finnegans Wake* demonstrates that Joyce's final work, for Wittgenstein, would qualify as "nonsense."[25] However, much of Wittgenstein's own work is also such nonsense, and this overlap emphasizes that their two apparently opposed projects share a similar goal: "to run against the boundaries of language."[26]

In order to bring head to head the differences between a positivist Tractarian and a Joycean approach to language, this chapter concludes by comparing some of Joyce's "nonsense," the Anna Livia Plurabelle (ALP) section from *Finnegans Wake*, to its 1932 translation into Basic English by C. K. Ogden in *Transition* magazine. Basic English, a re-imagined and simplified English language designed to facilitate global communication, is derived in part from ideas Ogden encountered when helping with the translation of the *Tractatus*, and "[t]hus Basic English brings down to earth Wittgenstein's project for a method of unmediated communication."[27] Therefore, although Wittgenstein and Joyce, unlike the other philosophers and novelists linked in this book, did not actually know each other, ALP and its Basic translation enact a kind of conversation between Joyce and Wittgenstein of the *Tractatus*. By limiting vocabulary to simple verbs and nouns through its vocabulary of 850 words, Basic aimed to make language simple, straightforward, and serviceable. If the world really were, as the *Tractatus* asserts, "the totality of facts," Basic would be extremely useful (*T* 1.1). Indeed, Basic had worldwide success before World War II, and by 1939 there were "some 200 titles in print in or about Basic English," as well as schools to teach Basic in over 30 countries.[28] Joyce invited Ogden to translate ALP into Basic and even, remarkably, enjoyed the final product. Critics, as I will discuss, are divided about the success of this translation and about what it even means to translate *Finnegans Wake*. I argue that the Basic translation had to fail because Joyce's ALP embodies the vagueness of language, the very characteristic that Basic aims to extinguish. Wittgenstein himself in his later writings derides Basic English as "cold, lacking in associations, and yet it plays at being 'language,'" which demonstrates his change of heart from logical and inert to vague but living languages.[29]

The virtual conversation between the early Wittgenstein and Joyce, through the *en face* publication of a section of ALP in Basic English and in the original *Wakese*, crystallizes a theme explored throughout this book: the chasm between early twentieth-century philosophical dreams of a logical language, universal and precise, and modernist fiction's exploration of ordinary language's vagueness. This book argues that in the modernist period the vagueness of ordinary language created the same problem for philosophical realism that it did for literary realism, thus resulting in new logical and literary languages. Basic English and *Finnegans Wake* are, therefore, two extreme and antithetical responses to the problem of vagueness.

2. Wittgenstein the Poet and Joyce the "Philosophist"

Philosophy. O rocks!

–James Joyce, *Ulysses*[30]

When critics turn to the topic of Joyce and philosophy, Joyce appears either a belated anti-modernist or a poststructuralist before his time; rarely is he contextualized among his philosophical contemporaries.[31] There is justifiable reason for this oversight, because "Joyce's reliance on philosophers like Aquinas and Aristotle, not to speak of Vico," sometimes seems to put him squarely with the reactionary "pre-modernists," as Jean-Michel Rabaté has argued, while Jacques Derrida's heralding of Joyce's influence cements his proto-deconstructionist pedigree.[32] Recent critics reveal that Joyce was more "up to date" in his linguistics reading than has previously been assumed and, in fact, there is a dispute about how well Joyce had read Ferdinand de Saussure, the French structuralist.[33] Derrida's sense that Joyce's texts "hypermnesically pre-program" the poststructural theories that follow him may stem from Joyce's own interest and exploration of Saussure.[34]

The advantages of looking at Joyce's writing in the light of Wittgenstein are threefold. First, this lens contextualizes Joyce's word play in a larger movement, suggesting why, in the same period, both Wittgenstein and Joyce – and Saussure, too – would envision language as a social game.[35] Benoit Tadié has shown that during Joyce's lifetime "linguistics had been partially reappropriated" by anthropologists such as Leonard Bloomfield, Edward Sapir, and Bronislaw Malinowski.[36] Wittgenstein believed he approached philosophy from an "anthropological point-of-view" and reading Joyce with Wittgenstein accentuates the ways that Joyce is interested in the relationship between cultural and linguistic estrangement.[37] Second, the later Wittgenstein's approach to philosophy as *therapy*, a way of clearing up misconceptions and philosophical humbug, resonates with Joyce's self-revisions and stylistic parodies in *Ulysses*. The growing irony toward Stephen, the former hero, forces readers to reconsider our assumptions about literary characterization, as well as acting as a kind of therapy for Irish xenophobia. Finally, juxtaposing *Finnegans Wake* with what I argue is the early Wittgenstein's progeny, Ogden's Basic English, emphasizes the constructive as well as the deconstructive spirit of Joyce's final project. "Aren't there enough words for you in English?" Joyce was asked. "'Yes,' he replied, 'there are enough, but they aren't the right ones,'" Richard Ellmann recounts (*JJ* 397). The accretive and omnivorous language of *Finnegans Wake* both influenced deconstruction and shared in its own time's vision of an international language; its fecundity parallels the encyclopedic styles of *Ulysses*.

While Joyce and Wittgenstein apparently never met or commented upon each other's work, both *Ulysses* and the *Tractatus* made a considerable splash in England after their publications in 1922.[38] Although Wittgenstein briefly lived across from Phoenix Park (the setting of HCE's crime in the *Wake*), he preferred reading American detective fiction to modernist literature during his years in Ireland.[39] Meanwhile Joyce's avowed philosophical preferences were for the classics, although his letters show that his years of cosmopolitan society in Paris were supplemented by wide-ranging reading. The fact that Joyce would suddenly ask after Alfred North Whitehead's latest works in a letter to Sylvia Beach, take notes on Russell's writing while revising *Ulysses*, or comment that C. K. Ogden had written *The Meaning of Meaning*, supports the idea that "Joyce was very likely far more aware of what was 'going on' than the extant evidence would suggest."[40] Indeed, the closeness of their social circles and literary projects is embodied in the figure of Ogden, who was a mutual friend and translated both the *Tractatus* into English and the ALP section of *Finnegans Wake* into Basic. In 1929–1930, both Wittgenstein and Joyce were corresponding with and working on projects with Ogden in England, and Ogden's main work even appears farcically in the *Wake*: "lote us see, light us find, let us missnot . . . the maymeaminning of maimoomeining!"[41]

There is startlingly little written comparing these two important twentieth-century figures, one who theorized the language game and one who created perhaps the most famously rebarbative example of one in *Finnegans Wake*.[42] Michael Bell briefly notes in "The Metaphysics of Modernism" that "Wittgenstein was like Joyce in being profoundly superficial."[43] If we remove the conventional negative valences from the word, it is true that both Wittgenstein and Joyce were fascinated by surfaces, or, more importantly, by the attempt to destroy the distinction between surface and content. Wittgenstein's statement that "the work of art does not aim to convey *something else*, just itself," parallels Samuel Beckett's explanation of *Finnegans Wake*: "[Joyce's] writing is not *about* something; *it is that something itself*."[44] The elliptical structure of the *Tractatus* has often been compared to a modernist poem, where the form of the text (the apparently logical numbering system) mirrors the argument for a "picture theory of language."[45] Wittgenstein's own comment that "I think I summed up my attitude to philosophy when I said: philosophy ought really to be written only as a *poetic composition*" supports Terry Eagleton's assertion that, as in a literary work, the structure also performs and informs the *Investigations*.[46]

Wittgenstein believed philosophy ought to be composed like poetry; similarly Joyce, like Stephen, often points to philosophers as evidence for his literary theories. In his early essay, "A Portrait of the Artist" (1904), "a sentence in Augustine" seems to offer "a philosophy of reconcilement" to Joyce's nameless hero, Stephen's predecessor.[47] One need only add Stephen's aesthetic theory redefining *integritas, consonantia*, and *claritas* from Aquinas in *Stephen Hero* and *A Portrait of the Artist as a Young Man* to his promotion of Aristotle over Plato in the National Library in the "Scylla and Charybdis" section of *Ulysses* in order to remember that Stephen claims to be highly influenced by Aristotle, Augustine, and Aquinas.[48] Stanislaus, Joyce's brother, asserted that Joyce had "an exalted opinion of philosophy," and "upholds Aristotle against his friends, and boasts himself an Aristotelian."[49] Joyce himself declared he was a "philosophist," and Ezra Pound noted that one of Joyce's elements of genius was that he could easily throw philosophical discussions into his fiction without their seeming out of place.[50] Joyce's cynicism toward philosophy, as toward many fields of knowledge, however, should not be overlooked. As he ironically warned Harriet Shaw Weaver: "I would not pay overmuch attention to these theories, beyond using them for all they are worth."[51]

Christopher Butler maintains that "Joyce thus enters the experimental mainstream of modernism by an extraordinary display of technique, and not by any anterior commitment to some avant-gardist doctrine."[52] But for Joyce, as for Wittgenstein, the emphasis on "technique" is in fact central to his doctrine and central to his desire to revolutionize his discipline. Both writers sought to change the entire method as well as the content of previous philosophers or novelists – the division between the two being a fallacy for both. Wittgenstein rebukes traditional philosophical analysis which states that the "*essence* of language" is "*hidden from us*," and that we ought to seek "something that lies *beneath* the surface." In contrast, Wittgenstein focuses on "something that already lies open to view": the "function" of words (*PI* §92). Similarly, a driving theory behind Joyce's writing in *A Portrait of the Artist as a Young Man* and *Ulysses* is that "*ways of doing things*" (as Wyndham Lewis put it) cannot be distinguished from "*things to be done*" in writing.[53] A "world-view" in Joyce always permeates a style.

The concluding image of the ladder in the *Tractatus* demonstrates Wittgenstein's frustration with the way earlier philosophy attempted to answer questions beyond the realm of what "could be said." Wittgenstein writes:

> My propositions are elucidatory in this way: he who understands me finally recognizes them as senseless, when he has climbed out through them, on them, over them. (He must so to speak throw away the ladder, after he has climbed up it.) (*T* 6.54)

Wittgenstein notes that those who understand his propositions, restricting what can meaningfully be said, will ironically recognize the *Tractatus* itself as something that is beyond the realm of sense. Philosophy like the *Tractatus*, that aims to investigate ethics, aesthetics, mysticism, the limits of the world, etc., ought to be discarded (like a used ladder). That is why Wittgenstein's own philosophy becomes "therapeutic," because its goal is to rid philosophy of "senseless" clutter, like the *Tractatus*.[54]

Wittgenstein's impatience with traditional philosophy looking *beyond* language for answers finds a parallel in Joyce's anger at the Romantic tradition in writing, as well as in the new school of psychoanalysis, for looking for truths *within* the human soul or subconscious. "What makes most peoples' lives unhappy is some disappointed romanticism, some unrealizable or misconceived ideal," Joyce commented to Arthur Power, "you may say that idealism is the ruin of man."[55] Similarly Joyce is dismissive about Freud: "Why all this fuss and bother about the mystery of the unconscious . . . What about the mystery of the conscious? What do they know about that?" (*JJ* 436). Joyce proudly proclaims that *Ulysses* is a realist work because "in realism, you get down to facts on which the world is based: that sudden reality which smashes romanticism into a pulp."[56] If Stephen is read as "a belated romantic," Joyce's aim to dissociate himself from his early Byronic tendencies is manifested in the gradual distancing of Stephen (from "A Portrait of the Artist," to *Stephen Hero*, to *A Portrait of the Artist as a Young Man*, to *Ulysses*). The diminishing size of Stephen's role, the increased irony with which he is treated, and the introduction of Bloom – the fact finder – as foil to Stephen – the soul seeker – further underscore Joyce's move away from his early Romanticism.[57] Through Bloom, for example, Joyce defines the nation as "the same people living in the same place" (*U* 317), rather than as an idealized and Romanticized Irish Republic where the ideal "citizen" declares "*Sinn fein!*" (*U* 293).

Indeed, my intention to read Joyce's writing as vague might seem compromised by Joyce's declared fixation on "facts." "I want," Joyce said about the world of *Ulysses*, "to give a picture of Dublin so complete that if the city one day suddenly disappeared from the earth it could be reconstructed out of my book," and famously would task his Aunt Josephine in Dublin to measure fences and check timetables in order to be sure that the events described in his writing were factually accurate.[58] His fury with a novelist like George Moore, who makes errors in what his characters would obviously know, is well documented (*JJ* 193). Ezra Pound, defending Joyce's early writing in the pages of *The Egoist*, notes that Joyce is "a realist" because he "writes a clear hard prose": "I can lay down a good piece of French writing and pick up a piece of writing by Mr. Joyce without feeling as if my head were being stuffed through a cushion," Pound declares.[59] "Exact" presentation, a lack of sentimentality, no "Dickensian caricature," and the fact that "he defines" these characteristics, according to Pound, set the realist writing of Joyce apart from the "boring" impressionists.

However, Joyce's "realist" writing is certainly of a peculiar bent, demonstrated by, for example, the liberation of the Nymphs from the painting over Bloom's bed to assault him in "Circe." Although one could propose a gulf between the "realist" fiction of *Dubliners* and *A Portrait of the Artist as a Young Man*, and the modernist verbal play of *Ulysses* and *Finnegans Wake*, Joyce's play with diction even in his earlier works bridges that divide. What Hugh Kenner has called the "Uncle Charles Principle" in Joyce's writing is Joyce's *style indirect libre*, his tendency to make diction and syntax, even in third person narration, bend to the thoughts of his characters.[60] David Lodge notes that bending to the voice of Stephen Dedalus in *A Portrait of the Artist as a Young Man* is what turns Joyce into a "fully-fledged modernist writer," in that he "varied his style to imitate various phases of his hero's development."[61] The seeds of Gertie MacDowell's fashion magazine narrative in "Nausicaa" were sown when Stephen's Uncle Charles "repaired" to the toilet in *A Portrait of the Artist as a Young Man* (*P* 62). *Ulysses* may "get down to facts on which realism is based" but these facts, Joyce asserts, must be "from eighteen different points of view and in as many styles, all apparently unknown or undiscovered by my fellow tradesmen."[62] Joyce's manipulation of syntax and diction in *A Portrait of the Artist as a Young Man* and *Ulysses* mirrors his willingness to create neologisms in *Finnegans Wake*; his varying narration mirrors his "vague speech" (*P* 108). Joyce's writing is vague not because it is romantic or aesthetic – what Joyce calls Oscar Wilde's "vague idea of delicate pastels, of life beautified with flowers" – but because it depicts facts through the vagueness of language and style.[63]

Even Pound was rather arbitrary in his diagnosis of Joyce's realism, because five months before declaring Joyce a "realist" in the pages of *The*

Egoist, Pound had heralded Joyce's distinction from realism in the pages of that same periodical. Right before the second installment of *A Portrait of the Artist as a Young Man*, Pound declared that "realism is dead":

> Realism in literature has had its run. For thirty years or more we have had in deluge, the analyses of the fatty degeneration of life. A generation has been content to analyse. They were necessary. My generation is not the generation of the romanticists. We have heard all that the "realists" have to say . . . To the present condition of things we have nothing to say but "*merde*" . . .[64]

Pound here dismisses both romanticism and realism as antithetical to new writing. Because Pound had in fact submitted the manuscript of Joyce's *A Portrait of the Artist as a Young Man* to *The Egoist*, his proclamation about "his generation" seems aimed to promote Joyce's new novel.[65] Joyce's writing according to Pound, therefore, appears to be saying "*merde*" to all the literary "isms," including romanticism and realism, which have preceded it.

Both Joyce and Wittgenstein's interest in surfaces connects to the vagueness they depict in language and, importantly, to pragmatism. If language is neither ahistorical nor transparent, but instead evolves in usage and is subject to social structures, then analyzing and depicting language games themselves, rather than the "ideas" behind words, becomes the right task for the novelist and the philosopher. Indeed, both demonstrate strongly anti-idealistic temperaments, whether in comments against Schopenhauer (for Wittgenstein) or Plato (for both).[66] In *Ulysses*, for example, Joyce has Stephen best AE's (George Russell's) idealism. AE insists:

> Art has to reveal to us ideas, formless spiritual essences. The supreme question about a work of art is out of how deep a life does it spring . . . Plato's world of ideas. All the rest is the speculation of schoolboys for schoolboys. (*U* 177)

Although AE reveres "Plato's world of ideas," Stephen merely "superpolitely" supports his own philosophical hero, replying, "Aristotle was once Plato's schoolboy" (*U* 177). Internally, though, he parodies the notion of the "Horseness is the whatness of allhorse," and exhorts himself to "Hold to the now, the here, through which all future plunges to the past" (*U* 178). Wittgenstein similarly questions reverence for Plato in *Culture and Value*:

> I read: " . . . philosophers are no nearer to the meaning of 'Reality' than Plato got, . . ." What a strange situation. How extraordinary then that Plato could have got even as far as he did! Or that we could not get any further! Was it because Plato was so *extremely* clever?[67]

Wittgenstein's italicized "*extremely*" adds a Dedalus-like flavor of mockery to his comment. For both Wittgenstein and Joyce, Plato's "Reality" errs in removing theory from the world of "facts."

Indeed, both Joyce and Wittgenstein can be seen as having pragmatic tendencies, and they were familiar with the writings of F. C. S. Schiller, the British pragmatist who argued with Bertrand Russell during Russell's "Vagueness" lecture in 1922. Wittgenstein's interest in the "use" of words sounds strongly pragmatic and he was conscious of, if uncomfortable with, this connection: "So I am trying to say something that sounds like pragmatism," he worried.[68] Although Wittgenstein dismissed Schiller's writings, the increasing pragmatic flavor of his own writings is often noted and connected to his friendship with F. R. Ramsey, the "acolyte" of Peirce.[69] Furthermore, William James's *The Varieties of Religious Experience* was one of his favorite books to recommend. "This book does me a *lot* of good," he noted, "I don't mean to say that I will be a saint soon, but I am not sure it does not improve me."[70] Wittgenstein praised James's analysis of the beneficial effect of religious "practice," just as he himself examined the practice of language games.

Joyce, too, championed elements of Schiller's pragmatism. In "Humanism" (1903), a review essay of Schiller's latest works, Joyce noted that:

> Pragmatism is really a very considerable thing. It reforms logic, it shows the absurdity of pure thought, it establishes an ethical basis for metaphysic, makes practical usefulness the criterion of truth, and pensions off the Absolute once and for all. In other words, pragmatism is common-sense.[71]

Pragmatism's lure for Joyce is crystallized in its ability to abolish the "Absolute once and for all," just as Stephen is "fond of saying that the Absolute is dead" (*SH* 206). The text of Schiller that Joyce was reviewing was dedicated to William James and calls out for pragmatism's praise of indeterminacy: "the indetermination which, as William James has urged, Pragmatism introduces into our conception of the world is essentially a gain."[72] Joyce, therefore, encountered pragmatism's indeterminacy early in his writing career. His review ends up critical of "Professor Schiller," primarily for Schiller's involvement with "Psychical Research," which Joyce finds to undermine the whole call to reform logic.[73] Although Joyce and Wittgenstein were uncomfortable with the pragmatic label, they both noted that the pragmatic approach, showing "the absurdity of pure thought," offered a "common-sense" escape from idealism. Joyce's and Wittgenstein's interest in vagueness was, therefore, connected to pragmatism's "re-instatement of the vague."

3. Learning Vague Language: *A Portrait of the Artist as a Young Man*

> Listen: a fourworded wavespeech: seesoo, hrss, rsseeiss, ooos. Vehement breath of waters amid seasnakes, rearing horses, rocks. In cups of rocks it slops: flop, slop, slap: bounded in barrels. And, spent, its speech ceases. It flows purling, widely flowing, floating, foampool, flower unfurling.
>
> –James Joyce, *Ulysses*[74]

At the beginning of *A Portrait of the Artist as a Young Man*, Stephen seeks the kind of certainty that a philosophy like Wittgenstein's *Tractatus* offers. An ordered world full of facts, principles, words with specific meanings, and questions with specific answers appeals to young Stephen. "It pained [Stephen] that he did not know well what politics meant" or "where the universe ended," writes Joyce, and Stephen wishes he were like the fellows with "big voices and big boots," who seem to know everything (*P* 14). However, just as a reconsideration of "vagueness" leads to Wittgenstein's revised depiction of language in the *Investigations*, so also does Joyce depict Stephen reluctantly accepting language's uncertainties. Stephen's disillusionment with language connects to his loss of faith, and the root of the "blasphematory spits" (*FW* 183:24) of *Finnegans Wake* is the "vehicle of a vague speech" Stephen imbibes in *A Portrait of the Artist as a Young Man* (*P* 108).

The *Tractatus* sets out a logical vision of a world where "the world is everything that is the case" (*T* 1.0), and "the world divides into facts" (*T* 1.2). "Logic fills the world" (*T* 5.61), Wittgenstein writes, and through the "*application* of logic" (*T* 5.557) the *Tractatus* re-examines the law of causality, the meaning of time, ethical propositions, and the laws of nature. Wittgenstein finished the *Tractatus* during World War I, mostly from a prison camp, and the only way he secured publication was by having his earlier mentor, Bertrand Russell, write an introduction. Russell's introduction explains to readers why the work is such "an important event in the philosophical world" (*T* 7). According to Russell, Wittgenstein's *Tractatus* is the apex of the "ideal language" tradition (*T* 8). "Mr. Wittgenstein," Russell writes, "is concerned with the conditions for a logically perfect language," and the *Tractatus* demonstrates "the whole function of language is to have meaning, and it only fulfils this function in proportion as it approaches to the ideal language which we postulate" (*T* 8). The "ideal language" acts like a "picture" of reality, and, as such, "in the picture and the pictured there must be something identical" (*T* 8, 10). The logical form of language mirrors the "logical picture of a reality":

> The gramophone record, the musical thought, the score, the waves of sound, all stand to one another in that pictorial internal relation, which holds between language and the world. To all of them the logical structure is common. (*T* 4.014)

The internal "logical structure" that governs language, music, and sound also governs the world; the purpose of philosophy is to "make clear and delimit sharply the thoughts which otherwise are, as it were, opaque and blurred" (*T* 4.112).

Although Russell's introduction is often read as clarifying the meaning of the *Tractatus*, Wittgenstein himself believed Russell had missed his main point. Wittgenstein refused to allow Russell's introduction to be published alongside the German edition of the text, and attempted to explain in a letter how Russell had missed the mark. "Now I'm afraid you haven't really got hold of my main contention, to which the whole business of logical prop [osition]s is only a corollary," Wittgenstein wrote, "[t]he main point is the theory of what can be expressed (*gesagt*) by prop[osition]s – i.e. by language – (and, which comes to the same, what can be *thought*) and what can not be expressed by prop[osition]s, but only shown (*gezeigt*)."[75] For Wittgenstein, significantly, ordinary language was already ordered and logical, which the *Tractatus* aimed to *show*; reform was only necessary for philosophical language. While Wittgenstein emphasizes the limits of language – a point to which I will return later in reference to his approach to what is mystical – Russell's introduction, in contrast, emphasizes the connections between Wittgenstein's picture theory and the ideal language tradition. Russell seems to read the *Tractatus* as a possible solution to the problem he investigated in his lecture "Vagueness," which (not surprisingly) he delivered at the same time he was writing the *Tractatus* Introduction.[76]

A "picture theory of language," in which the logic of language mirrors the logic of the world, would hold out much hope to the perplexed Stephen at the beginning of *A Portrait of the Artist as a Young Man*. To Stephen, language seems to offer the key to understanding the world around him, yet mastery of language, like answering the sum in math class or Athy's riddle, eludes him. "What did that mean, to kiss?' Stephen asks himself (*P* 11), and wonders how "belt" means not only "a belt round his pocket," but also "to give a fellow a belt" (*P* 5). Rather than having a single precise meaning, words have multiple meanings. Some of their definitions seem to make sense: Stephen's suit is his "belted grey suit" because there "was a belt round his pocket" (*P* 5). In contrast, "I'd give you such a belt in a second," is some sort of nasty action, but Stephen ought not to say it because, like giving "a toe in the rump," it is "not a nice expression" (*P* 5).

Stephen's desire to make sense of language's relationship to the world around him smacks of a version of nominalism, which is also evident in Wittgenstein's *Tractatus*. Andrew Thacker, discussing the *Tractatus*, notes that there "is a kind of extreme nominalism that haunts one form of modernism, where language is treated as a set of discrete entities or atoms, to be pinned onto objects in the world."[77] For Wittgenstein, this nominalism is evident in the assertion that "the name means an object. The object is its meaning" (*T* 3.203).[78] We see Stephen using a nominalist approach when he considers the words "cold and hot" and the lavatory sink: "There were two cocks that you turned and water came out: cold and hot. He felt cold and then a little hot: and he could see the names printed on the cocks" (*P* 8). The way the words are "printed" on the sink helps to pin down the meaning of the words, and Stephen can extrapolate from this cold and hot water to his own sensation of temperature. But this system fails to hold as he grapples with a "queer word" like "suck." "Suck" makes an "ugly" sound, which Stephen connects to the noise water makes going down a drain, but then why is the young Simon Moonan, a favorite of the prefect, called the prefect's "suck"? Stephen is flummoxed, and language to him seems hardly a picture of an orderly world but instead merely "a very queer thing" (*P* 8). Wittgenstein's later famous explanation of words as tools from *Philosophical Investigations* would help Stephen here. Words, in contrast to the *Tractatus*' theory, no longer *mean* a certain thing but *mean* according to their usage:

> Think of the tools in a tool-box: there is a hammer, pliers, a saw, a screw-driver, a rule, a glue-pot, glue, nails and screws. – The functions of words are as diverse as the functions of these objects. (*PI* §1:11)

Wittgenstein could explain that "suck" means different things according to its usage in the conversation, being a "tool" for a different function. But for the young Stephen, clinging to a less pragmatic and more ordered universe, the "queer" function of words remains puzzling.

Even Stephen's attempts to define himself (with his odd name) by fixing his place in the world only lead to further questions. Stephen writes on his geography book:

> *Stephen Dedalus*
> *Class of Elements*
> *Clongowes Wood College*

Sallins
County Kildare
Ireland
Europe
The World
The Universe

Stephen's list aims to define "himself, his name and where he was," yet reading it carefully makes him only more confused (*P* 12). "What was after the universe?" he asks, and "was there anything round the universe to show where it stopped before the nothing place began?" (*P* 13). Stephen, rather like a good theorist of vagueness, ponders the borders between linked terms and worries about fuzzy boundaries. He decides, somewhat arbitrarily, that there must be some sort of border between the "everything" in his list, and the "nothing" that comes after it: "It could not be a wall but there could be a thin thin line there all round everything" (*P* 13). Stephen's "thin thin line" protecting the borders of his universe begins to crumble when his religious faith begins to falter.

For Wittgenstein, the "grave mistakes" he notes in his earlier *Tractatus* are also connected to the problem of fixed boundaries; indeed, Wittgenstein directly addresses the sorites paradox in his later work. An examination of Wittgenstein's analysis of the "Problem of 'the heap'" in *Philosophical Grammar*, a transitional work between the *Tractatus* and *Philosophical Investigations*, underscores the "vagueness" of Wittgenstein's well-known definition of the "language-game."[79] In "The concept 'about,' Problem of the 'heap'" section of *Philosophical Grammar*, Wittgenstein treats Eubulides' paradox of the heap, concluding that "there exists no delimitation" to the size of a heap and "if we fix one, we are altering the concept."[80] If, in the *Tractatus*, Wittgenstein imagines a precise language that can specify that "the world is determined by the facts, and by these being *all* the facts" (*T* 1.11), in *Philosophical Grammar*, facts give way to "indeterminacy." "It is senseless to speak of a largest heaplet," Wittgenstein declares, "it is just that there are cases that we count as within the extension of the concept, and cases that we no longer count as within the extension of the concept." Wittgenstein uses charts to demonstrate that although the boundaries of a "heap" are "*blurred*," nonetheless the command, "Make me a heap of sand here," is absolutely comprehensible.[81] The sorites paradox fails to present a problem for Wittgenstein, because *use* defines meaning; the fact that "[m]ake me a heap of sand here" is followed demonstrates that "heap" has meaning. One critic, in fact, has argued that for Wittgenstein the sorites paradox is what Wittgenstein would call a "grammatical joke," because the paradox tries to treat "natural" language as if it were a logical one.[82]

In *Philosophical Investigations*, Wittgenstein's portrayal of the way words are used in ordinary discourse, "the language-game," mirrors his approach to the problem of the heap because all words' boundaries are similarly "blurred" (*PI* §71). He rejects his earlier view in the *Tractatus* – that "Philosophy should make clear and delimit sharply the thoughts which otherwise are, as it were, opaque and blurred" (*T* 4.112) – instead positing that philosophical exploration must examine the "vague boundaries" of language games (*PI* §71). A word, like the word "game," is "a concept with blurred edges" (*PI* §71) because games fail to all share in one definite meaning; rather, their uses demonstrate "family resemblances" (*PI* §67). However, the "indistinct" nature of words is not a problem because "*mastery*" of language merely means learning when and how words are used in various language games (*PI* §71). The "thin thin line" between Stephen's "Universe" and the "nothing" next to it does not exist, but, as long as Stephen can usefully communicate his terms to others, the difference is moot. Language, rather than being a logical process, is a social practice, and "*mastery*" is "something that *happens* while you are uttering the sentence" (*PI* §20). Wittgenstein insists that "[e]ach of the sentences I write is trying to say the whole thing, i.e. the same thing over and over again; it is as though they were all simply views of one object seen from different angles."[83] The rejection of the ideal language tradition, crystallized in Russell's positivist *Tractatus*, may be the central point he repeats throughout his later writing.

Stephen indeed learns language much as Wittgenstein sets it out in *Philosophical Investigations*. In "Riddles, Silence and Wonder: Joyce and Wittgenstein Encountering the Limits of Language," Thomas Singer argues that, in particular, Stephen's first thoughts accord with Wittgenstein's notion of language learning. Wittgenstein begins the *Investigations* with Augustine's paradigm of how children learn language from the *Confessions*. Rejecting Augustine's notion that one learns all language through "objects" being pointed out (ostensive learning), Wittgenstein notes that such a system requires that a child already recognize what is meant by pointing, as well as the exact boundaries of the object pointed out, "as if it already had a language, only not this one. Or again: as if the child could already *think*, only not yet speak. And 'think' would here mean something like 'talk to itself'" (*PI* §32). Singer adds that Wittgenstein's alternative is that "the child learns language as a form of life," and that the first words of *A Portrait of the Artist as a Young Man* – "Once upon a time a very good time it was there was a moocow" – enact this process.[84] No pointing to objects occurs; rather, Joyce depicts Stephen learning by listening to stories, listening to how language is *used*. Moreover, Stephen learns what it means to have his own identity, rather than privately "talking to" himself, through the story – "He was baby tuckoo" (*PI* §32, *P* 3). Joyce, therefore, "changes the Cartesian model from *Cogito, ergo sum* to *Fabulo, ergo sum*."[85]

Joyce portrays Stephen's faith in God, however, as Stephen's preservation against language's vagueness. Stephen thinks:

> It was very big to think about everything and everywhere. Only God could do that. He tried to think what a big thought that must be but he could think only of God. God was God's name just as his name was Stephen. *Dieu* was the French for God and that was God's name too; and when anyone prayed to God and said *Dieu* then God knew at once that it was a French person that was praying. But though there were different names for God in all the different languages in the world and God understood what all the people who prayed said in their different languages still God remained always the same God and God's real name was God. (*P* 13)

Stephen's world vision is made comprehensible by his belief in the existence of God. Contemplation threatens to be limitless, an endless regression to "everything and everywhere," until it is concretely capped by the thought of God. God therefore places a limit on knowledge – "Only God could do that" – so that the small boy's world can be contained by "think[ing] only of God." Stephen immediately connects the thought of God to another great power, that of language, connecting naming to God's naming power. The young boy admits contradictions in how names work. While Stephen has only one first name, in contrast, "*Dieu* was the French for God and that was God's name too." However, his belief in God's omniscience allows the boy to be dogmatic: "God's real name was God." Stephen acknowledges language's slippery quality, "there were different names for God in all the different languages in the world," yet his religious upbringing, entailing life with a purpose, naming rights, and God as creator-of-it-all, allows Stephen to state firmly, "still God remained always the same." God provides firm footing in the realm of language because "God's real name was God."

When Stephen's faith begins to falter, language falls from its state of certainty, and the existence of different languages is no longer explicable by a Biblical tower of Babel. Stephen realizes that English is not unquestionably his right language, and he understands this difference when speaking with the English dean of studies:

> The language in which we are speaking is his before it is mine. How different are the words *home, Christ, ale, master*, on his lips and on mine! I cannot speak or write these words without unrest of spirit. His language, so familiar and so foreign, will always be for me an acquired speech. I have not made or accepted its words. My voice holds them at bay. My soul frets in the shadow of his language. (*P* 205)

Whereas the younger Stephen allowed God to be the ultimate justification of the Word, Stephen realizes that without a firm faith in God there is no manifest reason for his allegiance to his own language. Stephen's word choices in describing his "unrest of spirit" and the fretting of his "soul" demonstrate that his linguistic crisis is ultimately a spiritual crisis. Whereas once "God's real name was God," because Stephen has "not made or accepted" English words, even the name of Christ has lost its reassuring sound. He has begun to resent Roman and English colonization – both incarnate in the English priest – and uncertainty falls in where surety once was.

Women catalyze Stephen's undoing, both in relationship to his faith and to his language. Just as Joyce himself writes, "How I hate God and death! How I like Nora!" so also he portrays Stephen as religiously "undone" by women and sexuality.[86] Women and Stephen's own body act as subversive or undermining forces against prudery and the hellfire religion he learns in school – is it right to kiss his mother? What does it mean for Eileen to be a "Protestant"? From his later encounter with the prostitute he not only learns to be "in mortal sin" against God, therefore toying with the idea *non serviam*, but also imbibes a new language that no longer reflects boyhood's linguistic certainty (*P* 105). Rather, the prostitute's lips, "pressed upon his brain as upon his lips as though they were the vehicle of a vague speech" (*P* 108). This vague speech flows into Stephen at the moment when he is sinning with his body against his Catholic faith.

Vagueness pervades the text after Stephen drinks in vague speech. The acts of the priests lose their purpose, becoming merely "vague acts" full of "vague pomp" (*P* 171–2), and paradise fades to "a scene on some vague arras, old as man's weariness" (*P* 181). Stephen twice admits that his "applied Aquinas" is "vague" (*P* 225, 227). Even as he tries to convince his friends of his "esthetic theory," he must admit that he finds "the connotation" of key words "rather vague" (*P* 230). Stephen's vagueness is especially connected with Emma; for example, "he knew vaguely that her figure was passing homeward . . . Vaguely first and then more sharply he smelt her body" (*P* 253–254). Stephen's new vagueness both connects to his new sexual rebelliousness and reveals that a new female and sexual language has invaded Stephen's linguistic sphere, undermining his youthful certainty. When he considers joining the priesthood, he "wondered vaguely" where he would live, then "he wondered at the vagueness of his wonder" (*P* 175). Vagueness has become not just a condition but also an object of speculation for Stephen.

Stephen's culminating writing to Emma, recalled in his diary at the end of the novel, appears to Stephen to be merely vague: "Vague words for a vague emotion" (*P* 274). What Stephen derides as now "vague" is the diary entry from April 10, which is a prose-poem of anticipation that Joyce culled from his earlier group of epiphanies. In *Stephen Hero*, Stephen notes that the "epiphany," the "sudden spiritual manifestation," can stem from "the vulgarity of speech or of gesture or in a memorable phase of the mind itself" (*SH* 211). The epiphanies are usually accordingly divided into two groups, the dramatic epiphanies ("the vulgarity of speech or of gesture") and the lyrical ones (the instance of a "memorable phase of the mind itself"). This lyrical epiphany recalls when Stephen hears horse hooves breaking the night silence and wonders where the horsemen are headed: "to what journey's end – what heart? – bearing what tidings?" (*P* 274). This moment can be termed a sort of Ur-epiphany, or an epiphany about the notion of the epiphany, because the question, "what tidings?" recalls the announcement of the birth of Jesus from the gospel of Luke: "Fear not: for behold, I bring you good tidings of great joy . . . for unto you this day is born in the city of David a Savior, which is Christ the Lord" (Luke 2:10–11). "Tidings" certainly has some sort of liturgical inflection in Joyce's works because in *Finnegans Wake* the "evangel of good tidings" makes an appearance (*FW* 551:15). This Ur-epiphany most closely connects the Catholic meaning of the epiphany – the vision of the Word made flesh – to Joyce's particular definition of the epiphany, where words can somehow truly manifest the "spirit" of an object or being. But this earlier belief in the epiphany, in a special connection between word and flesh or spirit, now seems merely "vague" to the more mature Stephen. His comment, "Vague words for a vague emotion," acts as an ironic criticism of the Catholic idea of epiphany, of Stephen's earlier theory of the epiphany, and also of Joyce's own earlier style and method of collecting epiphanies.

Significantly, this ironic self-criticism occurs when Stephen's story has changed format from a third person narrative to a set of diary entries. The novel's form mirrors the breakdown of Stephen's faith in language. Marilyn French argues that because Stephen learns the world through words, changing to a diary format demonstrates that he now controls his words, indivisible from his world.[87] But what kind of world is this if it appears merely "vague words for a vague emotion"? Indeed, early publisher's reports aimed the same criticism at the *A Portrait of the Artist as a Young Man* manuscript that Stephen aims at his writing: The novel is "too discursive, formless" and "we can only see a chance for it if it is pulled into shape and made more definite." Stephen senses his writing is merely "vague," just as early critics insisted that Joyce's manuscript needed to be "more definite."[88]

Stephen's journal entry about "vague words for a vague emotion" also occurs just before he returns to the question of the word "tundish," a paramount example of his frustration with language (*P* 274). Stephen remembers the English Dean who questioned him for using the word "tundish" – for funnel – claiming it must be a "most interesting" Irish word (*P* 204). Having realized "tundish" is, in fact, English, "and good old blunt English too," Stephen rails against his relationship with his teacher, with the English, and with their language: "Damn him one way or the other!" he writes (*P* 274). Stephen wants language to act like a tundish for his thoughts, distilling his ideas and channeling them to others. Instead, language becomes itself a barrier, the Tundish fails to work as a funnel, and Stephen's theories become lost in the materiality of language. Stephen's inability to find a language in which he is comfortable undermines his ability to voice his aesthetic theory, which is so central to artistic vocation. If language is learned through social practice as Wittgenstein argues, Stephen's consciousness of his "vagueness" seems drawn from his inability to find a social group with whom he can converse. His terminology is a Jesuit-Classical combination even as he strives to dethrone the Jesuit beliefs; "how your mind is supersaturated with the religion in which you say you disbelieve," even his "staunch" friend Cranly notes (*P* 261).

As early as *Stephen Hero*, Joyce underscores that Stephen's inability to communicate his "esthetic theories" effectively is tied to his unusual use of terminology. Stephen asserts to Cranly:

> If you were an esthetic philosopher you would take note of all my vagaries because here you have the spectacle of the esthetic instinct in action. The philosophic college should spare a detective for me. (*SH* 186)

The "vagaries" of Stephen's "esthetic instinct" stem from his desire to redefine terms. Cranly's frustration with Stephen's word "modern," for example, leads Stephen to exclaim, "Of course I know the word 'modern' is only a word. But when I use it I use it with a certain meaning ..."

(*SH* 186). Similarly, Stephen's defense of his paper about estheticism with the President of the College comes down to his definitions:

- I use the word "classical" in a certain sense, with a certain definite meaning, that is all. [Stephen]
- But you cannot use any terminology you like. [President]
- I have not changed the terms. I have explained them. [Stephen] (*SH* 97)

Stephen aims to force specific meaning into terms – including his idiosyncratic theory of the epiphany – which makes his theories appear mere "vagaries" to his peers and teachers.

In *A Portrait of the Artist as a Young Man*, Stephen's longing to find a precise vocabulary seems even stronger than in *Stephen Hero*: "One difficulty," Stephen bemoans, "is to know whether words are being used according to the literary tradition or according to the tradition of the marketplace" (*P* 203). Stephen's vocabulary is not quite suitable to either the literary tradition or the marketplace, and Davin's question nicely summarizes Stephen's difficulties: "One time I hear you talk against English literature. Now you talk against the Irish informers. What with your name and your ideas . . . Are you Irish at all?" (*P* 219). Stephen dismisses his Irish homeland, just as he dismisses the tradition of his English oppressors. In Wittgenstein's terms Stephen seems to be unwilling, or unable, to participate in his society's language game. Indeed, rather than growing up to realize he belongs firmly at the top of the list in his geography book, firmly in "Ireland" within the "Universe," Stephen as a young man seems absolutely at a loss to know where he belongs.

Joyce plays with the myth of Icarus to demonstrate how Stephen has "fallen" from his place at the top of creation to beneath the waves, emphasizing Stephen's new vagueness and highlighting the linguistic ties between the words "vague," "vagabond," and the French "*vague*" or "wave." In the myth, Icarus, son of Daedalus, flies too close to the sun and for his pride crashes into the sea. Stephen believes he is just about to venture on Icarus's flight at the end of *A Portrait of the Artist as a Young Man*: He envisions himself among his kinsmen "shaking the wings of their exultant and terrible youth" and calls upon his father to "stand me now and ever in good stead" (*P* 275–6). However, Joyce's pervasive water imagery after Stephen's encounter with the prostitute suggests that Stephen has already fallen beneath the waves. Stephen, son of Simon Dedalus, conscious of the "hawklike man whose name he bore" (*P* 244), finds himself, having sinned, in a new world: "dim, uncertain as under sea" (*P* 187). His "soul lay amid cool waters," Stephen muses, and his words, too, share in this subaqueous condition (*P* 235). Words appear submerged, "a soft liquid joy flowed through the words," and they flow in waves, "the soft long vowels hurtled noiselessly and fell away, lapping and flowing back" (*P* 245). Stephen is fallen – both in his Catholic faith and according to his mythic resonances – and his language is fallen beneath the waves too. Briefly, away from his sources of conflict, "my home, my fatherland or my church" (*P* 268), Stephen stops trying to make language submit to his precise definitions, or conform to his particular rules. He seems to have accepted the vagueness Wittgenstein depicts as constitutive of language. Stephen loves the "rhythmic rise and fall of words," and his writing, if writing there will be, comes out of this watery vagueness (*P* 180). Art again seems possible for Stephen under water: "The instant flashed forth like a point of light and now from cloud on cloud of vague circumstance confused form was veiling softly its afterglow" (*P* 235–236). Stephen's "instant" of inspiration is made possible by the new "vague circumstance" of his language. Albeit tinged with irony, Joyce's description seems to offer Stephen some hope for growth in his final planned departure.[89]

4. Throwing Away the Ladder, Losing the Key: Siopold and Boom in *Ulysses*

> Why was he doubly irritated?
>
> Because he had forgotten and because he remembered that he had reminded himself twice not to forget.
>
> –James Joyce, *Ulysses*[90]

Wittgenstein remarks, "if a man could write a book on Ethics which really was a book on Ethics, this book would, with an explosion, destroy all the other books in the world."[91] Of course, many read this as exactly the effect of *Ulysses*: "a novel to end all novels," or according to T. S. Eliot, "a book to which we are all indebted, and from which none of us can escape."[92] In *Ulysses*, Joyce demonstrates that literary characters, as well as the language by which they are constituted, are importantly vague. Just as Bloom attempts to find a "key" to the language-games of the city but instead finds himself with Stephen composing a "keyless couple" (*U* 621), so also for the reader Joyce's changing styles leave one searching, yet finally uncertain about whether he or she has found the "key." Indeed, Joyce's *Ulysses* may aim to be Wittgenstein's explosively therapeutic "book on Ethics," in that, in emphasizing the vague boundary between Stephen and Bloom, it undermines the conventions of traditional techniques of literary characterization. Moreover, in building to the climactic moment in "Ithaca" where Bloom and Stephen nearly acknowledge their connectedness – staring into "theirhisnothis fellowfaces" (*U* 655) – Joyce reveals the protagonists' homecoming is both to Molly and to the discomfiting realization of semantic vagueness.

In a discussion of the "Consequence of Blur" in art criticism, Jeffrey Perl posits that "We need a term, and *blur* will do, to indicate the relative unclarity that results from de-differentiating objects or qualities or states of affairs whose differences have been overstated."[93] A blurry aesthetics, that is, aims to break down boundaries or to topple traditional distinctions that may be blinding us to underlying similarities, affinities, or common origins. "Blurry" is a weighted term for discussing Joyce's aesthetic aim, as any critic who has seen Joyce's letters about his battles with his fading vision must note. In *Ulysses*, nonetheless, Joyce employs the blur, first differentiating, then de-differentiating Bloom and Stephen, a process that highlights their intertwined cultural and linguistic communities.

"So of course everyone had a laugh at Bloom" (*U* 317). This sentence from the "Cyclops" chapter of *Ulysses* could easily recur throughout the novel. From Molly's "mocking eye" first thing in the morning, to the relentless jeering – "(Laugh together) Ha ha ha ha" – at the "henpecked husband" in the wee hours in "Cyclops," Bloom remains an object of ridicule (*U* 62, 526, 524). As a Jew, even one born in Ireland, he is always an outsider, befuddled by questions about his "nation" as if he should know he does not belong: "What is your nation if I may ask, says the citizen" (*U* 317). For Gerty MacDowell, similarly, he is a "foreign gentleman" (*U* 365). At the end of "Hades," Bloom's confusion about the lawyer, John Henry Menton, is typical of many of his encounters with the other Dublin citizenry over the course of his day: "Why he took such a rooted dislike to me. Hate at first sight" (*U* 111). Bloom's attempts to fit in (working diligently, attending the funeral, wearing appropriate attire, watching out for Stephen) somehow make him stand out all the more. He fears the deep-seated anti-Semitism of his culture even as he distances himself from the idea that he could be its target. For example, Bloom recalls Judge Falkiner railing about Reuben J. Dodd – "Now he's really what they call a dirty jew" – but he refuses to take it personally, insisting to himself that the Judge was a "Wellmeaning old man." Nonetheless, Bloom's lurking fear of the "Power those judges have" suggests he realizes he is not as different from Dodd as he might pretend (*U* 174). "Safe!", the ending of "Lestrygonians," represents Bloom's goal for much of his day, mirroring his repeated attraction to the "idea behind" Agendath Netaim, a

Zionist colony (*U* 175, 58). Bloom embodies the wandering Jew, lost in the desert that is Dublin, and locked out of his house so that he cannot return home.

In *Philosophical Investigations*, Wittgenstein includes a culturally coded list of language games such as:

> Reporting an event –
> Speculating about the event –
> Forming and testing a hypothesis –
> Presenting the results of an experiment in tables and diagrams –
> Making up a story; and reading it – (*PI* §1:23)

These language games all have in common their "family resemblances," which, Dinda L. Gorlée explains, "[lie] perhaps first and foremost in their rule-governed nature, in the culturally established social situations in which they appear, and in the language (-like) symbols which are used in them."[94] The scientific aspect of these kinds of activities would certainly appeal to Bloom, the fact-finder, but the "culturally established social situations," which lead to their "rule-governed nature," perplex him. In *Ulysses*, Bloom's ability to report an event, speculate about an event, and test out hypotheses is both crucial to his mental preoccupation throughout his day, but also continuously challenged by the social rules with which he comes into conflict.

Bloom's inability to play a language game by his society's rules puts him particularly at risk. Bantam Lyons's famous misunderstanding of "throw it away" ("I'll risk it, he said. Here thanks" (*U* 82)), results in Bloom's physical harm at the hands of the citizen, which is nearly a "catastrophe" (*U* 329). Lyons understands Bloom's actual words but not their meaning, which is why he believes that Bloom is giving him a tip about a horserace. As Wittgenstein notes, words' meanings reside in their usage, resulting in the need to translate cultural cues. Bloom, however – and the reader with him, at least initially – remains befuddled by Lyons's meaning so that the rowdy chorus of voices condemning Bloom in Barney Kiernan's pub for failing to buy a round of drinks on his alleged winnings is completely incomprehensible. Bloom is as distant from the Catholic language game as he is from the pub one. Bloom's mistranslation of the markings on the cross "I. N. R. I." as "Iron nails ran in" (*U* 78) is merely funny when the thoughts are safely in his stream of consciousness, while he observes the Catholic mass as an anthropologist would, curious but distant. Later in the day, however, when he shouts out that "Christ was a jew like me" (*U* 327), words that are actually much closer to the correct translation of I. N. R. I. (the Latin initials for Jesus of Nazareth King of the Jews, *Iesus Nazarenus Rex Iudaeorum*), the citizen irately responds: "I'll brain that bloody jewman for using the holy name. By Jesus, I'll crucify him so I will" (*U* 327). Bloom dangerously taps into the Catholic terminology in a situation where cultural rather than religious affiliations are sacrosanct. He is a linguistic outsider, so that all day long "Flat Dublin voices bawled in his head" (*U* 75) while his words provoke and cause misunderstandings. Bloom does manage finally to regain his home ("as a competent keyless citizen he had proceeded energetically from the unknown to the known through the incertitude of the void" (*U* 650)) but his day is constantly one of "incertitude" as his attempts to communicate often miss their mark.

Like Bloom, the reader of *Ulysses* needs to surmount seemingly overwhelming obstacles to play the language games at work in the novel. Karen Lawrence notes that by constantly thwarting reader's expectations about narrative technique and character development, Joyce suggests that "*Ulysses* is about novel writing and novel reading."[95] However, early reviewers were not at all sure what *Ulysses* was "about," nor were they even convinced it deserved the name "novel."[96] For example, one 1922 reviewer contended that:

> "Ulysses" is a chaos. All the conventions of organised prose which have grown with our race and out of our racial consciousness which have been reverently handed on by the masters with such improvements as they have been able to make, have been cast aside as so much dross.[97]

Joyce's novel appeared to thwart "all the conventions of organized prose;" instead, resisting the canon's "improvements," *Ulysses* forces readers to relearn how to read each section, because each section's style and technique forms a game of its own.

In the *Philosophical Investigations* Wittgenstein shows how even when words are recognizable, our cultural and social estrangement can make us feel utterly at a loss: a phenomenon very familiar to the first-time reader of *Ulysses*. Wittgenstein writes:

> We also say of some people that they are transparent to us. It is, however, important as regards our considerations that one human being can be a complete enigma to another. One learns this when one comes into a strange country with entirely strange traditions; and, what is more, even given a mastery of the country's language. One does not *understand* the people. (And not because of not knowing what they are saying to themselves.) We cannot find our feet with them.[98]

Within *Ulysses*, the multiplicity of styles creates a novel game with constantly changing rules, where readers struggle to find footing. Eliot proclaimed that Joyce "had many voices but no 'style,'" emphasizing Joyce's unwillingness to commit to a single overriding voice.[99] Merely running through the pages of *Ulysses* demonstrates Joyce's panoply of surfaces, from the headlines and journalism of "Aeolus," to the "jingle jingle jaunted jingling" music of "Sirens," to Molly's extended monologue in "Penelope" (*U* 245). Colin MacCabe, in *James Joyce and the Revolution of the Word*, notes that *Finnegans Wake* "disrupt[s] the normal position assigned to a reader in a text."[100] *Ulysses*, similarly, repeatedly performs this disruption through its changing styles.[101]

The most jarring of Joyce's stylistic transformations occurs when he pointedly undermines the psychological stream-of-consciousness technique that he begins in the *Telemachiad*, thereby denying the reader's expectations for character development and portraying the vague boundary between Stephen and Bloom. Indeed, Wittgenstein's celebrated gesture of throwing away the ladder at the end of the *Tractatus* and thus declaring as "nonsense" everything that the entire book had carefully argued is echoed in Joyce's treatment of his characters and his styles in *Ulysses*.[102] Those who have forged their way through *Stephen Hero* and *A Portrait of the Artist as a Young Man* expect a certain continuation of Stephen's growth, perhaps his fulfillment into an artist or Homeric hero. Instead Joyce's text dissolves even the concept of "character" and reveals the conventions in even his own stream-of-consciousness technique. Not only does Joyce change characters' names ("Siopold," (*U* 265), "Boom" (*U* 602)), and alter their appearances (Bloom's multiple transformations in "Circe"), but also he blurs their unique streams of consciousness. When recalling Shakespeare, Bloom thinks, "In Gerard's rosery of Fetter lane he walks, greyedauburn. One life is all. One body. Do. But do" (*U* 265, 269). These thoughts are not actually Bloom's associations but Stephen's from seventy-six pages earlier. Furthermore, they are not even Stephen's remembered correctly, as Stephen thinks, "In a rosery of Fetter Lane of Gerard, herbalist, he walks, greyedauburn."[103] Joyce reveals that his characters' thoughts are not as unique as his stream-of-consciousness technique has taught the reader to expect.

What Stephen and Bloom do both think in exactly the same words is "One life is all. One body." Their words, drenched in the authority of liturgical resonance, unconsciously acknowledge the breakdown of the boundaries of their streams of consciousness. However, rather than the "One body" of Christ, it is their "inherited system of language" that binds them together.[104] When Joyce merges Bloom and Stephen, he makes suspect both literary characterization as well as the notion of distinct human subjectivity. If language blurs the psychological divisions between fictional characters, Joyce suggests, perhaps it acts the same way in human consciousness. Christine van Boheemen argues that *Ulysses* emphasizes that subjectivity and language are in "dialogic interdependence" and "raises the question of the relationship between the structures of our fictions and the structure of human identity."[105] Through his merging of Bloom and Stephen, therefore, Joyce suggests a general semantic vagueness in which language merely mirrors the vagueness of the world outside *Ulysses*.

Joyce's well-known explanation of *Ulysses* in a letter to Carlo Linati in 1920 emphasizes his intended vagueness:

> It is the epic of two races (Israel-Ireland) and at the same time the cycle of the human body as well as a little story of a day (life) . . . It is also a kind of encyclopædia. My intention is not only to render the myth *sub specie temporis nostri* but also to allow each adventure (that is, every hour, every organ, every art being interconnected and interrelated in the somatic scheme of the whole) to condition and even to create its own technique. Each adventure is so to speak one person although it is composed of persons – as Aquinas relates of the heavenly hosts.[106]

While critics often cite the beginning of this quotation in order to explain the way *Ulysses* acts as an epic, or to elucidate the Gilbert and Linati schemas (joining a color, organ, symbol, or technique to each section of *Ulysses*), most fail to note the reference to Aquinas. Within *Ulysses*, Joyce parodies Stephen's continued "applied Aquinas" when Buck Mulligan exclaims, "I'm not equal to Thomas Aquinas . . . Wait till I have a few pints in me first."[107] However, Joyce's explanation of *Ulysses* also connects to the overlap of his characters and follows the vagueness Aquinas outlines in the description of the Trinity. According to Aquinas, "There are some truths about God that exceed the capacity of human reason – for example the fact that God is three and one."[108] The overlap between the "three and one" of Aquinas explains the way each part of *Ulysses* is "one person although it is composed of persons," and both shed light on the relationship between Joyce's characters. Bloom and Stephen may have distinct persons but the boundaries between their persons, as between the characters and words of *Finnegans Wake*, are vague.

"Ithaca" builds to the climax where Bloom and Stephen realize their connectedness – if only in their mutual incomprehension.[109] Gazing at the light from Molly's window as they stand outside 7 Eccles Street, Stephen and Bloom are briefly united. "Both then were silent?" asks the pseudo-catechistic voice of the chapter, to which is replied: "Silent, each contemplating the other in both mirrors of the reciprocal flesh of theirhisnothis fellowfaces" (*U* 655). Stephen's earlier decision to turn down Bloom's offer of domicile and their later "dissimilar" patterns of urination emphasize the disconnectedness of Bloom and Stephen as characters. But, at this brief moment, "each" is nearly mirrored in the other's reflection. While they seem to see their dissimilarities their "nothis" face, in fact they see their own expressions of confusion mirrored back by the other's "fellowface." What they see is their mutual incomprehension about where they are joined and where they are distinct, a realization that their own limited self-knowledge is mirrored back in the face they contemplate. Joyce's linked words emphasize the characters' unity even as they consider their differences. Molly's illuminating lamp encourages them to see that despite their differences, they are nonetheless vaguely connected.

Joyce's desire for social change, or for his works to act as a kind of therapy for Ireland, is underscored by his vagueness of character and style. In an early letter, Joyce wrote:

> My mother was slowly killed, I think, by my father's ill-treatment, by years of trouble, and by my cynical frankness of conduct. When I looked on her face as she lay in her coffin – a face grey and wasted with cancer – I understood that I was looking on the face of a victim and I cursed the system which had made her a victim.[110]

Joyce expresses his anger at Irish society and the ways Roman Catholicism and patriarchy in general led to his mother's victimization. Society's glorification of the family is at the expense of women like "poor Mrs Purefoy" in *Ulysses* who have "to give the breast year after year all hours of the night" (*U* 153). His own "cynical frankness of conduct" and his "father's ill-treatment," as fictionalized in *A Portrait of the Artist as a Young Man*, *Ulysses*, and even through HCE in the *Wake*, are similarly the result of Irish pride mixed with dependency on England, where Ireland is "the old sow that eats her farrow" (*P* 220). Joyce's *Ulysses* can be seen to carry out his "curse" by subverting the systems – social, religious, philosophical – that entrap Ireland. Joyce's vagueness underscores what Wittgenstein calls the "arbitrary" rules of language, emphasizing the contingency of Ireland's apparently fixed social systems (*PI* §497). By changing the rules of the novel game in *Ulysses* and flouting the rules of recognizable language games in *Finnegans Wake*, Joyce's works force readers to be willing players. Moreover, if social systems, as well as the language that describes them, are based on malleable rules, there seems no reason why readers, or the citizens of his homeland, cannot choose to revise the rules. Joyce's vagueness therefore joins in Wittgenstein's philosophical revolt, hoping to change an outdated system. "At present we are combating a trend," Wittgenstein argues, "But this trend will die out, superseded by others."[111] Similarly, although *Ulysses* ends with Bloom pondering the "irreparability of the past," his optimism for the future, like Molly's final "yes," will not be destroyed, "because at the critical turningpoint of human existence he desired to amend many social conditions" (*U* 645–50).

5. Blasphemy and Nonsense: *Finnegans Wake* in Basic

> The Holy Roman Catholic Apostolic Church was built on a pun. It ought to be good enough for me.
>
> –James Joyce[112]

> Don't *for heaven's sake*, be afraid of talking nonsense! Only you must pay attention to your nonsense.
>
> –Ludwig Wittgenstein[113]

Joyce portrays Stephen at the end of *A Portrait of the Artist as a Young Man* as assailed by many voices. Stephen realizes that:

> While his mind had been pursuing its intangible phantoms and turning in irresolution from such pursuit he had heard about him the constant voices of his father and of his masters, urging him to be a gentleman above all things and urging him to be a good catholic above all things. These voices had now come to be hollowsounding in his ears . . . yet another voice had bidden him to be true to his country and help to raise up her fallen language and tradition. In the profane world, as he foresaw, a worldly voice would bid him raise up his father's fallen state by his labours. (*P* 88)

Stephen acknowledges the pressures of Catholicism, of a fallen father and language, and of an oppressed homeland, and he writhes under these combined responsibilities. All these voices have come to seem "hollow-sounding" to his ears, yet they press upon him unremittingly. Twenty-five years later James Joyce responds to these voices in the text that is *Finnegans Wake*. The *Wake* demonstrates the "labours" of Joyce, writing in the "profane world" about the subject of his "father's fallen state." However, rather than being "true to his country" and helping to "raise up her fallen language and tradition," Joyce celebrates this fallen state of language and land. *Finnegans Wake* revels in blasphemy against any mythic past, firmly engaging in what Wittgenstein would define as "nonsense."[114] This "nonsense" challenges the very idea of translation, especially translation into a logical language like that of C. K. Ogden's Basic English.

For Wittgenstein any kind of conversation about ethics, the mystical, and language itself is "nonsense," which means that the *Wake*, stridently blasphemous, is nonsense. *The Oxford English Dictionary* defines "blasphemy" as "impious irreverence against anything held sacred," and for Joyce such impiety propels *Finnegans Wake*.[115] *Finnegans Wake* can be seen as the ultimate in "blasphematory spits" (*FW* 183:24) for its subversive retelling of sacred myth, transforming, for example, Christ's crucifixion into a "cruelfiction" (*FW* 192:19), and for its irreverence toward a God-given language or "Logos" (*U* 178), preferring instead the "lagos of girly days" (*FW* 203:8). By numerous versions of the fall of HCE – "There extand by now one thousand and one stories, all told, of the same" (*FW* 5:28) – Joyce posits a circular view of history where the Fall has always already occurred and there is not an "Edenville" that can be remembered (*U* 38). Rather, by tearing apart traditional myth and emphasizing language's dependency on changing social practices, Joyce takes apart the "theocratic age," so familiar to Stephen Dedalus, and replaces the surety of "God's real name is God" with the ever-changing language and vision of ALP.[116]

In the *Wake*, history is "cyclewheeling history," thus any myth that claims to be founding is in fact merely a repetition (*FW* 186:2). The resounding fall – (bababadalgharaghtakamminarronnkonnbronntonnerronntuonnthunntrovarrhounawnskawntoohoohoordenenthurnuk!) (*FW* 3:15–7) – is "retaled" often but "Eve and Adam's" is just one more example of the Fall, none more significant than any other (*FW* 3:18). Whereas "christian minstrelsy" (*FW* 3:18) denotes the Fall in Genesis as central, the *Wake* happily blurs all Christian history together:

> For then was the age when hoops ran high. Of a noarch and a chopwife; of a pomme full grave and a fammy of levity; or of golden youths that wanted gelding; or of what the mischievmiss made a man do . . . Maye faye, she's la gaye this snaky woman! (*FW* 20:28–33)

This version of the Fall blurs together Noah and Adam and any other figure who would call himself a patriarch. Joyce transforms Eve into a "chopwife," and his version questions whether it was truly the "snaky woman" or merely the man's "mischievmiss" that led him to eat the "pomme full grave." "My faith!" has degenerated to merely "maye faye." When the washerwomen in ALP shout "Die eve, little eve, die!" they are not only ushering out the day, but also dismissing traditional concepts of Eve and the Garden of Eden (*FW* 215:4). The *Wake* rejects conventional narratives of the Fall by retelling the tale in various mocking guises: "not Edam reeked more rare" (*FW* 183:8). Ireland, a Catholic nation, becomes "Errorland," a place based on falsehood (*FW* 62:25).

Language is loosened from its signifying ties as "the buried life of language" is exhumed, and, as Stephen desired in *A Portrait of the Artist as a Young Man*, the "rhythmic rise and fall of words" are set free from their "associations of legend and colour."[117] *Finnegans Wake* posits ALP as a possible force to renew the wasteland of fallen myths and language. Anna the river is ever changing, exemplified in that she represents many ages of womankind from the "young thin pale soft shy slim slip of a thing" (*FW* 202:27) to "grannyma, gossipaceous Anna Livia" (*FW* 195:4). ALP cannot be stagnant; she is the ancestor as well to Derrida's "trace."[118] Acting as a mythic mother and language, she is both undeniably present and constantly transforming – "Anna was, Livia is, Plurabelle's to be" (*FW* 215:24). She is the fulfillment of vague language, the "turfbrown mummy" (*FW* 194:22), wearing her "alpheubett buttons" (*FW* 208:20), and bringing with her "alpilla, beltilla, ciltilla, deltilla" (*FW* 194:22–3). Whereas Stephen Dedalus once hoped to be the writer, even to write "alphabet books," it is ALP who has reclaimed the alphabet and contains letters within her waters (*U* 48). Joyce emphasized that *Finnegans Wake* represents "an attempt to subordinate words to the rhythm of water," returning to Stephen's vision of language submerged beneath the waves (*JJ* 564).

Finnegans Wake is the culminating expression of the "vague" language that Stephen imbibed from the prostitute. Stephen Dedalus in *Ulysses* never quite tears himself free from the mother/whore vision of women, never liberating himself from his mother's ghost or from the lyrics of "love's bitter mystery" (*U* 9). The boy of *A Portrait of the Artist as a Young Man* walks away into the early morning at the end of *Ulysses* freed or fallen from his relationship with God, yet still, apparently, trapped in a Catholic crisis. The final words (or thoughts) of Stephen reiterate the prayer of the dead that he refused to state for his mother, recalled already early in "Telemachus." These words "*Jubilantium te virginum. Chorus excipiat*" demonstrate not only that Stephen's mind is paralyzed by his refusal to pray, but also that he still envisions a heaven enthronged with a "glorious choir of virgins."[119] Although Stephen plays with language throughout *Ulysses* – for example, delighting in the sea's "Wavewhite wedded words shimmering on the dim tide" (*U* 9) – he remains committed to a Christian metaphorical and idealistic framework and stuck in his own crisis. He never seems to fully imbibe the wisdom of the "vehicle of vague speech."

The language of Molly Bloom, more than that of Stephen, foreshadows the punning technique of *Finnegans Wake*. Molly clings to the idea of God as the creator of it all: "it is as for them saying theres no God I wouldnt give a snap of my two fingers for all their learning why dont they go and create something I often asked him atheists or whatever they call themselves" (*U* 731). She also, however, foreshadows the *Wake*'s language with her puns and run-on sentences. When Bloom thinks of his wife, he remembers her puns:

> She used to say Ben Dollard had a base barreltone voice. He has legs like barrels and you'd think he was singing into a barrel ... Appetite like an albatross. Get outside of a baron of beef. Powerful man he was at storing away number one Bass. Barrel of Bass. See? It all works out. (*U* 147)

Molly's play with language, "base barreltone voice," joining base and barrel, prefigures the portmanteaux of the *Wake*. Molly's use of language, according to "Ithaca," could be equally applied to the Wake: "Unusual polysyllables of foreign origin she interpreted phonetically or by false analogy or by both: metempsychosis (met him pike hoses)" (*U* 639). The *Wake* extrapolates Molly's monologue in "Penelope" to its furthest extent, like "Penelope" having 'no beginning, middle, or end."[120] Like Stephen's vision of language that "flowed" beneath the waves in *A Portrait of the Artist as a Young Man* (*P* 245), Molly's language flows without periods (that is, except her period, which also flows).[121] For Molly the flow of language is not a problem but a source of creativity, for example, in "those beautiful words" (*U* 725) she plans to sing to Stephen, or in Bloom's funny sayings, which she might "write a book out of," she notes, "if I only could remember the one half of the things" (*U* 705).

In "A Lecture on Ethics," Wittgenstein particularly describes the limits of meaning, and his definition of "nonsense" would apply to writings like Joyce's *Finnegans Wake*.[122] Wittgenstein's lecture, his only "popular" speaking engagement, although given for a Cambridge association known as "The Heretics" – the same society where Woolf delivered her "Character in Fiction" talk in 1924 – sets topics like heresy outside the realm of meaningful "verbal expression." Nonetheless, *Finnegans Wake* could qualify as important "nonsense" because it aims to "run against the boundaries of language."[123] Wittgenstein admits that his "lecture" itself, in attempting to address the subjects of ethics, aesthetics, and religion, is a work of "nonsense."[124] And yet, he refuses to apologize for his nonsensical words: "For all I want to do with them was just *to go beyond* the world and that is to say beyond significant language":

> My whole tendency and I believe the tendency of all men who have ever tried to write or talk Ethics or Religion was to run against the boundaries of language. This running against the walls of our cage is perfectly, absolutely hopeless . . . But it is a document of a tendency in the human mind which I personally cannot help respecting deeply and I would not for my life ridicule it.[125]

For Wittgenstein, language is a cage that entraps discussions of aesthetics or ethics, but pushing against this boundary is what much of his philosophy aims to do. Similarly, "[r]unning against the boundaries of language" is a perfect description for Joyce's efforts in *Finnegans Wake*. For Wittgenstein, such an effort is "nonsense," not because it must be ridiculed, but because it is beyond the realm of logical analysis. Joyce, indeed, noted that language entraps like Wittgenstein's "cage." "I'd like a language which is above all languages," he wrote since, "I cannot express myself in English without enclosing myself in a tradition" (*JJ* 397). *Finnegans Wake* enacts Joyce's attempt to resist that "enclosing" in tradition, in the English literary tradition in particular. The *Tractatus*, the *Investigations*, "A Lecture in Ethics," and *Finnegans Wake* all share a similar aim to "go beyond significant language" and to push at the boundaries of what can meaningfully be said.

Wittgenstein would not necessarily have admired the nonsense of *Finnegans Wake*, of course, and not because it was blasphemous but because his literary preferences, unlike his architectural, tended away from modernism and verbal play.[126] In fact, if Wittgenstein's reaction to Basic English is any proof, he probably would have detested the *Wake*'s language. About Basic, Ogden's attempt to create a new universal language, Wittgenstein wrote: "Esperanto. The feeling of disgust we get if we utter an *invented* word with invented derivative syllables. The word is cold, lacking in associations, and yet it plays at being 'language.' A system of purely written signs would not disgust us so much."[127] For Wittgenstein, neologisms without associations rob language of beauty. Therefore *Finnegans Wake*, an "invented language" just as much as Basic, might indeed have filled Wittgenstein with "disgust." Moreover, Wittgenstein's choice to derisively note that Basic merely "plays at being" language is significant. Basic is a fake language game, without real players or a history of play. His scorn recalls his remark in the *Tractatus*: "In fact what solipsism *means*, is quite correct, only it cannot be *said*, but it shows itself" (*T* 5.62).

Wittgenstein's contempt for Basic is somewhat ironic, however, because Ogden's creation of Basic connected to his earlier project of editing and translating the *Tractatus*; Wittgenstein's skepticism about Basic English, therefore, demonstrates a change of opinion about logical languages.[128] In *Reading 1922*, Michael North yokes together Ogden's "project for a universal speech" and Ezra Pound's campaign for "complete clarity and simplicity" with Russell's logical positivism and Wittgenstein's *Tractatus*.[129] All of these kinds of linguistic reform movements aimed to stamp out the problem of vagueness, whether from a literary or a philosophical standpoint. Basic, for example, takes the *Tractatus*' theoretical limitations on language and puts them into practice. If the *Tractatus* really aims to argue that "the world is the totality of facts" (*T* 1.1), and those facts compose "the total reality [that] is the world" (*T* 2.063), then Basic's boiling down of English to 850 words, 600 of which are "names of things" is a useful language.[130] Joyce's decision to ask Ogden to translate a portion of "Anna Livia Plurabelle" into Basic, however, presents a true challenge to Ogden as translator and to Basic as a language. How is it possible to translate into the short Basic vocabulary what Ogden called the "word-ballet" of *Finnegans Wake*?[131] What would such a translation even aim to convey? And why did Joyce and Ogden think this was a good idea? Indeed, Joyce apparently helped Ogden with the translation into Basic just as he orchestrated the contentious translation into French.[132] By comparing a few key passages between the French and Basic translations of ALP, I will conclude this chapter by demonstrating that the Basic translation presents the great gulf between logical and natural languages for translating the *Wake*; the first aims to control language's vagueness, the second to liberate it.

Ogden's Basic English, like other universal language movements, such as Esperanto, Novial, Volapuk, Ido, and Isotype, had great hopes for improving international communication, particularly in the aftermath of the destruction caused by World Wars I and II.[133] Ogden came up with the idea for Basic while working with I. A. Richards on *The Meaning of Meaning* (1923). "This is a reconstruction book," Richards' first sentence in *Basic English and Its Uses* (1943) reads, and Basic will enable a "reasonable degree of communication spread out more evenly over the planet" (*Basic*, 5). Winston Churchill famously advocated Basic at a speech at Harvard in 1943, and he even wrote to Roosevelt encouraging the United States to take up the charge of Basic as a "great boon to mankind."[134] Basic was not meant to replace ordinary English but to be an addition, an "International Auxiliary Language." Richards admits that in an "artificial language" like Basic, "literature in the serious sense is all but impossible," or at least not "without centuries of wide and varied use" (*Basic*, 15). Basic, instead, aimed to facilitate global communication, stemming from the belief that an international language would help to secure world peace.

For, as Ogden wrote in *Debabelization* (1931), which sets out the case for Basic, "it is the business of all internationally-minded persons to make Basic English part of the system of education in every country, so that there may be less chance of war."[135]

The global impulse of Basic English was actually not so very different from Joyce's verbal experiments in *Finnegans Wake*, a similarity manifested by Joyce asking Ogden to write the preface for a selection from the *Wake* entitled *Tales Told of Shem and Shaun* (1929) and urging him to translate ALP into Basic. In the preface, Ogden calls himself "one whose approach is primarily linguistic" (*Tales*, iii), and laments that many readers will find Joyce and *Finnegans Wake* rebarbative because "whoever flouts, parodies, or evades linguistic conventions, will seem to the magistrature to have something in common with those whose inhibitions or social ties have broken down" (*Tales*, xi). Instead of portraying Joyce as a literary and social outcast, Ogden asserts that *Finnegans Wake* is urgently needed for de-homogenizing English literature: "Mr. Joyce appears as a promised liquidator where the machinery of literature has been clogged by the ministrations and minutiae of an ossified propaedeutic" (*Tales*, ii). English has become "overconventionalized," but Joyce's writing can help (*Tales*, i). Fascinatingly, given his own desire to simplify English for international communication, Ogden argues that greater linguistic complexity may be called for in literature. Ogden traces "two main tendencies" in writing:

> Chaucer, Elyot, Nash, Rabelais, Urquhart, and the literary practitioners of the last decade, are in contrast with a tradition which began with Bishop Wilkins and Leibnitz, and which led [...] even through Zamenhof and C. S. Peirce, to the makers of those latest notations and nomenclatures which are again revolutionizing the sciences. (*Tales*, xiv)

Having divided these writers into two groups, those who aim to write vividly in language and those who may kill language's evocative powers through "notations and nomenclatures," Ogden concludes: "The first may achieve the new Word-Orchestration, the second may destroy the old Word-Magic" (*Tales*, xiv). Ogden's own work creating Basic English, intriguingly, fits into the destructive latter camp, although his preface's diction and wordplay enthusiastically mirror the cadences of the *Wake* rather than of Basic. For Ogden both camps' approaches to language are currently necessary "to stimulate" a revitalized interest in language (*Tales*, xv).

Basic English and its Uses proclaims that Basic "took its start" from the desire to eliminate the "ambiguity, obscurity, and misunderstanding" in using colloquial English for communication (*Basic*, 106). In order to go about reducing this confusion, Ogden created his 850-word list, mostly concrete nouns ("Fruit, Glass, Gold, Government, Grain, Grass, Grip," for example), and created this patently nominalist (and secular) universe – tellingly, neither "heap" nor God, with all of their troublesome meanings are necessary words in Basic. Like young Stephen's word list in *A Portrait of the Artist as a Young Man*, which carefully positions himself in relationship to Ireland and the Universe, the Basic list makes of the world a seemingly concrete group of objects, which the subject can manipulate with a very simple group of verbs. Richards insists, "The reduction of the verbs to eighteen was the key to the discovery of Basic" (*Basic*, 33). The Basic word list carefully labels each word as a strict noun, adjective, or verb and their usage must follow firm rules ("Grip," listed above, may not be used as a verb, for example). This strict vocabulary and word patterning creates a language that Ogden claimed could be learned in merely seven weeks. Richards argues that one important goal of Basic was to protect the true English language. Basic can "serve our language as a fender" from "less expert users," such as those at a "Chinese university." He explains: "It can guard full English from those who will blur all its lines and blunt all its edges if they try to write and talk it before they have learned to read it" (*Basic*, 33). Such blurring and blending, however, is exactly the goal of *Finnegans Wake*, which takes English and blurs the idea of noun, verb, and adjective just as it blurs the relationship between expert and inept users. Similarly, the *Wake* rejects any firm rules: "In so far as *Finnegans Wake* is written in an 'invented language,' it is a language pointedly lacking in norms and clear rules."[136] The *Wake* highlights language's vagueness whereas Basic aims, like Wittgenstein's picture theory of language put into practice, to stamp it out. These opposing goals make the idea of ALP in Basic seem impossible.

In his introduction to the 1932 publication in *Transition* magazine of ALP in its original and in Basic English, Ogden noted, "In this way the simplest and most complex languages of man are placed side by side."[137] Joyce famously explained this section to an unconvinced Harriet Shaw Weaver: "a chattering dialogue across the river by two washerwomen who as night falls become a tree and a stone. The river is named Anna Liffey."[138] This was Joyce's favorite part of the entire enterprise – "Either the end of Part I Δ [*Anna Livia Plurabelle*] is something or I am an imbecile in my judgment of language"[139] – perhaps explaining why Joyce urged Ogden to translate this section after he recorded it for Ogden's audio version in 1929. The opposing goals of the different languages of Basic and the *Wake* are evident immediately, as the contrast between the following two passages demonstrates:

> Wait till the honeying of the lune, love! Die eve, little eve, die! (*FW* 215:03–4)
> Do not go till the moon is up love. She's dead, little Eve, little Eve she's dead.[140]

In the ALP passage, the two washerwomen's discussion of the ending of the day both mixes languages and changes words' conventional functions. Joyce combines the French word for moon ("lune") with the archaic usage of honey as a verb, so that the moon lights up the evening sky as it rises. While the Basic translation "simplifies" the vocabulary and conveys the basic plot points, it misses Joyce's meanings by sticking to its Basic vocabulary and rules.

Furthermore, the capitalization of "Eve" in the Basic translation means that even the "story" of the passage becomes obfuscated. In the introduction Ogden emphasizes that the translation aims to convey the "rhythm" at the expense of the "story" and as this passage demonstrates indeed the "story" is altered when adhering to the Basic rules.[141] What was merely an allusion to the biblical "eve" within the approaching "evening" in ALP, becomes stridently the reportage of the death of a woman named Eve in Basic. In *Modernist Heresies*, Damon Franke notes a similar difficulty about what makes for "the meaning" of Joyce's text. Many critics agree, he notes, that one of the most important "meanings" of ALP (as demonstrated most famously by John Bishop) is the accumulation of River names that "works to create the echoic effects of rushing waters or pulsating blood" of HCE.[142] The Basic translation leaves some of these river names in place, but needs to elide many other suggested names in Joyce's verbal play because they fail to be entire names, or are merely part of another more important "plot" word. As both the Eve and the rivers examples demonstrate, the important "plot" of ALP is contentious. To repeat what Beckett famously declared about Joyce's writing: It "is not *about* something; *it is that something itself*."[143] While this fact presents a challenge to any translator of ALP, the unity of the "story" and the style is particularly a challenge for the Basic translator where mirroring the verbal play at the word level is impossible.

Critics disagree about the success of ALP's translation into Basic, although most marvel at the strange idea of it. For Jean-Michel Rabaté, "the translation is surprisingly successful," whereas for Susan Shaw Sailer, "Though Basic English may be well suited to convey information among those for whom English is a second language, it is a completely inadequate tool for translating *Finnegans Wake*."[144] For Sailer, the Basic translation only convincingly communicates one feature of language, the "vehicular" feature, so that "Ogden is forced to combine silliness with distortion in his translation, because he sees the 'simple sense' of Joyce's language as one of transmitting information."[145] The silliness of the translation – crystalized in the deadpan tone of "She's dead, little Eve, little Eve she's dead," – is also due to an apparent lack of irony, where Basic's seemingly reverential attitude to the word from the Basic wordlist is in stark contrast to the *Wake's* neologisms and portmanteaux.[146]

In leaving the word sacrosanct the Basic translation misses the vast majority of Joyce's senses, which are conveyed, for example, in the French translation. Here, for comparison, are versions of ALP's evocative conclusion in the original, the French and Basic:

> Tell me, tell me, tell me, elm! Night night! Telmetale of stem or stone. Beside the rivering waters of, hitherandthithering waters of. Night! (*FW* 216:3–5)

> Dis-mor, dis-mor, dis-mor, orme. Nuit, nuit! Contemoiconte soit tronc ou pierre. Tant rivièrantes ondes de, couretcourantes ondes de. Nuit.[147]

> Say it, say it, tree! Night night! The story say of stem or stone. By the side of the river waters of, this way and that way waters of. Night! (*Basic ALP* 139)

As the earlier example of "lune" demonstrates, ALP frequently combines words from different languages; similarly, the French translation combines French and English in the phrase "dis-mor." "Dis-mor" combines "Dites-moi" (tell me) with "more" in English, reiterating the desire to be told, both through repetition and through the English request for "more." The musicality of the passage, key in the original, is similarly repeated in the mirroring rhythms of the French: "hitherandithering waters of" is echoed in the rhythm of "couretcourantes ondes de," and, for both these phrases, the quickly compressed words recall the waters' rushing movement. In the original ALP, in order to evoke the night's approach when sights become dim in the dusk, Shem and Shaun become "stem" and "stone" just as the washerwoman herself blends into the natural landscape. "Elm," one of the native trees of Ireland, also repeats the letters from "tell me," forming nearly a palindrome "[tel]l me, elm." The woman nearly becomes the elm as she asks her question in the fading light. The French translation also suggests this movement in "[dis-] mor, orme," because "orme" and "mor" are nearly the same letters merely moved slightly. In contrast, the rhythm of Basic's "say it, tree!" works in a different way. The sound is cacophonous with its hard consonants, and it glaringly distinguishes between the "tree" and the "it," both aurally and visually. According to W. V. Costanzo, most changes between the English and the French translation "have an effect of softening the prose. 'Dis-mor,' for example, is less sharp than 'dismoi,' and the elimination of two exclamation points makes the tone more gentle."[148] In contrast, the Basic translation sounds more aggressive. Whereas the French translation includes the near-homophone of love and death ("dis-mor" echoed in "l'amour" and "la mort"), the Basic contains strident commands: "Tell me, love," is quite opposite to "Say it, say it, tree!"

In a word-by-word comparison, the Basic English translation, if you can call it that, is closer to the original *Wakese*, because the words and word order are nearly interchangeable, with only a few simplifications (tree for Elm, story for tale). As a tool for conveying most major plot points, like a study guide such as Sparknotes, the Basic translation may have its uses, although even this, as Ogden noted, presents challenges. The French translation, in contrast, makes far greater linguistic changes and indeed, "story" changes. It is, however, more faithful to ALP's verbal play both in the incorporation of multiple languages and the punning and portmanteaux. Joyce stated with regards to *Finnegans Wake* that he would be willing to allow James Stephens, an Irish novelist and poet, to take over its creation: "As regards that book itself and its future completion I have asked Miss Beach to get into closer relations with James Stephens . . . If he consented to maintain three or four points which I consider essential and I showed him the threads he could finish the design . . . It would be a great load off my mind."[149] Fearing that his eyesight would make the writing of *Finnegans Wake* too taxing, Joyce allows that he could be willing to hand over his project. Furthermore, he observes that only "three or four points" would have to be agreed upon for Stephens to proceed. The "three or four points" may have related to revealing the musicality of language and irreverently deconstructing the word, both of which are conveyed in the French translation, although not in the Basic.

Of course Basic English cannot actually eliminate vagueness just because it sticks to nouns, nor can it avoid ambiguity because it follows strict rules. In the quotations cited above, Basic creates its own ambiguities. For example, "Do not go till the moon is up love. She's dead, little Eve, little Eve she's dead," seems to imply that the speaker is addressing "little Eve" herself, who is simultaneously declared dead (*Basic ALP* 139). Is this ambiguity the point: that we do not actually know whether the Eve/ning is alive or dead? In fact, reading the Basic translation of ALP and its play at the syntactical rather than word level evokes the writing of

Gertrude Stein. In this way Ogden's Basic project seems itself a version of literary modernist experimentation.

Perhaps sensing these experimental similarities, Joyce liked *Finnegans Wake* in Basic – "Yes, ALP in basic is all right," he wrote to Ogden, and expressed excitement about their en face publication in *Transition.*[150] Joyce "expressed a desire to see how far the effects at which he was aiming with a vocabulary of say 850,000,000 words could be conveyed with the 850 words of Basic English."[151] Perhaps Joyce enjoyed playing with the idea of the *Wake* in Basic, because although Basic aimed to convey the rhythm and plot of the original, the translation nonetheless manifestly demonstrated the limitations of a more straightforward language for conveying Joyce's own effects. Joyce's declared intention in the *Wake* was to draw in "that ideal reader suffering from an ideal insomnia" to be the other player in his complicated multilingual language game (*JJ* 703). Indeed, the number of *Wake* guides, websites, and reading groups demonstrates that Joyce's dream language is not a game he plays alone. This taps into the Utopian impulse behind both Basic English and *Finnegans Wake*: A new language could come into being, freed from hierarchies and international in scope. Basic intended to be "to the service of humanistic studies to society," allowing for universal comprehension and instruction: "the International Language," according to Ogden, "in which everything may be said."[152] *Finnegans Wake* similarly aimed to encompass all languages and all things that could be said; it would give voice to dreams, babble, and the thoughts of an international subject, a "Europasianised Afferyank" (*FW* 191:4). Of course, the projects internationalized in different ways, one by limiting, and one by expanding, the normal limits of language. In addition, the fact that "Henry Ford" was listed as one "convert," or that Churchill recommended Basic to FDR because of a "conviction" that Basic would be "a powerful support to the influence of the Anglo-Saxon peoples in world affairs," demonstrates strong historical ties among Basic, Anglo-American imperialism, and capitalism.[153] Basic stands for *B*ritish *A*merican *S*cientific *I*nternational *C*ommercial *E*nglish, which immediately highlights the difference between the *Wake* and Basic. If Joyce's language aimed to resist the yoke of British English, Basic, in contrast, worked to extend it.

Indeed, in the immediate aftermath of World War II, Basic became so popular that in his science fiction work *The Shape of Things to Come* (1933), H. G. Wells projected that "by 2020 there was hardly anyone in the world who could not talk and understand" Basic English. Wells's prediction for Joyce was not so rosy, however. Joyce will have "vanished at last from the pursuit of his dwindling pack of readers in a tangled prose almost indistinguishable from the gibbering of a lunatic."[154] The truth is rather the reverse, as Basic is now mostly only "an unacknowledged – even unconscious – part of teaching," particularly the instruction of English as a second language, whereas the Joyce industry thrives.[155] Joyce pinpointed the difficulties faced by an artificial language like Basic within the *Wake* itself:

> For if the lingo gasped between kicksheets, however basically English, were to be preached from the mouths of wickerchurchwardens and metaphysicians in the row and advokaatoes, allvoyous, demivoyelles, languoaths, lesbiels, dentelles, gutterhowls and furtz, where would their practice be or where the human race itself [. . .]? (*FW* 116:25–30)

In this quotation, Joyce questions where an unnatural "lingo," like "basically English," that needs to be "preached from the mouths of wickerchurchwardens and metaphysicians," would find practitioners: "where would their practice be." He demonstrates his knowledge of linguistics terminology, such as demivowels, labials, and dentals, and alludes to both Basic and Volapuk, while also questioning such International Auxiliary Language's purpose.[156] When Joyce wonders what would happen to humanity if Basic became popular – "where the human race itself" – he emphasizes his deep belief in the importance of a natural language like English, rich with associations and history.

The colorful history of the various efforts to translate the *Wake* into many languages, including French, Italian, Spanish, Japanese, Chinese, and Polish, suggests that in some ways this text acts as a test case for the art of translation; and here, again, Wittgenstein's comments about logical and natural languages shed light on the process of translation. Derrida famously argued that the *Wake* "resembles a too-powerful, outsize calculator incommensurable with any translating machine conceivable today," whereas Umberto Eco contended the converse, that Joyce's text is eminently translatable: "*Finnegans Wake* è anche – tra tutti – il testo piú facile da tradurre" (*Finnegans Wake* is even – above all others – the easiest text to translate).[157] For the Wittgenstein of the *Tractatus*, where language is a set of symbols standing for something else, all is translatable: "Every correct symbolism must be translatable into every other according to such rules" (*T* 3:343). However, Wittgenstein's change of opinion given language's vagueness makes translation much more challenging, as he noted nearly ten years after the *Tractatus*: "[T]he limit of language is shown by its being impossible to describe the fact which corresponds to (is the translation of) a sentence, without simply repeating the sentence."[158] Translation, when symbols no longer correspond to facts, may become impossible, or merely relegated to repetition.

Wittgenstein elaborates on the process of translation in a later work:

> Translating from one language into another is a mathematical task, and the translation of a lyrical poem, for example, into a foreign language is quite analogous to a mathematical *problem*. For one may well frame the problem 'How is this joke (e.g.) to be translated (i.e. replaced) by a joke in the other language?' and this problem can be solved; but there was no systematic method of solving it.[159]

For Wittgenstein, translating a lyrical poem needs to be seen as a task like translating a joke: a problem to be solved. One must recreate the cultural and social rules that make a joke funny, rather than merely translating the joke word for word. A group of translators, like Joyce's cohort for the French translation, may well be able to tackle this mathematical problem of translating ALP into French by determining how the English puns work and coming up with commensurate processes in French. Joyce's "nonsense" in the *Wake*, however, may be impossible to translate into Basic, a language whose strict rules, aimed precisely at eliminating vagueness and confusion, cannot allow for the verbal play it requires.

In *Modernism as a Philosophical Problem*, Robert B. Pippin argues that bourgeois self-hatred, a philosophical stance endemic in modernity, stems in part from the backlash against a former optimism for all things scientific and rational.[160] Basic English seems a perfect example of such a naïve enthusiasm. But as projects as diverse as Wittgenstein's *Tractatus* and Ogden's Basic English show, the desire to tap down language's vagueness, to believe in some sort of ideal, transparent, or isomorphic tool for communication to unite disparate nations or to further philosophical knowledge was ubiquitous in early twentieth-century Europe. Two world wars put such scientific enthusiasm to the test, but not before, as the next chapter will argue, its ramifications spread to a new type of literary criticism.

CHAPTER 4

Conclusion: To Criticize the Criticism: T. S. Eliot and the Eradication of Vagueness

Words strain,
Crack and sometimes break, under the burden,
Under the tension, slip, slide, perish,
Decay with imprecision, will not stay in place,
Will not stay still.

–Eliot, "Burnt Norton."

The verbal disease above noticed may be reserved for diagnosis by and by.

–Eliot, "The Perfect Critic."[1]

1. Eliot's Critical Influence

"I really think that I have far more *influence* on English letters than any other American has ever had," Eliot humbly wrote in 1919, "unless it be Henry James."[2] Eliot's proclamation in terms of modernist criticism ends up not far off the mark, because he is often said "to exemplify English modernism," labeled "by far the most important critic of the twentieth century in the English-speaking world," and even hailed, hyperbolically, as a modernist "God."[3] Eliot's reputation is undergoing exciting reconsideration with the ongoing publication of his collected works, and even as the field of modernist studies expands both horizontally and vertically, he remains central, as either an influential poet, critic, or both.[4] He persists to this day, however, as a figure whom critics love or love to hate. He is particularly chastised for his alleged fathering of New Criticism, which, it is often argued, through its ahistorical and purely formalist methods, misrepresented and "domesticated" modernism.[5] This book concludes by simultaneously supporting and dismissing that characterization of Eliot. On the one hand, although he never championed ahistoricism, I do agree that Eliot's early influential essays fostered an instrumental approach to understanding modernist writing, like that of James, Woolf, and Joyce, that focused on its precise structure and formal exactitude in the face of modernity's chaos. I aim, throughout this project, to revise these standard accounts of modernism by emphasizing that vague, subjective, and imprecise are similarly essential descriptions of this fiction. On the other hand, however, I also hope to illuminate the evolution of Eliot's relationship to vagueness; looking at the long arc of Eliot's career, it is clear that his enthusiasm for Russell's scientism and analytic approach was brief and measured. Indeed, Eliot's transformations as a literary critic in his attitude toward language's vagueness mirror the movement that this book has charted from Frege's *Begriffsschrift* to Wittgenstein's "Blur."

This conclusion is divided into two further discrete sections. In the first, I treat Eliot as the cumulative case of this book: Like James, Woolf, and Joyce, Eliot was an important early twentieth-century literary figure reacting to and against movements in contemporary philosophy, although his situation is unique because he was himself training to be an academic philosopher. In this section, I will argue that we have underestimated the influence of Bertrand Russell on Eliot's powerful version of modernism. I will demonstrate that debates about vague language significantly affected Eliot's early literary criticism and that Eliot's interest in the methods of Russell's analytic philosophy motivated his influential essays in *The Sacred Wood*. This part looks backward, intending to shed light on Eliot's relationship to the linguistic turn. In the final section, I will shift the focus forward in order to demonstrate how Eliot's interest in eradicating literary vagueness in the early years shaped his own response to Henry James, Joyce, and Woolf, as well as the response of the literary critics in his wake, particularly Empson and the New Critics. If early twentieth-century Cambridge philosophy can be characterized as clearing "away the metaphysical clutter of the Victorians so that knowledge could be re-defined in the epistemologically more secure terms of linguistic logic," so also the Cambridge literary critics (Eliot and Richards, with Empson and the New Critics in their wake) aimed to place literary criticism on firmer logical and anti-aesthetic footing.[6] The final section of the conclusion will argue for a renewed "fuzzy" approach to literary criticism, which allows for the vagueness of language, warning against an overzealous "return to empiricism" called for by some contemporary literary criticism (for example, by some digital humanities, distant readings, or cognitive scientific approaches).[7]

"[P]hilosophising," Eliot lamented to a friend, merely results in "a perversion of reality," which makes "the world appear as strange as

Bottom in his ass's head."[8] As Harold Bloom has made clear, literature and literary criticism also pervert and manipulate reputations in order to make way for new approaches and readings.[9] I will admit, as a lifelong admirer of Eliot's poetry *and* criticism, that one additional goal of this conclusion is to reanimate Eliot as a critical thinker, because he often seems petrified as the archetypical conservative formalist in modernist studies, a claim that is sometimes, but not always, accurate.[10] Although Eliot's early essays were instrumental in the formation of literary criticism as a professionalized "cultural science," he himself was no advocate for the rigorous empiricism afoot in our current academic climate.[11] "When a subject matter is in its nature vague," Eliot warned, "clarity should consist, not in making it so clear as to be unrecognisable, but in recognising the vagueness [. . .] and in checking analysis and division at the prudent point."[12] Eliot may have launched the New Criticism, illustrated by his essays on James, Woolf, and Joyce, which value structure, precision, and unity, but we also see in Eliot the seeds for another way: a fuzzier, more pragmatic way.

2. Eliot and Russell: "Wobbliness" and "The Scientific Paradise"

> So I assumed a double part, and cried
> And heard another's voice cry: 'What! are *you* here?'
>
> –Eliot, "Little Gidding"[13]

Late in life, according to Eliot's widow Valerie, Eliot liked to recount the following anecdote about a conversation with a London cab driver:

> "You're T. S. Eliot, aren't you?"
> "Ah."
> "Just last week, do you know who was sitting where you're sitting now? Bertrand Russell!"
> "Ah."
> "So I said, 'Well, Lord Russell, what's it all about?' And, you know, he couldn't tell me!"[14]

Eliot was clearly entertained by the image of Russell's predicament. As Hugh Kenner puts it, Eliot's story shows "how self-assumed Omniscience got confronted by a man with a simple wish for one clarifying sentence . . . which Omniscience was powerless to formulate."[15] For Eliot, philosophy itself, and with that Russell, erred in thinking it could answer the question, "What's it all about?" Eliot's move to focus solely on poetry, social and literary criticism, and his embrace of the Anglican faith demonstrate his disenchantment with the false "omniscience" of academic philosophy. However, his early years, the years preceding his first book of literary criticism, *The Sacred Wood,* were spent immersed in philosophy.

In the Introduction to Eliot's *Selected Prose,* Frank Kermode writes, "Eliot was clearly right in supposing that the most influential of his essays were among the earliest" (*SPTSE* 13). "Tradition and the Individual Talent," "Hamlet," "The Metaphysical Poets," "Henry James," and "*Ulysses,* Order and Myth," were all written by 1923, five years before his declaration "as classicist in literature, royalist in politics, and anglo-catholic in religion," and with over forty years of social and literary criticism still to come.[16] Many of these early essays contain Eliot's well-known pronouncements and were collected into *The Sacred Wood* (1920), *Selected Essays* (1932), and finally in *Selected Prose* (1975). In *To Criticize the Critic* (1965), Eliot admitted these early essays had a "warmth of appeal" that the later essays were missing.[17] Part of this "warmth of appeal" derives from Eliot's self-consciously precarious balance of literary proclamation – what he later called "an assumption of pontifical solemnity" – with self-doubt.[18] Eliot decrees, for example, that the "style of [Swinburne] is essentially a prose style; and Mr. Symons' prose is much more like Swinburne's poetry than it is like his prose" (*SPTSE* 52). However, he quickly admits when he attempts to propound this theory, "here one's thought is moving in almost complete darkness" (*SPTSE* 52). Eliot's prose style has a kind of doubleness about it, which is particularly evident in his analysis of language.[19]

This doubleness stems from the changes in Eliot's philosophical outlook during the period. Ever since Eliot's doctoral thesis in philosophy, *Knowledge and Experience in the Philosophy of F. H. Bradley,* was published in 1964, studies of the relationships among Eliot's philosophy and his poetry and prose have flourished.[20] "By the centennial of his birth," Jeffrey Perl wittily notes, "Eliot had been associated with nearly every school or category of philosophy with which he could conceivably have been familiar."[21] Certain critics, such as Ann Bolgan and Michael Levenson, have sought to demonstrate the thoroughgoing influence of Bradley's idealism, particularly on Eliot's holistic notion of Tradition.[22] Other critics, notably Walter Benn Michaels and Donald Childs, citing Eliot's own assertion that the revised dissertation aimed to be "entirely destructive," contend that Eliot's skepticism led to a kind of pragmatism; still other critics add that his eventual abandonment of philosophy for literary criticism and orthodox Christianity is foretold in the early poetry and essays.[23] I believe that the number of these mutually incompatible interpretations of the dissertation demonstrates that Eliot's dissertation is divided between endorsing and criticizing Bradley's idealism (his later comment that philosophy felt like "cramming both feet into one shoe" supports this discomfort).[24] Moreover, and to return my focus to Eliot's literary criticism, I maintain that the influence of Russell, an early friend and mentor, is responsible for much of the new analytic tone in Eliot's early literary critical essays.

With Richard Shusterman, the author of *T. S Eliot and the Philosophy of Criticism*, I agree that Eliot's dissertation strongly differs in style from his early criticism. Shusterman maintains that the influence of Bertrand Russell instigated Eliot's "revolt against the Hegelian idealist tradition represented by Bradley," resulting in a move toward "scientific realism and positivistic objectivism."[25] I would temper Shusterman's claims only to point out that as early as his undergraduate course notes and graduate dissertation Eliot expressed strong reservations about Russell's symbolic logic and scientific realism, which later flowered into a full dismissal of Russell as a merely scientific philosopher.[26] Nonetheless, I aim to demonstrate that Russell's methods presented a breath of fresh air to the young Eliot in his fight against impressionistic literary criticism.[27] Even as Eliot parodied Russell's realism as a new kind of Romanticism, he was still continually attracted to Russell's style and method. Although Eliot's philosophy continued to evolve throughout his career, in his early years in London – the years of *The Sacred Wood* – his reading of and relationship with Russell led to Eliot's absorption of Russell's logical atomism and its passion for logical analysis and hatred of vagueness. Indeed, the best way to make sense of Eliot's renowned although somewhat obscure coinage of the "objective correlative" is by reading it in light of his temporary adoption of elements of Russell's philosophy. For Eliot, however, although Russell's realist framework presented a useful approach for criticism, it was, nonetheless, always just another fiction. Throughout Eliot's earlier criticism phrases like "the objective correlative" and "the historical sense" yearn for scientific precision, while his theories of "the dissociation of sensibility" and the "verbal disease" emphasize that such precision in language lies just out of reach.[28] Although Eliot's critical statements often aimed to stamp out "verbalism" (*SPTSE* 54), vagueness, like the return of the repressed, haunts his critical attempts to make modern literature cohere.

The more commonly accepted reason for the new austerity of Eliot's tone is tied to the influence of T. E. Hulme, the charismatic writer whom Eliot grandly described as "the forerunner of a new attitude of mind, which should be the twentieth-century mind."[29] Hulme himself radically revised his opinion about vagueness as he moved from an earlier Bergsonian phase to his enthusiastic neo-Classicism, where he indicted Bergson as a Romantic. Hulme's influence on the school of Imagism and on Eliot's pro-Classicist proclamations is well known, and both Eliot and Hulme "follow a similar intellectual trajectory," as Erik Svarny notes, "from an enthusiasm for Henri Bergson's implicitly liberal, irrationalist and vitalist philosophy towards a gradual alignment with the authoritarian ideas of [Charles] Maurras and the *Action Française*."[30] Hulme's change of opinion about vagueness is tied to this political and literary reversal. In his early "Lecture on Modern Poetry," which was most likely delivered in 1908, Hulme argued that "[w]e are no longer concerned that stanzas shall be shaped and polished like gems, but rather that some vague mood shall be communicated." A "vague mood," not entrapped in "cramping, jangling, meaningless, and out of place" meter, would be the new voice of modern poetry.[31] In his switch to "Classicism," however, his opinion about vagueness reversed, as vagueness became aligned with the enemy, Romanticism, and he called for "classical revival" of "dry" poetry. His belief that for poetry "[t]he great aim is accurate, precise and definite description" influenced Eliot enough that he would conclude *The Use of Poetry and the Use of Criticism* by quoting and analyzing these words.[32] Hulme clearly tied vagueness to Romanticism, lamenting that "[s]o much has romanticism debauched us, that, without some form of vagueness, we deny the highest."[33] He believed "the highest" form of poetry would avoid sentiment and vagueness altogether, but stern standards and critics were needed to enlighten readers who had been "debauched" by Romanticism. Eliot, who it is now believed knew of Hulme's writings as early as 1916, responded to his call and began lecturing on Hulme's views on Romanticism, tying Romanticism to "vague emotionality" and outlining the new Classicism.[34] Hulme himself, meanwhile, as evidenced in his posthumous collection *Speculations*, admitted the influence of Moore and Russell, and his antipathy to vague language mirrors theirs.[35] Furthermore, Eliot received the influence of analytic thought both indirectly, through Hulme, and directly, through Russell.

The story of Eliot's fraught personal link to Russell is well documented, perhaps so well documented that we forget that Eliot and Russell had a kind of father-son relationship before it turned sour. His relationship with Russell actually began at Harvard in 1914 when Russell, as a visiting professor sixteen years senior to Eliot, gave a course Eliot attended in Symbolic Logic. Russell's philosophy at that time seemed to Eliot, the president of the University Philosophical Society, to lack "anything to do with reality."[36] Indeed, Eliot's early skepticism is evidenced by his derisive comments on both pragmatism and Russell's symbolic logic in an address to the Philosophical Society: "James's philosophical writings constitute an emotional attitude more than a body of dogma," Eliot notes, "and we observe Mr. B. Russell with passionate enthusiasm directing his unearthly ballet of bloodless alphabets."[37] Eliot's caricature of Russell as "Mr. Apollinax," collected in *Prufrock and Other Poems* (1917), similarly highlights Russell's "dry and passionate talk," while emphasizing his other passions, which make him appear "unbalanced" during his time as a visiting professor (*CPP* 31). "He laughed like an irresponsible fœtus," Eliot writes, paralleling Russell to an oversexed Greek fertility god: "Priapus in the shrubbery / Gaping at the lady in the swing" (*CPP* 31). Eliot's depiction of the great man undone by his sexuality mirrors Woolf's recollection that Russell claimed his philosophy failed him when "my passions got hold of me" (*DVW* 2:148).

Russell's "passions," as Ronald Schuchard has shown us in *Eliot's Dark Angel*, led to the end of both Eliot's marriage and Eliot's and Russell's relationship, but when Eliot initially moved to London in 1915 Russell's influence seemed a godsend.[38] It was to Russell, the respected philosopher, that Eliot turned to act as a kind of ambassador when he needed his mother to understand his career decisions, and Eliot also depended upon Russell's hospitality and financial generosity.[39] Russell helped to introduce the young Eliot to London's intellectual and literary circles. And although Russell could be critical of Eliot, whom he described as "altogether impeccable in his tastes" but without "vigor or life – or enthusiasm," he also confessed, "I have come to love him, as if he were my son."[40]

The disintegration of their relationship ought not to cancel out the fact that, in his early years as a critic, Eliot expressed enthusiasm for both Russell and his philosophical method. Eliot wrote from England, "I do enjoy [Russell] quite as much as any man I know," and he spent time "absorbed" in *Principia Mathematica*, examining Russell's symbolic logic.[41] In 1918, reviewing Russell's "Mysticism, Logic, and Other Essays" in *The Nation*, Eliot heralds Russell "as one who has invented a new method."[42] "[H]e is also a philosopher who has invented a new point of view," Eliot notes, "and a new point of view is style."[43] He praises this style, this "language in which it is possible to think clearly and exactly on any subject"; moreover, he emphasizes the possible influence such exactitude could have on literary language. "The *Principia Mathematica* are perhaps a greater contribution to our language than they are to mathematics," he concludes.[44] Exactitude, for Eliot, was a virtue symbolized by the *Principia Mathematica*, and an alternative to the vagueness of abstract literary language, like that of both the Romantics and their descendants, the Georgian Poets. "In the Georgian poets we observe the same attitude [as in Wordsworth]," Eliot lamented, and "[o]nly in something harder can great passion be expressed." He maintained: "[T]he vague is a more dangerous path for poetry than the arid."[45] Similarly, literary criticism must strive for strict analysis and avoid vague appreciations; he concludes the introduction to *The Sacred Wood* with the example of Johnson "as a model to critics who desire to correct some of the poetical vagaries of the present age."[46] Throughout *The Sacred Wood* and Eliot's other early writings, vagueness and abstraction are the enemies of good literary criticism and art, whereas solidity, objectivity and the technique of "analysis" – all Russell's virtues – are Eliot's positive keywords for literary and critical techniques.[47]

Russell calls out for "logical analysis" to rid philosophy of terms such as "mind, matter, consciousness, knowledge, experience, causality, will, time," which are "essentially infected with vagueness" and therefore "incapable of forming part of any exact science."[48] Similarly, Eliot consistently emphasizes the need for precise definitions of literary terms and for a strong analytical technique in literary criticism. In fact, it is a characteristic move of Eliot's essayistic style to begin with a term whose meaning he attempts to pin down to initiate the essay.[49] (One thinks of J. Alfred Prufrock, fixed in a "formulated phrase" and "pinned and wriggling on the wall."[50]) As Eliot argues in "The Perfect Critic" (1920), good criticism must pin words down, must move "in the direction of analysis and construction," and should carefully avoid "comment and opinion" and "new emotions which are vaguely applied" (*SPTSE* 52–3). Earlier modes of literary criticism, such as "aesthetic criticism" and "impressionistic criticism," have their use, but they are merely incomplete first steps, and the "perfect critic" will "begin to analyse and construct, to 'ériger en lois'" (*SPTSE* 52), or put into laws, his original impressions. "Comparison and analysis," Eliot repeats in "The Function of Criticism" (1923), "are the chief tools of the critic" (*SPTSE* 75). In "Reflections on *Vers Libre*" (1917), Eliot uses analysis to define *vers libre* out of existence. "*Vers libre*," or free verse, is an impossible oxymoron according to Eliot, because no "positive definition" exists and "there is no freedom in art" (*SPTSE* 32). Criticism and art must have structure, just as poetry must have some kind of meter: "[*V*]*ers libre* does not exist, for there is only good verse, bad verse, and chaos" (*SPTSE* 36).

Just as Russell aims to move philosophy away from language and toward mathematic and scientific precision, Eliot praises science – "the scientific mind," Eliot notes, "might better be called the intelligent mind" *(SPTSE* 56) – and uses scientific metaphors for the artistic process, particularly in his "single most important essay": "Tradition and the Individual Talent."[51] Eliot explains his claim that "[t]he emotion of art is impersonal" by means of "a suggestive analogy" to describe what occurs when "a bit of finely filiated platinum is introduced into a chamber containing oxygen and sulphur dioxide" (*SPTSE* 40, 44). The poet's mind, or the platinum, will remain unchanged by and external to art, the chemical reaction, and will act as a mere catalyst for creativity; hence, "the more perfect the artist, the more completely separate in him will be the man who suffers and the mind which creates" (*SPTSE* 41). Science elevates the creative process for Eliot, who declares, "It is in this depersonalization that art may be said to approach the condition of science."[52] Indeed, Eliot's greatest praise for Joyce's creation of the "mythical method" similarly echoes this elevation of science: "It has the importance of a scientific discovery" (*SPTSE* 177).

Where Eliot most resembles Russell is in his famous description of the "objective correlative" in "Hamlet and His Problems," and comparing this idea with Russell's ideal language sheds overdue light on the meaning of this long-debated phrase.[53] I do not claim Eliot took the term "objective correlative" from Russell, but rather that Russell's "Celestial Language" explained in "Vagueness" works just like Eliot's ideal art. The "objective correlative" aims for a scientific objectivity and, indeed, smacks of a "picture theory of meaning" akin to Russell's "special language" of sign notation or that of Wittgenstein's *Tractatus*.[54] For Eliot, *Hamlet* and even the Mona Lisa, another cherished work of high European culture, are failures because, although they are "interesting," they contain "an emotion which is inexpressible." Eliot explains:

> The only way of expressing emotion in the form of art is by finding an "objective correlative"; in other words, a set of objects, a situation, a chain of events which shall be the formula of that *particular* emotion; such that when the external facts, which must terminate in sensory experience, are given, the emotion is immediately evoked. (*SPTSE* 48)

Eliot's attempt to echo scientific theorizing is evident in his use of terms like "formula" and "sensory experience." The "objective correlative" itself resounds with "that familiar vague suggestion of the scientific vocabulary which is characteristic of modern writing" for which he later chastises Arthur Symons (*SPTSE* 50). Significantly, the precise way in which a particular set of words will instigate a "*particular* emotion" for the reader mirrors the way a precise word should signify a particular object or emotion in an ideal language, like that which Russell outlines in "Vagueness." For Russell, to recall his example, "a representation is *vague*," he argues, "when the relation of the representing system to the represented system is not one-one but one-many. For example, a photograph which is so smudged that it might equally represent Brown or Jones or Robinson is vague" (*V* 66). Just as in a smudged photograph, the problem with language is that it is one-many, because a word does not have one specific bounded meaning. For Eliot, emotion should be exactly invoked by the object, it should be a one-to-one ratio, but in Hamlet the emotion is "in *excess* of the facts as they appear" (*SPTSE* 48). Art should strive to work like a perfect language for Eliot. There will be no vagueness in successful art, because talented artists will create objects that precisely correlate to the art emotions they desire to communicate. It is not surprising that Eliot was another admirer of Basic English, even as he admitted its inadequacy for translating poetry.[55]

In "The Perfect Critic" (1920), however, Eliot notes that words lack the "exactness" of science, and in fact he blames this tendency of abstraction, what he calls "the verbal disease," on philosophy itself, his erstwhile profession (*SPTSE* 51–4). Eliot claims not to be criticizing philosophy in general, but merely "the unscientific ingredients of philosophy," which actually compose "the greater part of the philosophic output of the last hundred years" (*SPTSE* 54). Russell is again the ideal for Eliot, as Eliot sets up "certain remarks of Pascal and Mr. Bertrand Russell" to symbolize mathematical "exactness," as a foil to Hegel and those who came after him, whose verbal "corruption has extended very far." The problem with this latter group is that they "have as a rule taken for granted that words have definite meanings" and therefore been sloppy in their usage in philosophy (*SPTSE* 54). Words "have changed their meanings," Eliot argues. "What they have lost is definite," and, lamentably for Eliot, "what they have gained is indefinite" (*SPTSE* 55). Eliot implies, as he will again one year later in "The Metaphysical Poets," that there was a time when language was not vague, but this time of being "definite" is long past.

As early as the 1920s, Eliot appears to acknowledge that something like the linguistic turn is occurring, and, while he is uncertain about its ramifications for philosophy, he is certain that its influence on literary criticism is dangerous. He emphasizes that the "verbalism" of contemporary philosophy is due to those philosophers who believe they deal "with objects" that are "of the same exactness as the mathematician's" *(SPTSE*

54). Instead, philosophy is moving away from asking about "objects," and he fails to believe philosophers are precise enough in their usage of language. It is doubtful whether the vagueness of William James's pragmatism or the blur of Wittgenstein's language games in *Philosophical Investigations* would have satisfied Eliot's desire for exactitude. Instead, for Eliot, philosophy, and with it "modern criticism," has become "degenerate":

> The vast accumulations of knowledge – or at least of information – deposited by the nineteenth century have been responsible for an equally vast ignorance. When there is so much to be known, when there are so many fields of knowledge in which the same words are used with different meanings, when every one knows a little about a great many things, it becomes increasingly difficult for anyone to know whether he knows what he is talking about. (*SPTSE* 55)

Modernity itself, and its surplus of knowledge, is also to blame for the current linguistic crisis. Whereas Wittgenstein's speakers effectively communicate through following the rules of a language game, Eliot fears this blurred sense of knowledge because so "many fields of knowledge" mean everyone might be playing a different game. For Eliot, modernity could result in meaningless cacophony; hence his desire for a single unified tradition and his need for a "closely-knit and homogenous society" to foster artistic "perfection" (*SPTSE* 36). Eliot continues to call out for "facts" and "objectivity" even as he acknowledges that in modernity even the expression of "facts" must change since "the same words are used with different meanings" (*SPTSE* 55).

By *To Criticize the Critic* in 1965, Eliot sounds much more as if he has accepted the pragmatist approach to language, when he states that that "wobbliness of words is not something to be deplored."[56] In an essay entitled, "Can 'Education' Be Defined?" Eliot notes that words' "meanings interpenetrate each other" and insists that "we must remember that the meaning of a word is never wholly represented by its definition." The "current use" of a word, Eliot writes, sounding very much like Wittgenstein, J. L. Austin, or Stanley Cavell, is the only way a word like "education" can be defined.[57] In contrast to his earlier fear of verbalism, he writes that "[w]e should not try to pin a word down to one meaning, which it should have at all times, in all places, for everybody." Eliot unconsciously echoes Virginia Woolf's radio broadcast's language when he states that *pinning* a word down, like one of Woolf's moth-like words, will cause language to die. Indeed, he emphasizes there are "many words which *must* change their meaning, because it is their changes in meaning that keep a language *alive*, or rather, that indicate the language *is* alive."[58] Jeffrey Perl notes that Eliot read Wittgenstein's writings later in life and argues that Eliot "may well have met with a sense of *déjà vu* Wittgenstein's opinion that reality is a convention, defined by a common language."[59] Eliot's later approach to "wobbliness" does come much closer to Wittgenstein's analysis of vagueness.

In keeping with his evolving pragmatic approach to language, Eliot's pointed criticism of Russell also increases in his later years. By the 1950s, when it had become evident that Eliot's and Russell's political, social, and religious beliefs were entirely opposed, their comments about each other changed tone. Eliot moves from merely chastising Russell's tendency to bow down to "the demagogy of science" to writing scathingly about Russell's early methods.[60] He asks in an introduction to a book "Where are the great philosophers?" :

> To those who pine for philosophy in this ampler sense, logical positivism is the most conspicuous object of censure. Certainly, logical positivism is not a very nourishing diet for more than the small minority which has been conditioned to it. When the time of its exhaustion arrives, it will probably appear, in retrospect, to have been for our age the counterpart of surrealism: for as surrealism seemed to provide a method of producing works of art without imagination so logical positivism seems to provide a method of philosophizing without insight and wisdom.[61]

Logical positivism's use of rigorous formal logic to examine an empirically knowable world derives from Russell's and Wittgenstein's early work.[62] Eliot's comment about the lack of great philosophers demonstrates he has changed from lauding Russell's methodology, with its rigorous symbolism and analytic methods – and even using it as a model for literary criticism – to declaring it utterly useless. Russell, meanwhile, denies their mutual influence, perhaps predictably given his messy involvement in Eliot's first marriage and Vivienne Eliot's eventual institutionalization. Russell's move to distance himself from any relationship with the Eliots is patently rewriting history: "The suggestion sometimes made," Russell argued in his autobiography, "that one of us influenced the other is without foundation."[63]

It is important to remember, however, that in his early most-anthologized essays, Eliot is not nearly so critical of Russell's method, nor welcoming to language's vagueness. Eliot's early essays aim to demonstrate that literary criticism can make sense of the difficulty of modern works, and indeed his "*Ulysses*, Order, and Myth," is a classic academic introduction to Joyce's difficult work.[64] The potentially destructive energies of vagueness, "verbalism," and the "revolution in the English language," must be quelled, and Eliot's search for unity and structure has been characterized, not altogether kindly, as "a kind of aesthetic heroism."[65] Because "the critic and the creative artist should frequently be the same person" (*SPTSE* 58), critics too must acquire the "historical sense" of "Tradition and the Individual Talent." If writers think with "the whole of literature from Europe to Homer" on their minds, critics must approach their works with a scholarly as well as an analytic eye (*SPTSE* 38). Although it may require sweat and hard work, the "perfect critic" must "simply elucidate" (*SPTSE* 56), and the "presentation of relevant historical facts which the reader is not assumed to know" will clarify modern *difficulty* (*SPTSE* 46). Eliot argues that literary criticism itself should not be castigated for "building theoretical scaffolds" because "in a really appreciative mind" perceptions should "form themselves as a structure; and criticism is the statement in language of this structure" (*SPTSE* 57–8). As Michael Levenson notes in *A Genealogy of Modernism*, Eliot's early essays set up the way the difficulty of modernism was understood: "English modernism achieved its decisive formation in the early twenties – not only because of legitimizing masterworks such as *Ulysses* or *The Waste Land* but because there developed a rhetorically effective doctrine to explain and justify that body of work."[66] According to Eliot's "rhetorically effective doctrine," structure, order, and form are the keynotes of modern fiction and criticism, and vagueness, characterized as modern "corruption" inflicted by philosophy, must be eliminated.[67]

3. "Fuzzy Studies" and Fuzzy Fictions

> Finished, it's finished, nearly finished, it must be nearly finished. (*Pause*.) Grain upon grain, one by one, and one day, suddenly, there's a heap, a little heap, the impossible heap.
>
> –Beckett, *Endgame*[68]

My final epigraph from Beckett's *Endgame* emphasizes something "impossible" about the idea of concluding a book. How is it that we add page upon page and somehow make a book? How many pages make a book? More than fifty but less than 800? Precisely 227? We are back to where we began with the sorites paradox. We can blame language for its vagueness or we can marvel at the efficiency of language games – either way the sorites paradox, as Beckett's Clov notes, points to the need for a kind of humility. Suddenly, we have a heap, "the impossible heap," but we cannot really fathom why.

Among the various ways that critics have contended with language's vagueness, this book will end by tracing one path – I'll call it analytic criticism – but gesturing toward another.[69] As the last section discussed, Bertrand Russell strongly influenced the young Eliot's ideas about vagueness. From Russell, through to Eliot, through to the New Critics (and even, in an inverse way, on to deconstruction), one way critics have dealt with the problem of vagueness for literature was to seek to eliminate it – to claim that ambiguities could be resolved, that readings could be final, and that unity, structure, and objectivity should be the greatest virtues of works of art. Taking a rigorously logical, quasi-scientific approach to literature, this approach saw vagueness, whether of style or of reference, as a fault.[70] Given, as this study has aimed to demonstrate, modernist fiction's own engagement with the problem of vagueness, this kind of criticism ends up ignoring or devaluing essential elements of these texts. Another path, with which this project is deeply resonant, follows what Jeffrey Perl has heralded as a kind of "fuzzy studies" that deny the idea that analytic virtues need to set the standards of criticism or fiction.[71] "Fuzzy studies" blur disciplinary boundaries, examine terminological overlap rather than distinction, and even must admit, humbly, the occasional vagueness of their own key terms and object of study. "Fuzzy studies" have much in common with what Wai Chee Dimock and Eve Kosofsky Sedgwick, following Silvan Tomkins, have called "Weak Theory," which is "a weaker, lower-level kind of theorizing," that focuses on "hanging threads and out-of-focus blurriness."[72] From my point of view, "fuzzy studies" differ from deconstruction in that they are not satisfied by simply pointing out language's vagueness but use vague terms to *get somewhere*.[73] Such terminological humility, as Richard Poirier also notes in *Poetry and Pragmatism*, is an essential inheritance of pragmatism, and, I believe, is key to approaching the novels of James, Woolf, and Joyce in their examination of language's vagueness.[74]

Eliot himself connected the New Criticism to Russell, and in his desire to stamp out vagueness, he became a crucial link in this chain.[75] Part of the power of Eliot's early essays was historical, as Peter Ackroyd notes: "Eliot provided literature with an order and certainty all the more potent because these were the qualities lacking in social and political life after the First World War."[76] Indeed, in looking at his influential essays on James, Woolf, and Joyce, it becomes clear that Eliot values "order," "unity," and "exactitude" as hallmarks of strong modern literature, whereas the "abstract" and "verbalism" mark failures.[77] In contrast to emphasizing the vagueness of modernist fiction as embodied in these three writers' works – as this book has aimed to do so far – Eliot's critical essays, I will argue, set the pattern for approaching these works by looking for how they use structure, unity, or some sort of metanarrative to offset modernity's chaos.

"*Ulysses*, Order, and Myth" (1923) is the most well known of Eliot's critical essays on any modernist writer, and it drives home his emphasis on unity and coherence as fundamental qualities of modern literature. Joyce himself liked it so much that he hoped Eliot would hurry up and write another essay on him.[78] Rather than depicting Joyce as a "prophet of chaos" or part of "the flood of Dadaism" (*SPTSE* 175), Eliot emphasizes the "structure" and "order" that Joyce has found in his "parallel use of the *Odyssey*" (*SPTSE* 177). Eliot declares that the "novel ended with Flaubert and with James," but that Joyce's "discovery" in the "mythical method" has taken "a step toward making the modern world possible for art," by finding an "order and form" to provide the "something stricter" that "the expression of an age" requires (*SPTSE* 177–8). Readers will learn to trace parallels to the *Odyssey* in order to understand Joyce's master work, and although the word "novel" may no longer suffice, the "order" of Eliot's essay's title will be the key feature of modern writing. Joyce's apparent difficulty can be (mostly) explicated, because his method offers "a way of controlling, of ordering, of giving a shape and a significance to the immense panorama of futility and anarchy which is contemporary history." Joyce rightly feared when a negative review appeared in Eliot's *Criterion* that Eliot might turn against *Finnegans Wake* because of its less obvious structure.[79]

Twenty years after "*Ulysses*, Order and Myth," Eliot still emphasizes the "construction" of Joyce's works. In *Introducing James Joyce*, Eliot writes that Joyce's later works are "too closely constructed, and depend too much upon cumulative effect, for any extracts to be more than those parts easiest to grasp in isolation."[80] Joyce appears a master craftsman according to Eliot's characterization, and even the selection of the *Wake* that Eliot chooses to complete his Introduction is telling: "a passage which becomes, deliberately, more lucid as the dreamer of the book approaches waking consciousness."[81] Eliot decides to focus on Joyce's lucidity and deliberation, although the section focusing on the awakening consciousness is a tiny fraction of the overall "dream language" of *Finnegans Wake*.[82] In a radio broadcast for *The Listener* the following year, Eliot continues to focus on both Joyce's early "simple, bare, and straightforward" style and his later mythic parallels.[83] It seems telling that although he praises both *Ulysses* and

Finnegans Wake as "great" books, he fails to discuss the *Wake* and mentions that reading *Ulysses* now "present[s] no difficulty at all."[84] Joyce has many virtues for Eliot but, as with his earlier essays, he prioritizes Joyce's early strict realism and his later orderly mythic parallels over his experimentalism or new vague language in the *Wake*.[85]

In Eliot's notes for the lectures he delivered on "The Contemporary Novel" in 1933, his praise for Joyce's "concrete" writing is particularly clear. In juxtaposing Joyce to D. H. Lawrence, Eliot finds Joyce the better and more moral novelist – although he admits one should "discount my preference for Joyce: Friend of Joyce and never knew Lawrence" (*LCN*). Specifically, Eliot admires that Joyce "sees the particular from the general; the concrete from the abstract," while D.H. Lawrence does the opposite (*LCN*). Joyce's ability to take lofty ideas and pin them down to specific details makes him the stronger writer, whereas Lawrence's style is itself one of abstraction, even if the ideas behind them end up being concrete. For Eliot, Joyce's specificity of style is actually "Catholic" in that the big ideas that govern life are crystallized in specific details, whereas Lawrence's "Protestant" writing emphasizes individual interpretations over truth. Eliot makes his preference for the concrete clear: "I must be with Joyce" (*LCN*).

Eliot's early critical essays on Henry James, who was arguably formative in Eliot's own vision of the American writer abroad, similarly highlights James's clear and unified depiction of society at the expense of his interest in "the deeper psychology" and stylistic experimentation. Repeatedly, Eliot emphasizes the unity of James's novels, indeed of his entire *oeuvre*. In "A Prediction Regarding Three Authors" (1924), Eliot clarifies James's importance for "our future," and asserts, "[o]ne thing is certain, that the books of Henry James form a complete whole," adding, "their lesson is one lesson."[86] Six years earlier Eliot explains what James's main "importance" will be. While James excels at portraits of Americans – "I do not suppose that anyone who is not an American can *properly* appreciate James," Eliot asserts, showing some patriotic stripes – James's true "intelligence" involves his creation of a single "social entity" in which his characters are mere parts.[87] "The general schema is not one character, nor a group of characters in a plot or merely in a crowd," Eliot argues; instead, the "real hero, in any of James's stories, is a social entity." Eliot uses scientific metaphors that foreshadow those of "Hamlet" the following year in order to emphasize that "[c]ompared with James's, other novelists' characters seem to be only accidentally in the same book" (*SPTSE* 151). For Eliot, unlike Leavis, the later James's ambiguous morals and abstract conversations are not a problem because James focuses on a cohesive depiction of society. Through a special "chemistry," like alchemy, James's fiction appears to create an entire society.[88]

Eliot's astute analysis focuses on James's dense social fabric and yet ignores James's focus on the missed vague innuendos of conversations that highlight those social entities' decay. The marriage of modern American business with European class structure makes it tricky to catch the right "tone" or "note," just as it becomes more difficult for readers to know exactly what is meant when a character "hangs fire" in James's later novels. Similarly, Eliot only gestures to the "deeper psychology" of the novels, because, for Eliot, James is all about "trim, definite outlines," and "solid atmosphere."[89] Eliot notes:

> The example which Henry James offered us was not that of a style to imitate, but of an integrity so great, a vision so exacting, that it was forced to the extreme of care and punctiliousness for exact expression.[90]

Although Eliot argues that James did not present a "style to imitate," James's influence is certainly remarkable in Eliot's own "Portrait of a Lady" and in the country estate setting of plays like *The Family Reunion*.[91] In "Portrait of a Lady," for example, Eliot recasts the "velleities and carefully caught regrets" of conversation as threatening to the young speaker.[92] In his critical essays, however, Eliot maintains that James's "New England Genius" resides in his "punctiliousness" and exactitude.

If Eliot praises Joyce and James for their clear order and style, his evaluation of Woolf is more measured, because he alternates between paralleling his own process to hers and aligning her works with the "verbalism" that afflicts modern philosophy and literature. "But you do not make it easy for critics," Eliot wrote to Woolf, and this unease beautifully captures Eliot's response, both in his published essays and in his private correspondence, to Woolf's work.[93] In a "London Letter" to the *Dial*, for example, Eliot's notorious comment that he distrusts "the Feminine in literature," is mirrored by his faint praise for Woolf's "more feminine type" of writing.[94] Unlike Joyce, who can create an "articulate external world," Woolf's kind of writing:

> makes its art by feeling and by contemplating the feeling, rather than the object into which the feeling has been made . . . A good deal of the secret charm of Mrs. Woolf's shorter pieces consists in the immense disparity between the object and the train of feeling which it has set in motion.[95]

While Eliot succinctly describes what I have called Woolf's "circular technique," the "secret charm" that Eliot praises in Woolf is hardly equivalent to his declaration of Joyce's genius. Furthermore, the discrepancy between his characterization of Woolf's technique and his notion of the "objective correlative" (to return to my discussion from the previous section) further indicates his lukewarm response.[96] Woolf's art fails to provide a suitable object to correlate to her "train of feeling," and the lack of an "objective correlative" implies that Eliot's censure of *Hamlet* would equally apply to Woolf. Woolf's art, unlike Russell's ideal language, is vague. Similarly, Vivienne Eliot's review of "Mr. Bennett and Mrs. Brown," which Eliot apparently edited, criticizes Woolf's failure to value objective facts. While calling Woolf's essay "brilliant," Vivienne Eliot nonetheless contends that Woolf's modern view of representing human character is "wrong," because Bennett's technique of observation is necessary for fiction. She argues that "if you observe accurately a vast number of the facts surrounding a character – if you observe *enough* of the facts – you reach the character itself." She contends that Woolf undervalues facts and overvalues "flight of imagination."[97] Woolf herself sensed that when Eliot called her writing "characteristic &c" he means it exhibits "wordiness, feebleness, & all the vices" (*DVW* 3:49).

However, Eliot also published many of Woolf's essays and short stories and urged her to write more articles for the *Criterion*, and he often compared their techniques in their friendly private letters.[98] For example, Eliot called "Character in Fiction" (1924), Woolf's essay that was first delivered as a talk before the Heretics before being printed in Eliot's *Criterion*, "a most important piece of historical criticism." He added:

> It also expresses for me what I have always been very sensible of, the absence of any masters in the previous generation whose work one could carry on, and the amount of waste that goes in one's own work in the necessity, so to speak, of building one's own house before one can start the business of living. I feel myself that everything I have done consists of tentative sketches and rough experiments. Will the next generation profit by our labours?[99]

Eliot's sense that their generation was creating "tentative sketches and rough experiments" mirrors Woolf's feeling that "[w]e must reconcile ourselves to a season of failures and fragments." She declares that in novels like *Ulysses*, "the smashing and crashing" the "breaking up the old traditional form of the novel" must occur.[100] (Intriguingly, in the version revised for publication in Eliot's magazine, she adds Eliot as a valued contemporary, a detail Eliot admitted gave him "great pleasure."[101])

Eliot's image of modern fiction building its "own house" is ironic in relation to the destructive imagery in Woolf's essay, even as it foreshadows

Eliot's criticisms of Woolf's lack of structure. In "Character in Fiction," Woolf castigates the Edwardians for exactly their excess of houses. In the notes for the talk this emphasis is particularly clear:

> [The Edwardians] have laid an enormous stress upon the fabric of things, the appearance of things [;] they have given us a house, in the hope that we may be able to deduce the human being who lives there. And if you hold, as I hold that novels are ~~founded upon character, that is a very clumsy way of~~ about people and not about the houses they live in, that is the wrong way to set about it. (*EVW* 3: 513)

Writers like Bennett, Woolf argues, try to depict "[c]haracter, life, humanity" through their houses because they are agreed in a "vast and unanimous way Old women have houses" (*EVW* 3:514). All these houses are metaphors for the structure of the traditional novel that, Woolf argues (and thematically demonstrates in *Jacob's Room*), fails to capture human character. Instead, in modern novels, Woolf argues, "there is a ~~more~~ vaguer force at work – a force which is sometimes called the Spirit of the Age or the Tendency of the age" (*EVW* 3:504). This vague force will break down excessive "artifice" and will not, as Woolf puts it elsewhere, "sacrifice so devoutly at the shrine of form" that "truth" or "Mrs. Brown" is lost.[102] Yet for Eliot, as he argues in *La Nouvelle Revue Française* (1927), Woolf's lack of "structure" means that although she has a "remarkable gift for description," her writing feels somehow "superficial."[103]

As these three examples demonstrate, Eliot's devotion to "unity" and "structure," at the expense of abstraction or "verbalism," is quite consistent throughout his criticism of James, Woolf, and Joyce. This critical emphasis bore fruit in New Criticism, and particularly in the pedagogical technique of analyzing verbal ambiguities in order to demonstrate how they contribute to, rather than shatter, literary works of art. It is not surprising that Eliot links Russell to Ogden, Empson, and Richards, because all of them approach literature in a scientific or analytic temperament (*LCN*). From essays such as "*Ulysses*, Order and Myth," and "Hamlet and his Problems," as well as the influence of Russian formalism, the New Critics are said to have found their focus upon reading a literary work as a discrete object for analysis. "The influence of T. S. Eliot was obviously decisive," writes René Wellek in his explanation of New Criticism, while Richard Calhoun calls Eliot's *The Sacred Wood*, as well as I. A. Richards's *Principles of Literary Criticism*, the "starting points" for New Criticism.[104] Eliot, along with Richards and Yvor Winters, composed the group John Crowe Ransom outlined in his 1941 *The New Criticism*, although the group usually is taken to include also Empson, F. R. Leavis, Cleanth Brooks, Robert Penn Warren, Allen Tate, and others.[105] Ransom, however, notes that Eliot is premier among his peers: "It is likely that we have had no better critic than Eliot."[106] Eliot himself was not a fan of what he called New Criticism – he labeled it the "lemon-squeezer school" of criticism – and Eliot's emphasis on the "historical sense" contrasts with some New Critics' tendencies of reading the artwork ahistorically.[107] However, Eliot's insistence on seeing literature, "not as a collection of the writings of individuals," but instead as "'organic wholes,'" was certainly influential on New Critical notions of organic form and the ensuing analysis of ambiguity (*SPTSE* 68). Resolving ambiguity was the New Critical solution to vagueness, just as explicating *difficulty* was Eliot's answer to the "verbal disease."

"Ambiguity," I. A. Richards notes in *Practical Criticism*, "is systematic"; however, "the rival meanings can be worked out."[108] Working out rival meanings, for example, famously in Keats's "Ode on a Grecian Urn," allowed New Critics to make sense of Keats's ambiguities in order to keep the urn intact. Wellek, outlining New Critical practices, explains that "the New Critics reject the distinction of form and content: they believe in the organicity of poetry and, in practice, constantly examine attitudes, tones, tensions, irony, paradox, all psychological concepts partly derived from Richards."[109] However, Louis Menand argues that the analysis of ambiguity not only supported organicism, but also effectively erased belief or content: by "developing an aesthetic that took a good poem to be one in which the 'views' or 'beliefs' expressed in it, in effect, cancel each other out – thus the well-known critical lexicon of 'irony,' 'paradox,' and 'ambiguity,' all of which name techniques for neutralizing content."[110] In "neutralizing content," readings could ideally focus on the discrete work, rather than examining the beliefs it espoused. Such techniques aimed to demonstrate that "Modernist works were organic, unified, and self-contained despite a fragmented and chaotic appearance."[111]

Although New Critical techniques were primarily directed at poetry, with an implied hierarchy elevating poetry above prose, Eliot himself argued that there is no "sharp distinction between 'poetry' and 'prose.'"[112] When New Critics, for example William Empson, wrote about fiction, they tended to praise, like Eliot, novels with strong structures, where ambiguities could be resolved in terms of form. Indeed, in Empson's analysis of Virginia Woolf, "problems of form" are what it "is necessary in talking about Mrs Woolf to consider," and her altogether "inadequate" technique merely gives sensations as a "substitute for telling a story." Empson calls this her "Vase of Flowers method" and concludes that her method fails: "[I]f only these dissolved units of understanding had been co-ordinated into a system; if only, perhaps, there was an index, showing what had been compared with what."[113] Empson's index sounds a lot like Eliot's notes appended to *The Waste Land* or Joyce's schema for *Ulysses*. The unified "system" Empson seeks is thwarted by Woolf's tendency to "dissolve." R. P. Blackmur similarly focuses on the structure of James in "The Loose and Baggy Monsters of Henry James," while Eliot's critical approach to Joyce can be traced through Stuart Gilbert's *James Joyce's Ulysses* (1930) to Richard Ellmann's *Ulysses on the Liffey*, and onward through numerous structural studies.[114]

That vagueness was an enemy of New Criticism is evident in arguably one of its key texts, *Seven Types of Ambiguity* (1930).[115] It is not surprising, given his desire to explicate ambiguities and annihilate vagueness, that Empson was another fan of Basic English. "For myself at least," he argued, "it has become a fixed process on reading something deeply true to see if it is still good sense in Basic."[116] In *Seven Types of Ambiguity*, Empson, like Eliot before him, blames modernity for the "increasing vagueness" of English, which, "from the scientific point of view," he aims to eliminate as he parses the categories of linguistic ambiguity.[117] Wanting to get to the root of poetic beauty – "unexplained beauty arouses an irritation in me," he humorously confesses (*E* 9) – Empson energetically divides ambiguity up into seven manageable kinds, with increasing levels of "logical disorder" (*E* 48). He explains:

> As for the immediate importance of the study of ambiguity, it would be easy enough to take up an alarmist attitude, and say that the English language needs nursing by the analyst very badly indeed. (*E* 236)

Journalism in particular is blamed for this vagueness, because in journalism, "the word is used, as at a distance, to stand for a vague and complicated mass of ideas and systems which the journalist has no time to apprehend" (*E* 236). "A brief study of novels" shows the infection of this journalistic "flatness" as well as the "further disturbing influence" of scientific jargon (*E* 236). Empson asserts that studies like his will become more necessary with increasing modernity: "I want to suggest that the machinery I have been using upon poetry is going to become increasingly necessary if we are going to keep the language under control" (*E* 237).

Vagueness, or "the cult of vagueness" (*E* 187), is mentioned as the ugly stepsister of ambiguity. While careful ambiguities are the strength of poetry, what Empson means by vagueness (although he is not always precise about it) is clearly not favorable. Empson includes "[t]he cult of vagueness" in the sixth type of ambiguity in which "a statement says nothing, by tautology, by contradiction, or by irrelevant statements" (*E* 176). Because of these irreconcilable statements, "the reader is forced to invent statements of his own and they are liable to conflict with one another" (*E* 176). Although occasionally such "vagueness," Empson admits (as in Yeats's "Who goes with Fergus?"), can be used for powerful effect, mostly vagueness is to blame for the "wavering and suggestive indefiniteness of nineteenth-century poetry," which, he decrees, "is often merely weak" (*E* 190). "The cult of vagueness" also "produced the nonsense writers like Lear and Lewis Carroll," who refuse the strength of ambiguity, engaging in writing that ultimately "says nothing." According to Empson, vagueness is a weak refusal of the concrete alternatives of ambiguity.

However, vagueness is not so easily dismissed, for even Empson admits the vagueness of his categories of ambiguity:

> "Ambiguity" itself can mean an indecision as to what you mean, an intention to mean several things, a probability that one or other or both of two things has been meant, and the fact that a statement has several meanings. It is useful to be able to separate these if you wish, but it is not obvious that in separating them at any particular point you will not be raising more problems than you solve. (*E* 5–6)

Because of the lack of clear-cut distinctions among the categories of ambiguity, Empson concludes, "I shall often use the ambiguity of 'ambiguity'" (*E* 6). Such a second-order ambiguity comes close to his own definition of vagueness, undermining the strength of its categories through tautology. Moreover, Empson admits, "In wishing to apply verbal analysis to poetry the position of the critic is like that of the scientist wishing to apply determinism to the world," because "[i]t may not be valid everywhere" (*E* 17). Empson notes that his techniques might not work for writers who "write with the whole weight" of language upon them, fixed upon the way "a word is regarded as a member of the language" (*E* 6). He emphasizes that a writer like "Miss Gertrude Stein, too, at this point, implores the passing tribute of a sigh" (*E* 7). The categories of ambiguity are not discrete, nor are their classifications wholly adequate, particularly to the range of modernist fiction.

Immediately, critical responses to Empson's *Seven Types of Ambiguity* repeatedly foregrounded Empson's own vagueness even as they admired his wit and daring. While some of his contemporaries lauded his "dissection" for "a clearer idea of the effects, often premeditated, of language, syntax, grammatical structure," more often critics responded that in many cases he "obscures rather than explains."[118] Empson himself chose to include a critical review in the Preface to the second edition of his book, which highlights his "vagueness as to the nature and scope of ambiguity" (*E* xii). Empson admits and emphasizes for his future readers that there is "vagueness about ambiguity" (*E* xv). By including a self-criticism, he succinctly foreshadows poststructural critiques of the New Critics' failure to resolve ambiguities. Empson has therefore been seen as one of the ancestors of deconstruction because, in his frustrated discovery that language's ambiguities cannot, finally, be resolved in some satisfactory way, he foreshadows the deconstructionists' move that all language points to the vagueness of meaning.

Paul de Man himself pointed to Empson's influence in "The Dead-End of Formalist Criticism." He argues that "[a]fter the writings of an Empson, little is left of the scientific claims of formalist criticism. All of its basic assumptions have been put into question: the notions of communication, form, [...] and objective precision."[119] Empson appears to de Man to have pushed the boundaries of formalist analysis as far as they could go, revealing in his own failure to maintain categories of ambiguity the essential slippage in language. In "New Criticism and Deconstructive Criticism, or What's New?" Shuli Barzilai and Morton Bloomfield similarly argue that poststructuralists were shown the way to "indeterminacy" through New Critical ambiguity.[120] While the ambiguity of ambiguity points to indeterminacy, the attitudes of the New Critics and their deconstructionist successors like de Man towards such indeterminacy, of course, are pointedly different. The New Critics seek to make sense of ambiguities, while many poststructuralists argue that the inability to restrict play, or to determine closure, is exactly the point. Hence, Eliot, for example, has been called the "primary theoretical whipping boy of deconstruction" for his insistence on reading literature as unified wholes.[121]

Therefore, one path of modernist literary criticism, originating in Frege's and Russell's work on logic (although of course with many other influences along the way), stretches from Russell to Eliot to Empson and aims to root out vagueness; its thorny stepchild is deconstruction.[122] If deconstruction has really had its day, now a theoretical truism, what kind of literary criticism will engage with language's vagueness while refusing to accept that it is itself the final answer?[123] We may need another kind of criticism to read these texts: one that neither argues science or logic can vanquish vagueness nor that language's vagueness places meaning always already out of reach.

As I was concluding my project, I was excited to see a kind of call-to-arms for "fuzzy studies" in the 2011–2014 issues of *Common Knowledge*, which places my work in a vibrant new conversation. In introducing the first issue of the "Fuzzy Studies Symposium," Jeffrey Perl begins:

> Anyone who has studied the arts or humanities (or the qualitative social sciences) on a campus where quantitative disciplines are dominant will have memorable experience of the term "fuzzy studies" and its deployment. Words like *soft* as in "soft sciences," have had likewise dismissive but comparatively adolescent uses. The opposite of *hard* in the sense of *difficult* would be, not *soft* but *easy*; so the jibe is not that humanists have lighter workloads than scientists but that, by comparison with the sciences, the humanists are flaccid. One response to disrespect of this kind is self-subordination – the acquiescence of "soft" disciplines to the criteria of "hard" ones, as, for example, in the application of cognitive research to the criticism of literature and the arts. "How Rembrandt Saw Brown," however, is not everyone's idea of a suitable research topic. (*CK* 441–2)

Perl implies that such a scientific approach to art history, mapping how neurons underscore Rembrandt's vision of his subject, seems somewhat strange. In literary studies, I believe, we see this approach crystallized in books such as Lisa Zunshine's *Strange Concepts and the Stories They Make Possible* (2008) and William Flesch's *Comeuppance* (2009), or digital humanities manifestos such as Erez Aiden and Jean-Baptiste Michel's *Uncharted* (2013). They provide fascinating cognitive science or statistical insights into literature, but what do they miss? If all literary criticism began mirroring the scientific approaches to literature (as they well might, given current budgetary demands), what would be lost? Perl urges, instead, the wider adoption of a "fuzzy" approach to academic studies, embodied in the humanities by neo-pragmatists, most famously Richard Rorty, and in the sciences by engineers, computer scientists, and mathematicians, most famously Lotfi Zadeh.

Rorty asks why we fail to realize that truth is not "clear, hard, defined," but instead "that fuzziness is a fine state in which to be"? He contends:

> What prevents us from relaxing and enjoying the new fuzziness is perhaps no more than cultural lag, the fact that the rhetoric of the Enlightenment praised the emerging natural sciences in a vocabulary which was left over from a less liberal and tolerant era. This rhetoric enshrined all the old philosophical oppositions between mind and world, appearance and reality, subject and object, truth and pleasure.[124]

Rorty argues that when our rhetoric catches up to our new pragmatic beliefs, the binaries that are still inherent in "old philosophical oppositions" will break down, instead allowing for "blur" between "mind and world, appearance and reality, subject and object, truth and pleasure" (*CK* 443). The new "fuzzy studies," according to Perl, will derive their motivation both from pragmatism, and "at the same time (and on the other hand), a significant body of mathematicians, hard scientists, and engineers [. . .] coming to conclude that fuzziness is in the nature of things – or at least *some* things" (*CK* 444). This originates from "fuzzy set theory," which is based on "degrees of truth" rather than binaries, arguing for "a large range of truth values between 0 and 1, where 0 means 'completely false,' 1 'completely true,' and all other values are intermediate degrees of truth."[125] Zadeh, the Berkeley mathematician and author of "Fuzzy Sets," used the sorites paradox to argue for the necessity of fuzzy logic; "[s]ome 15,000 articles" have derived from his work (*CK* 444). Encouraging fuzzy logic was not initially an easy battle for Zadeh:

> I encountered skepticism, derision and sometimes outright hostility. There were two principal reasons: the word "fuzzy" is usually used in a pejorative sense; and, more importantly, my abandonment of classical, Aristotelian, bivalent logic was a radical departure from deep-seated scientific traditions. (*CK* 445)

Admitting "fuzzy studies" will continue to encounter similar challenges, Perl nonetheless posits two examples for what "fuzzy studies" as a "practical application" to academic studies would look like. First, in the sciences the response is simple: Zadeh's work has led to applications in software, consumer-goods design, and artificial intelligence. (I imagine that, for example, teaching Siri, the iPhone voice controlled system, to interpret commands required her to understand the vagueness of natural languages.) For the humanities, Perl turns to history to examine the ways that thinking of a fuzzy world could impact the ways historians approach their discipline. Natalie Zemon Davis, for example, emphasizes the way that in a "global frame" history must be fuzzy (*CK* 446). It is not only that "African Studies now flourish in Norway," but also that the "boundaries around any one of these groups are often fuzzy and porous" (*CK* 446–7). "[H]istorians like myself," she notes, "have increasingly been turning their attention to forms of cultural mixture, *métissage*, and exchange – whether occasioned by the movement of peoples, by trading networks and diasporas, or by the coexistence in the same region of peoples with different customs and languages" (*CK* 447). Fuzzy studies' approaches to history would focus on cultural mixing, rather than divisions, overlap, rather than distinction, and coexistence, rather than the desire for mutual destruction.

With these qualities in mind, I ask, what would "fuzzy studies" look like for literature? *Modernist Fiction and Vagueness* resonates in many ways with the challenges posed by "fuzzy studies," and not surprisingly, because the recognition and reevaluation of vagueness is at the heart of both projects. My project is "fuzzy" in two fundamental ways. First, it emphasizes that the borders between philosophy and literature in the early twentieth century were porous. I see the fictions of these philosophies and the philosophies of these fictions as integrally related. Second, I am fascinated by what Woolf described in *Orlando* as the "crepuscular half-lights" of modernity, where what had seemed firm and fixed suddenly seemed fuzzy and subject to context (*O* 20). I have traced many of the different ways that this vagueness registers. For Henry James, the vagueness, tied to pragmatism, connects to the unresolvable secrets of his plots, his flowering, unresolvable clauses, and his rewriting of the marriage plot in new vague terms. His upending of moral absolutes while stridently clinging to fiction's sacred purpose makes him a powerful influence on Woolf and Joyce in his wake. For Woolf, vagueness is more specifically gendered female, and it constitutes her literary response to the traditional philosophical problem of subject and object relations. For Joyce, in turn, vagueness is first a metaphor for Stephen's new language, freed of the yokes of British and Catholic imperialism, then the motivation behind the *Wake*'s recognizable style. Because one of my primary contentions throughout this book is that in the early twentieth century the problem of modernity's vagueness transformed literary realism just as it shook the principles of philosophical realism, I aim to resituate modernist experimentalism in the face of the novelists' new "fuzzy" beliefs. The far reaches of stylistic vagueness, particularly in the experimental texts with which each of my chapters nearly ends – *The Sacred Fount*, *The Waves*, and *Finnegans Wake* – may have courted solipsism, and they certainly antagonized some early readers. And yet, in their effort to engage with vagueness, these works in particular continue to speak to the questions that "fuzzy studies" raise today.

To a certain extent, literary studies have always been somewhat shamefacedly "fuzzy," much to Eliot's dismay, and the interests in cosmopolitan studies, transnationalism, and ecocriticism in New Modernist Studies take on specific inquiries that we could link to "fuzzy studies." But we also need to remember to welcome the "fuzzy," to acknowledge the "impossible heap," and to be wary of placing higher value on scholarly work modeling "hard-hat" science. Some (but not all, of course) proponents of affect theory and neo-materialism point to neuroscience as the basis for their definitive knowledge about the human body and mind. Bertrand Russell's contention that vague knowledge is less worth having than precise knowledge is the opposite of Zadeh's argument that "high precision is incompatible with high complexity" (*CK* 445). In fiction, high complexity might risk vagueness in losing its audience. In literary criticism, high complexity might sometimes risk vagueness in gestures to style, atmosphere, and aesthetics whose meanings are not quite possible to pin down. But from Russell's analytic methods, we move to early Eliot, to the New Critics, and, with deconstruction passé, there is a renewed danger of ignoring vagueness and returning to the continued evaluation of literary works based on criteria derived from science. And really, does anyone believe that *Hamlet* is a failure?

Notes

Introduction

1 Virginia Woolf, *Orlando* (1928), ed. Brenda Lyons (London: Penguin Books, 1993), 20.

2 T. S. Eliot, "*Ulysses*, Order, and Myth" (1923), rpt. in *Selected Prose of T. S. Eliot*, ed. Frank Kermode (New York: Farrar, Straus and Giroux, 1975), 175–178, hereafter cited as *SPTSE*.

3 W. B. Yeats learned to be "definite and concrete" from Ezra Pound, qtd. in Richard Ellmann, *Eminent Domain: Yeats Among Wilde, Joyce, Pound, Eliot and Auden* (Oxford: Oxford University Press, 1967), 66; E. M. Forster encourages plots to be "spare" in *Aspects of the Novel* (1927), (London: Edward Arnold, 1974), 61; in "Hamlet and His Problems" (1919), T. S. Eliot famously praised the "objective," and "particular," in *SPTSE*, 48; Katherine Mansfield praised Forster's "fine precision of expression," rpt. in *The Critical Writings of Katherine Mansfield*, ed. Clare Hanson (New York: St. Martin's Press, 1987), 69; similarly for Pound, the "watchword" was precision, "Status Rerum," *Poetry* 1.4 (Jan. 1913): 126, and Joseph Conrad praised his own "precision of images and analysis," qtd. in *Joseph Conrad on Fiction*, ed. Walter F. Wright (Lincoln: University of Nebraska Press, 1964), 37; Williams seeks "to refine, to clarify, to intensify," William Carlos Williams, *Spring and All, The Collected Poems of William Carlos Williams*, eds. A. Walton Litz and Christopher MacGowan, 2 vols. (New York: New Directions, 1986), 1:178; Ford Madox Ford insisted upon "unity" in "Thus to Revisit," (1919), rpt. in *Ford Madox Ford: Critical Essays*, eds. Max Saunders and Richard Stang (Manchester: Carcanet, 2002), 187; the Imagists strove "to employ always the *exact* word, not the nearly-exact . . . we believe that poetry should render particulars exactly and not deal in vague generalities," *Some Imagist Poets* (1915), in *Modernism: An Anthology of Sources and Documents*, ed. Vassiliki Kolocotroni, Jane Goldman, and Olga Taxidou (Chicago: University of Chicago Press, 1998), 269.

4 James Joyce to Carlo Linati, 21 September 1920, *Selected Letters of James Joyce*, ed. Richard Ellmann (London: Faber and Faber, 1975), 271.

5 Virginia Woolf, *The Diary of Virginia Woolf*, eds. Anne Olivier Bell and Andrew McNeillie, 5 vols. (London: Hogarth, 1977–1984), 2:13–14, hereafter cited as *DVW*.

6 All records of this event follow Russell's diary in stating that the lecture occurred on the 22nd of November. According to the minutes of the Oxford Society, however, "the hon. Bertrand Russell read a paper on 'vagueness'" on the 25th of November, Jowett Society Minutes, MS. Top. Oxon. d. 359, folio 25, Bodleian Library, Oxford.

7 Bertrand Russell, "Vagueness," *Australasian Journal of Philosophy and Psychology* 1 (1923): 84–92. Rpt. in *Vagueness: A Reader*, eds. Rosanna Keefe and Peter Smith (Cambridge: Massachusetts Institute of Technology Press, 1996), 61–68, hereafter cited as *V*.

8 Russell, "The Philosophy of Logical Atomism" (1918), in *Essays on Language, Mind and Matter, Collected Papers of Bertrand Russell*, ed. John G. Slater, vol. 9 (London: Unwin Hyman), xix–xx, hereafter cited as *CPBR*.

9 Before the early twentieth century, the vagueness paradox was known only as the sorites paradox. For discussion of vagueness in classical times, see M. F. Burnyeat, "Gods and Heaps," *Language and Logos*, ed. Malcolm Schofield and Martha Nussbaum (Cambridge: Cambridge University Press, 1982), 315–338; Jonathan Barnes, "Medicine, Experience and Logic," *Science and Speculation*, ed. Jonathan Barnes (Cambridge: Cambridge University Press, 1982), 24–68; and Timothy Williamson, *Vagueness* (London: Routledge, 1994).

10 Galen, *On Medical Experience XVII*, qtd. in Burnyeat, "Gods and Heaps," 315–316.

11 Burnyeat, "Gods and Heaps," 315–316.

12 Rosanna Keefe, *Theories of Vagueness* (Cambridge: Cambridge University Press, 2000), 1.

13 For Gottlob Frege, of course, the concern was how to set up logical axioms avoiding such vague terms, rather than whether such vague terms function usefully in daily life.

14 See Williamson, *Vagueness*, 8–12.

15 Thomas Rickets, "Frege," *The Cambridge Dictionary of Philosophy*, ed. Robert Audi (Cambridge: Cambridge University Press, 1999), 328.

16 Richard Poirier, *Poetry and Pragmatism* (Cambridge: Harvard University Press, 1992), 41–2, 139.

17 Stanley Cavell, *Must We Mean What We Say? A Book of Essays* (Cambridge: Cambridge University Press, 2002), 43. For discussion of literary modernism and the drive to reconceptualize the ordinary, see Liesl Olson, *Modernism and the Ordinary* (New York: Oxford University Press, 2009).

18 Richard Rorty, *The Linguistic Turn: Recent Essays in the Philosophical Method* (Chicago: University of Chicago Press, 1967), 3. While there is some disagreement about the contours and members of the linguistic turn, Rorty's influential work remains prevalent in discussions of early twentieth-century Anglo-American philosophy. For discussion see Michael Losonsky, *Linguistic Turns in Modern Philosophy* (Cambridge: Cambridge University Press, 2006).

19 G. E. Moore, *Principia Ethica* (Cambridge: Cambridge University Press, 1959), 6–8. Moore, Russell, and Wittgenstein are the "common source" of the later linguistic turn movement. See Gustav Bergmann, "Logical Positivism, Language, and the Reconstruction of Metaphysics," *The Linguistic Turn*, 63.

20 F. C. S. Schiller, *Formal Logic* (London: Macmillan, 1912).

21 Henry James, *Autobiography: A Small Boy and Others; Notes of a Son and Brother; The Middle Years*, ed. Frederick W. Dupee (New York: Criterion Books, 1956), 412; Woolf, "Modern Fiction" (1925), rpt. in *The Essays of Virginia Woolf*, ed. Andrew McNeillie, 4 vols. (London: Hogarth, 1986–1994), 4:159, hereafter cited as *EVW* (this essay was originally entitled "Modern Novels," published in the *TLS* (10 April 1919), and revised and published as "Modern Fiction" in *The Common Reader* (1925)); Joyce, *A Portrait of the Artist as a Young Man* (1916), ed. Seamus Deane (London: Penguin, 1992), 108, hereafter cited as *P*.

22 Ian Watt, *The Rise of the Novel: Studies in Defoe, Richardson and Fielding* (London: Penguin Books, 1963), 11–12.

23 For discussion of the "revolt against positivism," see H. Stuart Hughes, *Consciousness and Society* (New York: Alfred A. Knopf, 1961), 33–66.

24 William James, *Principles of Psychology* (1890), (New York: Dover Publications, 1950), 254, hereafter cited as *PP*.

25 William James to Henry James, 22 October 1905, *The Correspondence of William James: William and Henry*, eds. Ignas K. Skrupskelis and Elizabeth M. Berkeley, 3 vols. (Charlottesville: University Press of Virginia, 1992–4), 3:301.

26 Watt, *The Rise of the Novel*, 13–15, and Michael McKeon, *The Origins of the English Novel: 1600–1740* (Baltimore: Johns Hopkins University Press, 1987), 2.

27 For "modernism" as a "mode of interruption," see Astradur Eysteinsson, *The Concept of Modernism* (Ithaca: Cornell University Press, 1990), 208, 238.

28 William to Henry James, 4 May 1907, *The Correspondence of William James*, 3:338.

29 For connections between analytic philosophy and modernism, see Andrew Thacker, "A Language of Concrete Things: Hulme, Imagism and Modernist Theories of Language," *T. E. Hulme and the Question of Modernism*, ed. Edward P. Comentale and Andrzej Gasiorek (London: Ashgate, 2006), 39–55. For this kind of approach see also Michael North, *Reading 1922* (Oxford: Oxford University Press, 1999), and Michael LeMahieu, "Nonsense Modernism: The Limits of Modernity and the Feelings of Philosophy in Wittgenstein's *Tractatus*," *Bad Modernisms*, ed. Douglas Mao and Rebecca Walkowitz (Durham, NC: Duke University Press Books, 2006), 68–93. Richard Shusterman declares that "the debt of modern literature to analytic philosophy is very much greater than has hitherto been acknowledged," *T. S. Eliot and the Philosophy of Criticism* (New York: Columbia University Press, 1988), 39, while Dora Zhang argues that "in general early analytic philosophy remains a neglected corpus among literary critics," "Naming the Indescribable: Woolf, Russell, James, and the Limits of Description," *New Literary History* 45.1 (2014): 54. See also issues 3 and 4 of nonsite.org.

30 See https://books.google.com/ngrams/graph?content=vague&year_start=1800&year_end=2000&corpus=16&smoothing=3&share=&direct_url=t1%3B%2Cvague%3B%2Cc0

31 Sianne Ngai, *Our Aesthetic Categories: Zany, Cute, Interesting* (Cambridge: Harvard University Press, 2012), 1.
32 Steven Best and Douglas Kellner, *The Postmodern Turn* (New York: The Guilford Press, 1997), 256.
33 F. R. Leavis, *The Great Tradition* (New York: George W. Steward Publishers, 1948), 158.
34 Henry James, *The Ambassadors* (1903), ed. Christopher Butler (Oxford: Oxford University Press, 1985), 419, hereafter cited as *A*; "The Beast in the Jungle" (1903), *Collected Stories (1892–1910)*, ed. John Bayley, 2 vols. (London: Everyman's Library, 1999), 2:762, hereafter cited as *Beast.*
35 Henry to William James, 17 October 1907, *The Correspondence of William James*, 3:347.
36 Woolf, "The Tunnel" (1919), a review of Dorothy Richardson, in *EVW*, 3:12.
37 Russell B. Goodman argues that because Wittgenstein and James are from two different philosophical traditions, "Their relationship has not often been taken into account" (5). By finally linking these two, Goodman reveals, "A classical American Presence in analytic philosophy running not only through C. I. Lewis, Morton White, W. V. O. Quine, and Hilary Putnam – Americans all – but, a generation earlier, through the work of an Austrian who worked in England and visited America only in the last years of his life" (6). See Russell B. Goodman, *Wittgenstein and William James* (Cambridge: Cambridge University Press, 2002). My book similarly works to bridge both two distinct philosophical traditions – pragmatism and analytic philosophy – *and* two distinct literary traditions. While there are many excellent works on pragmatism and American literature (see Poirier, Schoenbach, etc.), few books, if any, have linked literary modernism in general to this American philosophical tradition. A central aim of this project is to fill in that gap.
38 Eliot, *Four Quartets* (London: Faber and Faber, 1944), 21.
39 Shuli Barzilai and Morton Bloomfield, "New Criticism and Deconstructive Criticism, or What's New?" *New Literary History* 18.1 (1986): 154.
40 Eliot, "The Perfect Critic" (1920), in *SPTSE*, 51, 54; "The Metaphysical Poets" (1921), in *SPTSE*, 64.
41 See "Fuzzy Studies: A Symposium on the Consequence of Blur, Part 1," Jeffrey M. Perl, Natalie Zemon Davis, and Barry Allen, *Common Knowledge* 17.3 (2012): 444–445.
42 See Raymond Williams, *The Politics of Modernism* (London: Verso, 1989), 77–8, and for a rewriting of Williams taking on the "global" dimensions of this question, see Michael North, *Reading 1922*, 11–19.
43 See Vincent Sherry, *The Great War and the Language of Modernism* (Oxford: Oxford University Press, 2003).
44 C. K. Ogden, introduction to James Joyce's *Tales of Shem and Shaun* (Paris: The Black Sun Press, 1929), 1.
45 Frank Lentricchia, *After the New Criticism* (Chicago: University of Chicago Press, 1980), 205.
46 Ford Madox Ford, qtd. in Ian Watt, *Conrad in the Nineteenth Century* (Berkeley: University of California Press, 1979), 169–75.

47 Margery Sabin, "James's American Dream," *The Cambridge Companion to Henry James*, ed. Jonathan Freedman (Cambridge: Cambridge University Press, 1998), 214.
48 Jesse Matz, *Literary Impressionism and Modernist Aesthetics* (Cambridge: Cambridge University Press, 2001), 15.
49 Jonathan Holden, "Postmodern Poetic Form: A Theory," *New England Review* 6 (1983): 22.
50 For further discussion see Poirier, *Poetry and Pragmatism*, 44.
51 Woolf, "Craftsmanship" (1937) *Collected Essays*, ed. Leonard Woolf, 4 vols. (London: Chatto & Windus, 1966), 2:245–251, hereafter cited as *C*; Joyce, *Ulysses* (1922), ed. Jeri Johnson (Oxford: Oxford University Press, 1993), 49, hereafter cited as *U*; Joyce, *P*, 108.
52 William James, *A Pluralistic Universe* (1909), (Cambridge: Harvard University Press, 1977), 70.
53 For discussion of modern writing and Einstein's theories, see Derek Ryan, "Woolf and Contemporary Philosophy," *Virginia Woolf in Context*, ed. Bryony Randall and Jane Goldman (Cambridge: Cambridge University Press, 2012); Michael H. Whitworth, *Einstein's Wake: Relativity, Metaphor and Modernist Literature* (Oxford: Oxford University Press, 2001); Alan J. Friedman, "Ulysses and Modern Science," *Seventh of Joyce*, ed. Bernard Benstock (Bloomington: Indiana University Press, 1982); Peter Francis Mackey, *Chaos Theory and James Joyce's Everyman* (Gainesville: University Press of Florida, 1999).
54 Bertrand Russell, "Einstein's Theory of Gravitation," *Athenaeum* (14 November 1919), qtd. in Michael Whitworth, "Pièces d'identité: T. S. Eliot, J. W. N. Sullivan and Poetic Impersonality," *English Literature in Transition* 39.2 (1996): 152.
55 *The Holy Bible*, King James Version (Oxford: Oxford University Press, 1998).
56 Rorty, "How Many Grains Make a Heap?" *The London Review of Books*, 20 January 2005, 12 September 2012 <www.lrb.co.uk/v27/n02/rort01_.html>. For a recent excellent (and readable) approach to the problem of vagueness, particularly for Artificial Intelligence, see Kees Van Deemter, *Not Exactly: In Praise of Vagueness* (Oxford: Oxford University Press, 2010). According to the recent "Symposium on Fuzzy Studies" in *Common Knowledge*, more than 15,000 articles have recently been devoted to the subject of "Fuzziness is in the nature of things." See "Fuzzy Studies: A Symposium on the Consequence of Blur," Jeffrey M. Perl, Natalie Zemon Davis, and Barry Allen, *Common Knowledge* 17.3 (2012): 444–445.
57 Rorty, "How Many Grains Make a Heap?" and see Scott Soames, *Philosophical Analysis in the Twentieth Century*, 2 vols. (Princeton: Princeton University Press, 2003–2005). For a recent overview of theories of vagueness see Diana Raffman, *Unruly Words: A Study of Vague Language* (New York: Oxford University Press, 2014).
58 Gottlob Frege, *Posthumous Writings*, qtd. in Christopher Hookway, "Vagueness, Logic and Interpretation," *The Analytic Tradition*, eds. David Bell and Neil Cooper (Oxford: Basil Blackwell, 1990), 61; also see Williamson, *Vagueness*, 37.

59 For further discussion, see J. Van Heijenoort, "Frege and Vagueness," *Frege Synthesized*, eds. Leila Haaparanta and Jaakko Hintikka (Boston: Kluwer Academic Publishers, 1986), 31–45.

60 Russell, "Introduction," *Tractatus Logico-Philosophicus*, trans. C. K. Ogden (London: Routledge & Kegan Paul, 1996), 7, hereafter cited as *T*. See Chapter 3 for the competing approaches to reading the *Tractatus*.

61 Ogden was considered Peirce's English disciple. See C. K. Ogden and I. A. Richards, *The Meaning of Meaning*, ed. John Constable (London: Routledge, 2001), 287–99.

62 Russell, "The Philosophy of Logical Atomism," in *The Philosophy of Logical Atomism and Other Essays: 1914–9, Collected Papers of Bertrand Russell*, 8:161.

63 Charles Sanders Peirce, *Collected Papers of Charles Sanders Peirce*, eds. Charles C. Hartshorne et al., 8 vols. (Cambridge: Harvard University Press, 1931–60), 5:446, hereafter cited as *CP*.

64 Peirce, *The Dictionary of Philosophy and Psychology*, ed. James Mark Baldwin, 2 vols. (New York: Macmillan, 1902), 2:748.

65 Hookway, "Vagueness, Logic and Interpretation," 74.

66 William James, *The Meaning of Truth: A Sequel to "Pragmatism"* (1909), rpt. in *Pragmatism* and *The Meaning of Truth* (Cambridge: Harvard University Press, 1975), 148, hereafter cited as *PMT*.

67 Russell, "Introduction," to *T*, 8 and Wittgenstein, *T*, 63.

68 "It is a commonplace that Wittgenstein's later work has a 'pragmatist flavor,'" Hookway, "Vagueness, Logic, and Interpretation," 62. For discussion of William James's influence on Wittgenstein, see Hilary Putnam, "Was Wittgenstein a Pragmatist?" in *Pragmatism* (Oxford: Blackwell, 1995); for Peirce's influence on Wittgenstein, see Charles S. Hardwick, "Peirce's Influence on Some British Philosophers: A Guess at the Riddle," *Peirce Studies* 1 (1979): 25–30.

69 Wittgenstein, *PI* §98, *Vagueness*, ed. Justin Needle, 7 July 2012 <www.btinternet.com/~justin.needle/>.

70 For the current reassessment of the importance of Frank P. Ramsey to early twentieth-century analytic philosophy, see *Ramsey's Legacy*, eds. Hallvard Lillehammer and D. H. Mellor (Oxford: Clarendon Press, 2005), and *F. P Ramsey: Critical Reassessments*, ed. María J. Frápolli (London: Continuum Studies in British Philosophy, 2005).

71 Ann Banfield also notes this as a possible source for Ramsay's name. See Banfield, *The Phantom Table: Woolf, Fry, Russell and the Epistemology of Modernism* (Cambridge: Cambridge University Press, 2000), 404.

72 Frank P. Ramsey, *The Foundations of Mathematics and Other Logical Essays*, ed. R. B. Braithwaite (London: Kegan Paul, 1931), 194.

73 For discussion see Hardwick, "Peirce's Influence on Some British Philosophers," 25–30, and Russell B. Goodman, *Wittgenstein and William James*, 16.

74 Ramsey, *Foundations*, 263–269.

75 Michael Clark, *Paradoxes from a to z* (London: Routledge, 2002), 71.

76 James, "The Minor French Novelists" (1876), rpt. in *Henry James: Literary Criticism*, ed. Leon Edel, 2 vols. (New York: Library of America, 1984), 2:170, hereafter cited as *HJLC*.
77 R. M. Sainsbury and Timothy Williamson, "Sorites," *A Companion to the Philosophy of Language*, eds. Bob Hale and Crispin Wright (Oxford: Blackwell, 2001), 446; Francis Jeffry Pelletier and István Berkeley, "Vagueness," *The Cambridge Dictionary of Philosophy*, 946. For a further distinction between semantic and epistemic vagueness in philosophical terminology, see Sainsbury and Williamson, 465–7.
78 For discussion see Karen Barad, *Meeting the Universe Halfway: Quantum Physics and the Entanglement of Matter and Meaning* (Durham: Duke University Press, 2007).
79 For discussion, see Banfield, *The Phantom Table*, 10.
80 Peter Nicholls, *Modernisms: A Literary Guide* (Berkeley: University of California Press, 1995), 1, and Michael Levenson, *A Genealogy of Modernism* (Cambridge: Cambridge University Press, 1984), vii.

Chapter 1

1 Henry James, *Autobiography*, 412.
2 Louis Menand, *The Metaphysical Club* (New York: Farrar, Straus and Giroux, 2001), xi. For discussion of Peirce's status in this club, see Joseph Brent, *Charles Sanders Peirce: A Life* (Bloomington: Indiana University Press, 1993), 86–87.
3 Henry James, *The American Scene* (1907) rpt. in *Henry James: Collected Travel Writings: Great Britain and America*, ed. Richard Howard (New York: Library of America, 1993), 351.
4 Henry James to Charles Eliot Norton, 4 February 1872, *Henry James Letters*, ed. Leon Edel, 4 vols. (Cambridge: Harvard University Press, 1974–84), 1:273.
5 Henry to William James, 18 July 1909, *The Correspondence of William James*, 3:391–4.
6 Henry James to Frederick Macmillan, 1 August 1878, *Henry James: A Life in Letters*, ed. Philip Horne (London: Penguin Books, 1999), 93–94.
7 Henry James, "The Minor French Novelists" (1876), rpt. in *HJLC*, 2:176; Henry James, "The Art of Fiction" (1884), rpt. in *HJLC*, 1:46.
8 Ross Posnock, *The Trial of Curiosity* (Oxford, UK: Oxford University Press, 1991), viii. Many scholars have noted William James's interest in vagueness but I believe I am the first to connect it to both Charles Peirce and to Henry James. My project provides a new answer, therefore, to the debate about what Henry James meant by having "unconsciously pragmatised." For discussion, see Posnock, 92–93, and Richard A. Hocks, *Henry James and Pragmatistic Thought* (Chapel Hill: University of North Carolina Press, 1974). William James scholarship, particularly William Joseph Gavin, *William James and the Reinstatement of the Vague* (Philadelphia: Temple University Press, 1992) and Frederick Ruf, *The Creation of Chaos: William James and the Stylistic Making of a Disorderly World* (Albany, NY: State University of New York Press, 1991),

has noted William James's preoccupation with vagueness. Richard Poirier's *Trying it Out in America* (New York: Farrar, Straus and Giroux, 1999) importantly noted the importance of vagueness for both James brothers. In a chapter entitled "In Praise of Vagueness: William and Henry James," he writes, "There is . . . a predilection shared by both brothers with earlier American writers, like Emerson and Thoreau, and later ones, like Frost and Stevens, for what each of them at some point gets to call 'vagueness'" (243). Poirier drops his examination there, however. Andrew Taylor posits that the James brothers may have inherited an appreciation for vagueness from their father; see Taylor, *Henry James and the Father Question* (Cambridge, UK: Cambridge University Press, 2002), 200. Joan Richardson connects Jamesian vagueness to Hermann von Helmholtz, the nineteenth-century physicist; see Richardson, *A Natural History of Pragmatism* (Cambridge, UK: Cambridge University Press, 2007), 125–130.

9 Henry to William James, 17 October 1907, *The Correspondence of William James*, 3:347.

10 F. R. Leavis, *The Great Tradition* (New York: George W. Steward Publishers, 1948), 127.

11 For discussion of the disaster of Henry James's staging of *Guy Domville*, see Leon Edel, *Henry James: A Life* (New York: Harper & Row, 1985), 414–20.

12 William to Henry James, 25 October 1920, *The Correspondence of William James*, 3:220.

13 Ian Watt, "The First Paragraph of *The Ambassadors*" (1960), rpt. in *Henry James: A Collection of Critical Essays*, ed. Ruth Bernard Yeazell (Englewood Cliffs, NJ: Prentice Hall, 1994), 122.

14 Henry James to Augustin Daly, 3 December 1893, *Henry James: A Life in Letters*, 268; Henry James to William Dean Howells, 30 March 1877, *Henry James: A Life in Letters*, 83.

15 William to Henry James, 25 October 1920, *The Correspondence of William James*, 3:220.

16 Henry James to Julian Russell Sturgis, 20 September 1886, *Henry James: A Life in Letters*, 188.

17 Posnock, *The Trial of Curiosity*, 55.

18 See Posnock, "Affirming the Alien: The Pragmatist Pluralism of *The American Scene*," in *The Cambridge Companion to Henry James*, ed. Jonathan Freedman (Cambridge, UK: Cambridge University Press, 1998), 224.

19 Henry James declared, "I am a realist," Henry James to Elizabeth Boott, 26 May 1877, *Henry James: A Life in Letters*, 91.

20 Leon Edel, *The Master: 1901–1916* (New York: Avon, 1978). See for recent examples of the queer and global James: Kevin Ohi, *Henry James and the Queerness of Style* (Minneapolis: University of Minnesota Press, 2011); Eric Haralson, *Henry James and Queer Modernity* (Cambridge, UK: Cambridge University Press, 2003); *Henry James's New York Edition: The Construction of Authorship*, ed. David McWhirter (Cambridge, UK: Cambridge University Press, 1999); and the special "Global James" edition of *The Henry James Review*, 24.3 (2003).

21 Henry James, Preface to Roderick Hudson (1907), in *HJLC*, 2:1041.

22 William James, *A Pluralistic Universe* (1909), 9.
23 Henry James, "Project of Novel [*The Ambassadors*]" (1 September 1900), in *The Complete Notebooks of Henry James*, eds. Leon Edel and Lyall H. Powers (Oxford, UK: Oxford University Press, 1987), 544, and *A*, 401.
24 Henry to William James, 23 November 1905, *The Correspondence of William James*, 3:303–6.
25 Susan Howe, *Peirce-Arrow* (New York: New Directions, 1997), 72.
26 Peirce, "How to Make Our Ideas Clear" (1878), rpt. in *Writings of Charles S. Peirce*, ed. Christian J. W. Kloesel, Vol. 3 (Bloomington: Indiana University Press, 1986), 3:257–276; For William James's declaration of the "birth certificates," see Brent, *Charles Sanders Peirce*, 138.
27 Peirce, "The Fixation of Belief" (1877), rpt. in *Writings*, 3:246.
28 Peirce, "How To Make Our Ideas Clear," *Writings*, 3:260.
29 Peirce, "How To Make Our Ideas Clear," *Writings*, 3:265–6.
30 Henry James, *The Golden Bowl* (1904), (New York: Penguin Books, 1987), 310.
31 Peirce, "Pragmatism," *The Dictionary of Philosophy and Psychology*, 2:321.
32 See Bertrand Russell's Foreword to James Feibleman, *An Introduction to Peirce's Philosophy* (New York: Harper and Brothers, 1946), xv–xvi.
33 Peirce later asserted of "How to Make Our Ideas Clear" that its "principal positive error is its nominalism," qtd. in Brent, *Charles Sanders Peirce*, 326.
34 The letters containing this debate occur on 3 October 1904 (Peirce to W. James) and 10 March 1909 (W. James to Peirce), rpt. in Ralph Barton Perry, *The Thought and Character of William James* (1948), (Nashville, TN: Vanderbilt University Press, 1996), 288, 292.
35 For discussion see Jill M. Kress, *The Figure of Consciousness: William James, Henry James and Edith Wharton* (New York: Routledge, 2002), 31.
36 William James, *Pragmatism: A New Way for Some Old Ways of Thinking* (1907), in *PMT*, 106–7. For discussion see Hilary Putnam, "James's theory of truth," in *The Cambridge Companion to William James*, ed. Ruth Anna Putnam (Cambridge, UK: Cambridge University Press, 1997), 166–85.
37 William James, *PMT* 37.
38 William James, "On Some Omissions," *Mind* (January 1884), and "The Stream of Thought," Chapter IX, *PP*, 1:239.
39 See also Gerald Myers, "Pragmatism and Introspective Psychology," in *The Cambridge Companion to William James*, 16–17.
40 Gavin, *William James and the Reinstatement of the Vague*, 17.
41 William to Henry James, 12 December 1875, *The Correspondence of William James*, 1:246.
42 James, "The American Journals" (24 Nov. 1881), in *The Complete Notebooks of Henry James*, 216.
43 James, *The Complete Notebooks of Henry James*, 216.
44 Henry to William James, 3 December 1875, *Henry James Letters*, 2:13.
45 Henry to William James, 14 March 1876, *Henry James Letters*, 2:32.
46 Peirce to William James, 16 December 1875, in Brent, *Charles Sanders Peirce*, 103–104.

47 Henry to William James, 15 February 1885, *Henry James: A Life in Letters*, 172.
48 T. S. Eliot, "Henry James" (1918), in *SPTSE*, 151.
49 Henry James to H. G. Wells, 10 July 1915, *Henry James: A Life in Letters*, 554.
50 In *The American*, James's arguably most melodramatic novel, he uses the word "vague" forty-five times. See David Higdon and Todd Bender, *A Concordance to Henry James's The American* (New York: Garland, 1985). This number only seems to grow with the longer later works, and vague appears over sixty times in *The Ambassadors*, sixty times in *The Portrait of A Lady* and over ninety in *The Golden Bowl*, according to my own admittedly rough count.
51 James, "The Jolly Corner," *Collected Stories*, 2:957–58.
52 James, *The Portrait of a Lady* (1881), ed. Geoffrey Moore (New York: Penguin Books, 1986), 624.
53 James, *The Portrait of a Lady*, 204, 299, 280.
54 James, *The Portrait of a Lady*, 363.
55 James, *The Notebooks of Henry James*, ed. F. O. Matthiessen and Kenneth B. Murdock (New York: George Braziller, Inc., 1955), 18.
56 Horne, *Henry James: A Life in Letters*, 403.
57 James, *The Complete Notebooks of Henry James*, 112.
58 *Louisville Courier-Journal* (9 March 1901), in *Henry James: The Contemporary Reviews*, ed. Kevin J. Hayes (Cambridge, UK: Cambridge University Press, 1996), 347.
59 Henry James to John St. Loe Strachey, 6 May 1896, *Henry James: A Life in Letters*, 291.
60 Henry James, "The Question of Our Speech" (1905), rpt. in *Henry James on Culture: Collected Essays on Politics and the American Social Scene*, ed. Pierre A. Walker (Lincoln: University of Nebraska Press, 1999), 53.
61 James, *Watch and Ward* (1878), rpt. in *Henry James: Novels 1871–1880*, ed. William T. Stafford (New York: Library of America, 1983), 15, hereafter cited as *WW*.
62 Martha Banta, "The Excluded Seven," *Henry James's New York Edition: The Construction of Authorship*, 240.
63 James, Preface to Roderick Hudson, in *HJLC*, 2:1040.
64 See for example, Michelle D. Nelson, "*Watch and Ward*: James's Fantasy of Omnipotence," *Style* 29.3 (1995), 373–88, and B. R. McElderry, "Henry James's Revision of Watch and Ward," *Modern Language Notes* 67.7 (1952), 457–61.
65 Stuart Johnson, "Germinal James: The Lesson of the Apprentice," *Modern Fiction Studies* 31.2 (1985), 237.
66 Henry James, "The New Novel" (1914), in *The Art of Fiction and Other Essays* (Oxford, UK: Oxford University Press, 1948), 186.
67 Henry James to William Dean Howells, 24 October 1876, and 30 Oct. 1878, *Henry James: A Life in Letters*, 73–74, 96–97.
68 Edel, *Henry James: A Life*, 125. A 1966 reader's guide even suggests that such passages make Roger "endearing" (!); see S. Gorley Putt, *A Reader's Guide to Henry James* (London: Thames and Hudson, 1966), 27–33.

69 Ellis Hanson, "Screwing with Children in Henry James," *GLQ: A Journal of Lesbian and Gay Studies* 9.3 (2003), 367–391.
70 James to Charles Eliot Norton, 9 August 1871, *Henry James Letters*, 1:262. Note also the conclusion to this letter: "I believe I never close a letter without saying I have left the heart of the matter untold. So it must be this time. I seem to see a great vague surplus – chiefly sentimental, perhaps – lying unhonored and unsung – but quite 'unwept,' doubtless by you."
71 Lindsey Traub similarly suggests that *Watch and Ward* acts as a parody of popular novels of the time, in "'I Trust You Will Detect My Intention': The Strange Case of *Watch and Ward*," *Journal of American Studies* 29.3 (1995), 367–78.
72 For discussion of the melodramatic genre with regards to *Watch and Ward*, see Richard Henke, "The Embarrassment of Melodrama: Masculinity in the Early James," *Novel: A Forum on Fiction* 28.3 (1995), 257–84.
73 Tzvetan Todorov, *The Poetics of Prose*, trans. Richard Howard (Ithaca: Cornell University Press, 1971), 145.
74 Edel, *Henry James: A Life*, 125.
75 Henry James wrote to his father of his minute corrections: "If I get any fame my early things will be sure to be rummaged out," and therefore he "lately gave great pains to patching up *Watck* [sic] *and Ward*," 19 April 1878, *Henry James Letters*, 2:167.
76 Charles Peirce, qtd. in Brent, *Charles Sanders Peirce*, 51
77 Henry James, *Beast*, 750.
78 Peirce, "How to Make Our Ideas Clear," *Writings*, 3:257–76; "birth certificates," Brent, *Charles Sanders Peirce*, 138.
79 Peirce, "How to Make Our Ideas Clear," *Writings*, 3:261.
80 Brent, *Charles Sanders Peirce*, 51.
81 Paul J. Lindholdt, "Pragmatism and 'The Beast in the Jungle,'" *Studies in Short Fiction* 25.3 (1988), 275.
82 Critics have ranged from presenting Henry James himself as the source for John Marcher's character to William James to literary figures such as Nathaniel Hawthorne or Edgar Allan Poe. For discussion see Lyndall Gordon, *A Private Life of Henry James* (London: Chatto & Windus, 1998), and Lindholdt, "Pragmatism and 'The Beast,'" 275.
83 Richard A. Hocks, *Henry James and Pragmatistic Thought* (Chapel Hill: University of North Carolina Press, 1974), 182–3. For pragmatic resonances, see Posnock, *The Trial of Curiosity*, 3–53; Sharon Cameron, *Thinking in Henry James* (Chicago: University of Chicago Press, 1989), 76–82; and, for an excellent summary of works relating the James brothers, Richard A. Hocks, "Recollecting and Reexamining William and Henry," *The Henry James Review* 18.3 (1997), 280–7.
84 James, *The Complete Notebooks of Henry James*, 143–4.
85 William to Henry James, 24 January 1869, *The Letters of William James*, edited by his son Henry James, 2 vols. (Boston: Atlantic Monthly Press, 1920), 1:149.
86 William James to John Shaw Billings, 28 June 1902, *William James: Selected Unpublished Correspondence (1885–1910)*, ed. Frederick J. Down Scott (Columbus: Ohio State University Press, 1986), 289.

87 William James, *The Will To Believe* (New York: Longmans, Green & Co, 1897), and William James to F. C. S. Schiller, 10 May 1901, *William James: Selected Unpublished Correspondence*, 256.
88 A further germ of "The Beast in the Jungle" appears in his notebook on August 27, 1901; by 1902 James had published the critical introduction to *Madame Bovary*, and in 1903 he published "The Beast in the Jungle." See *The Complete Notebooks of Henry James*, 199.
89 See *William James, Selected Unpublished Correspondence (1885–1910)*, 287–305.
90 Peirce, "Evolutionary Love" (1893), rpt. in *CP*, 6:289.
91 Gert Buelens, "In Possession of a Secret: Rhythms of Mastery and Surrender in 'The Beast in the Jungle,'" *Henry James Review* 19 (1998), 17–18. The initial critical consensus that May is a selfless victim to Marcher's blind egotism (although still a force in potent arguments such as those of Yeazell and Sedgwick) has moved to the far opposite extreme and reads May herself as the vampire of Marcher's life. The best balance is in Buelens's assertion that although a "moralizing" reading provides a pleasing "allegorical simplicity," the relationship between Marcher and May is less easily diagrammed, and instead through their "twin desire for mastery and surrender," we see "a particularly poignant illustration of the interpersonal and rhythmical constitution of identity in James," Buelens, 18–31. See also Herbert Perluck, "The Dramatics of the Unspoken and Unspeakable in James's 'The Beast in the Jungle,'" *Henry James Review* 12.3 (1991), 246; Ruth Yeazell, "The Imagination of Metaphor," and Eve Kosofsky Sedgwick, "The Beast in the Closet" in *Henry James: A Collection of Critical Essays*, ed. Ruth Yeazell (Englewood Cliffs, NJ: Prentice Hall, 1994), 154–89; Leda Montgomery, "The Lady Is the Tiger," *The Finer Thread, The Tighter Weave*, ed. Joseph Dewey and Brooke Horvath (West Lafayette, IN: Purdue University Press, 2001), 139–48.
92 Yeazell, "The Imagination of Metaphor," 171.
93 Yeazell, "The Imagination of Metaphor," 182.
94 Peter Brooks, *The Melodramatic Imagination* (New Haven, CT: Yale University Press, 1976), 175–6. Brooks directs the reader to James Guetti, *The Limits of Metaphor* (Ithaca, NY: Cornell University Press, 1967).
95 Milton R. Konvitz and Gail Kennedy, *The American Pragmatists* (Cleveland: Meridian Books, 1967), 79. Although, of course, the current flourish of interest in Peirce in a variety of disciplines, "logic, epistemology, metaphysics, philosophy of science, semiotics, computer science, literary criticism, film studies," suggests Peirce avoided Marcher's fate after all. See *The Rule of Reason*, eds. Jacqueline Brunning and Paul Forster (Toronto: University of Toronto Press, 1997), 3.
96 Eve Sedgwick, "The Beast in the Closet," 164.
97 Eve Sedgwick, "The Beast in the Closet," 170.
98 Eve Sedgwick, "The Beast in the Closet," 163.
99 Henry to William James, 14 March 1876, *Henry James Letters*, 2:32.
100 William to Henry James, 12 December 1875, *Correspondence of William James*, 1:246–7. For further discussion about the erotics of the James-Peirce

relationship see Cheryl B. Torsney, "An Exchange of Gifts in *The American*," *Henry James and Homo-Erotic Desire*, ed. John R. Bradley (New York: Macmillan, 1999), 83.

101 James's "obscure hurt" that prevented his service in the Civil War presents a similar "beast" hunt for Jamesian critics. See Edel, *Henry James: The Untried Years* (New York: Avon, 1978), 173, and Posnock, *The Trial of Curiosity*, 183.

102 Hugh Stevens, "The Resistance to Queory: John Addington Symonds and 'The Real Right Thing,'" *Henry James Review* 20.3 (1999), 256.

103 Henry James, *Autobiography*, 412.

104 For discussion, see Poirier, *Poetry and Pragmatism*, 44.

105 See Ohi, *Henry James and the Queerness of Style*, 2–3.

106 William to Henry James, 22 October 1905, *Correspondence of William James*, 3:301.

107 Poirer, *Poetry and Pragmatism*, 41–42.

108 Henry to William James, 17 October 1907, *The Correspondence of William James*, 3:347.

109 Henry James, "Is There Life After Death?" in *In After Days* (New York: Harper & Brothers, 1910), 233.

110 James, *PP*, 1:6.

111 Edith Wharton to Sara Norton, March 1901, *The Letters of Edith Wharton*, ed. R. W. B. and Nancy Lewis (New York: Scribners, 1988), 45.

112 William James, *The Letters of William James*, 1:47. For discussion of why James chose not to include *The Sacred Fount* in the New York Edition, see Julian B. Kaye, "*The Awkward Age*, *The Sacred Fount*, and *The Ambassadors*: Another Figure in the Carpet," *Nineteenth Century Literature* 17 (1963): 343. Elliot M. Schrero argues in "The Narrator's Palace of Thought in *The Sacred Fount*," that "the narrator's vision of life and his method of inquiry into its realities" should be viewed as "middle terms" between "scientific materialism" and "pragmatic humanism," *Modern Philology* 68.3 (1971): 287–8.

113 Rebecca West, qtd. in Leon Edel, "Introduction," *The Sacred Fount* (1901), (New York: New Directions, 1995), 3, hereafter cited as *SF*.

114 James, *Pragmatism, PMT*, 28–29.

115 James, qtd. in Edel, "Introduction," *SF*, 14.

116 Cameron, 160. Michael Wood also argues that the factual barebones of the story, such as May's improvement, must be an "objective" truth for the story to function. See Wood, "The Museum of What Happens," *The Henry James Review* 26.3 (2005): 256–64.

117 James also suggests a connection between this "May" and the heroine of "The Beast in the Jungle." Part of the origin of the narrator's theory is that May appears to him "beastly unhappy," and James reiterates this description throughout the novel. Moreover, in *The Sacred Fount*, the hunt is once again figured as a riddle. Mrs. Brissenden finds herself "thinking how to name such mysteries," *SF*, 66.

118 *SF*, 130. There is a large body of criticism that seeks to comprehend the meaning of this famous ekphrastic moment. For my own reading, what

matters is that his fellow houseguests are as much fodder for the narrator's obsessive interpretation as art is and that his desire to fix them in a role robs them (like the death mask) of vitality. For discussion see Thomas J. Otten, *A Superficial Reading of Henry James: Preoccupations with the Material World* (Columbus: Ohio State University Press, 2006), 127–9; Adeline Tintner, *The Museum World of Henry James* (Ann Arbor: UMI Research Press, 1986), 138; and Marcus Klein, "Henry James's *Sacred Fount*: The Theory, The Theorist, and The Lady," *Arizona Quarterly* 62.3 (2006): 100–2.

119 Henry and William James were not the only James family members to equate vagueness with life. In her diary, when Alice James finally receives her diagnosis of breast cancer, a fate that she has been awaiting, she writes, "To any one who has not been there, it will be hard to understand the enormous relief of Sir A.C.'s [the doctor, Sir Andrew Clark's] uncompromising verdict, lifting us out the formless vague and setting us within the very heart of the sustaining concrete," *The Diary of Alice James*, ed. Leon Edel (Boston: Northeastern University Press, 1999), 207.

120 Otten, 122.

121 Klein, 93.

122 James, *The Complete Notebooks of Henry James*, 142.

123 James, "Project of Novel [*The Ambassadors*]" (1 September 1900), *The Complete Notebooks of Henry James*, 562.

124 James, *The Complete Notebooks of Henry James*, 551; *A*, 403.

125 Critics have read the narrator of *The Sacred Fount* as a nasty version of Lambert Strether, where the tendencies latent in Strether (living vicariously, voyeurism, abstruse theorizing) become manifest and sadistic in the unnamed narrator of *The Sacred Fount*. See Posnock, *The Trial of Curiosity*, 325, and Marcus Klein, "Henry James's *Sacred Fount*: The Theory, The Theorist, and The Lady," 96.

126 James, *The Complete Notebooks of Henry James*, 543, 553, 554.

127 James, *The Complete Notebooks of Henry James*, 555.

128 Joan Richardson has also noted the preponderance of "vagueness" in *The Ambassadors* and connects it to William James's "key figure" of "the 'vague,'" which stems from "Helmholtz's work on optical activity." Relevant to my argument is her emphasis on "Henry James's pervasive use of the trope of navigating a vessel of some sort on a stream, river, in a current, at sea (connected with this figure, as well, are figures of mooring, bridges, sinking, shipwreck, the 'abyss'); the dominant use of the word 'vague' with its variations 'vaguely,' 'vagueness,' 'waves' and 'wavering,'" Richardson, *A Natural History of Pragmatism*, 145. However, I find her reading of *The Ambassadors* as an anamorphic text mirroring Hans Holbein's skull intriguing, but less relevant to my own argument than David Lodge's in *Language of Fiction* (London: Routledge and Kegan Paul, 1966).

129 Todorov, "The Secret of Narrative," 145.

130 Annie R. M. Logan, review in *The Nation*, LXXVIII (4 February 1904): 95.

131 James, *The Complete Notebooks of Henry James*, 548; *A*, 146.

132 Paul Grimstad similarly emphasizes that "the novel's privileging of relations between characters – its being more about relations than fixed terms" connects Henry to William James's philosophy, specifically William's radical empiricism. See Grimstad, *Experience and Experimental Writing: Literary Pragmatism from Emerson to the Jameses* (Oxford, UK: Oxford University Press, 2013), 94.
133 Ian Watt, "The First Paragraph of *The Ambassadors*," 134, 127.
134 Watt, "The First Paragraph," 124, 122.
135 Henry James, *A*, xxxix. James does not actually strictly follow this plan, as critics have gleefully noted for over fifty years. See John E. Tilford, Jr., "James The Old Intruder," *Modern Fiction Studies* 4 (1958): 157–64.
136 Lodge, *Language of Fiction*, 193–4.
137 Lodge, *Language of Fiction*, 204.
138 Christopher Butler, "Introduction," *A*, xvi.
139 Posnock, *The Trial of Curiosity*, 258 and 284.
140 James is happy to reverse this formula and attribute vagueness to the new American nation and fixity to the European class system. See for one example in *The American Scene*: "The vagueness was warm, the vagueness was bright, the vagueness was sweet, being scented and flowered and fruited . . . the Florida of that particular tone was a Florida adorable," *Collected Travel Writings*, 732.
141 Julie Rivkin, "The Logic of Delegation in *The Ambassadors*," *Henry James: A Collection of Critical Essays*, 135.
142 Eric Haralson, "Lambert Strether's Excellent Adventure," *The Cambridge Companion to Henry James*, 172.
143 James, *Henry James Letters*, 3:244.
144 James to Jocelyn Persse, 28 October 1903, *Henry James Letters* 4:286.
145 W. H. Auden, who similarly bridged America and Britain, wrote, "James thought, and I agree with him, that if you *are* called to the intellectual life, then you had better remain single and, if possible, celibate," although he didn't follow this maxim himself. "Henry James and the Dedicated" (1944), rpt. in *The Complete Works of W.H. Auden: Prose*, ed. Edward Mendelson, Vol. 2 (Princeton: Princeton University Press, 2002), 242–4.
146 See also Rebecca Walkowitz, *Cosmopolitan Style: Modernism Beyond the Nation* (New York: Columbia University Press, 2006), 40.
147 Arnold Bennett, *The Savour of Life* (1928), rpt. in *Twentieth Century Interpretations of The Ambassadors*, ed. Albert E. Stone, Jr. (Englewood Cliffs, NJ: Prentice Hall, 1969), 28.
148 Cornell West, *The American Evasion of Philosophy* (Madison: University of Wisconsin, 1989), 206.

Chapter 2

1 Virginia Woolf, *EVW*, 3:30–37.
2 Woolf to Violet Dickinson, 25 August 1907, *The Letters of Virginia Woolf*, eds. Nigel Nicolson and Joanne Trautmann, 6 vols. (London: Hogarth, 1975–1980), 1:306. Hereafter cited as *LVW*.

3 Woolf, *To The Lighthouse* (New York: Harcourt Brace, Jovanovich, Inc., 1927), 249–50, hereafter cited as *TTL*.
4 Ann Banfield, in her important study of Woolf and Russell, also notes this as an example of Ramsay's "analytic spirit," *The Phantom Table*, 188.
5 For Woolf's "circular tendency," see "Modern Fiction" and "The Mark on the Wall," *The Complete Shorter Fiction*, ed. Susan Dick (New York: Harcourt, 1989), 85, 83–89, 112–121.
6 This term is borrowed from Jaakko Hintikka, whose article, "Virginia Woolf and Our Knowledge of the External World" (1979), was a ground-breaking examination of the importance of philosophy to Woolf. Hintikka writes, "Philosophical ideas are not the subject matter of her novels, but they are part and parcel of their texture" and focuses on how "external time," like external events, loses its hegemony in Woolf's novels. See Hintikka, *The Journal of Aesthetics and Art Criticism* 38.1 (1979): 5–14.
7 "Modern Fiction," 160. *EVW* 3:30–37, *EVW* 4:157–165.
8 Woolf, *Night and Day* (1919), ed. Julia Briggs (London: Penguin Books, 1992), 34, hereafter cited as *ND*.
9 Woolf, *Mrs. Dalloway* (1925), (New York: Harcourt Brace Jovanovich, 1981), hereafter cited as *MD*, and "Modern Fiction," *The Common Reader* (New York: Harcourt, 1925), 212, hereafter cited as *CR*.
10 Gillian Beer implies this inversion, comparing the two texts and noting that "*Orlando* is exterior" while *The Waves* brings "into question what gets left out when life is described," in *The Common Ground* (Ann Arbor: University of Michigan Press, 1996), 62, 76.
11 Woolf to Goldsworthy Lowes Dickinson, 27 October 1931, *LVW*, 4:397.
12 Woolf to Ethel Smyth, 12 July 1930, *LVW*, 4:357.
13 Mark Hussey calls for "a new field of inquiry: the philosophical implications of Woolf's art, and thus the implications for our lived experience in the world," in *The Singing of The Real World* (Columbus: Ohio State University Press, 1986), xiv. There is actually a limited, although important, history of scholarship on Woolf and philosophy. S. P. Rosenbaum's article, "The Philosophical Realism of Virginia Woolf," *English Literature and British Philosophy* (Chicago: University of Chicago Press, 1971), explicates the connection between G. E. Moore's "Refutation of Idealism" and Woolf's depiction of the "obduracy of matter." Rosenbaum's later works on Bloomsbury continue to examine the relationship between Bloomsbury and Moore's philosophy. Tom Regan, author of *Bloomsbury's Prophet: G. E. Moore and the Development of his Moral Philosophy* (Philadelphia: Temple University Press, 1986), and "Moore and Bloomsbury: The Myth and the Man," *The British Tradition in Twentieth-Century Philosophy*, eds. Jaakko Hintikka and Klaus Puhl (Vienna: Verlag Hölder-Pichler-Tempsky, 1995), similarly emphasizes the connection between Moore's "naturalistic fallacy" and Bloomsbury values, claiming that "What Bloomsbury's Cambridge core also found in the *Principia* was a philosophical justification for their anti-authoritarian and anti-conventional tendencies" (48). He contests Paul Levy, who argues in *G. E. Moore and the Cambridge Apostles*

(London: Weidenfeld and Nicolson, 1979) that Bloomsbury was "influenced by Moore's charismatic personality but by his moral philosophy not at all" (57). Russell denied Moore's influence on Bloomsbury, stating Bloomsbury embraced an elitist and aesthetic "doctrine, [which] quite unfairly, they fathered upon G. E. Moore, whose disciples they professed to be," *The Autobiography of Bertrand Russell*, vol. 1 (London: George Allen and Unwin Ltd., 1967), 71. In *The Common Ground*, Gillian Beer demonstrates how, through her father, Woolf imbibed the idea of "the fictitiousness of the separation between object and subject" (30) and argues that in Woolf people "survive . . . in a kind of writing which eschews permanence" (47). Rosenbaum's "Wittgenstein in Bloomsbury: 1911–1931," and Martha Nussbaum's "The Window: Knowledge of Other Minds in Virginia Woolf's *To The Lighthouse*," both collected in Hintikka and Puhl, are two Wittgensteinian readings of Woolf; the former a historical essay, describing the Apostles and Russell's influence on Wittgenstein, the latter arguing that Woolf's "approach can in some respects be fruitfully compared with some interpretations of the later Wittgenstein, particularly that in Stanley Cavell's *The Claim of Reason*" (28), and that *To The Lighthouse* depicts the possibility of knowing the other *as* other. Banfield's *Phantom Table*, Hussey's *Singing of the Real World* and Beer's *Virginia Woolf: The Common Ground* are the most pertinent texts to my discussion of Woolf, Russell, and vagueness, and provide the foundational texts for anyone working in the interdisciplinary field of Woolf and Philosophy.

14 Woolf, *The Waves* (1931), eds. Michael Herbert and Susan Sellers (Cambridge, UK: Cambridge University Press, 2011), 148–149. Hereafter cited as *W.*

15 Woolf, *A Room of One's Own* (London: Hogarth, 1929; New York: Harcourt Brace, 1929), 108. Hereafter cited as *R.*

16 Woolf, "The Novels of George Meredith" (1928) rpt. in *Collected Essays*, ed. Leonard Woolf, 4 vols. (London: Chatto & Windus, 1966–7), 1:230, hereafter cited as *CE.* See also Woolf, "Philosophy in Fiction" (1918), rpt. in *EVW*, 2:208.

17 "Old Bloomsbury," rpt. in *Moments of Being*, ed. Jeanne Schulkind (London: Hogarth, 1985), 190. Hereafter cited as *MOB.*

18 "A Sketch of the Past" (1939), *MOB*, 72.

19 See, for Hume, David Dwan, "Woolf, Scepticism and Manners," *Textual Practice* 22.2 (2008): 249–268; for Heidegger, Heidi Storl, "Heidegger in Woolf's Clothing," *Philosophy and Literature* 32.2 (2008): 303–314; for Benjamin, Angeliki Spiropoulou, *Virginia Woolf, Modernity and History: Constellations with Walter Benjamin* (Basingstoke: Palgrave Macmillan, 2010); for poststructuralism, Pamela L. Coughie's *Virginia Woolf & Postmodernism: Literature in Quest & Question of Itself* (Urbana, IL: University of Illinois Press, 1991).

20 Hussey, *The Singing of the Real World*, xi, and Matz, *Literary Impressionism and Modernist Aesthetics*, 176.

21 I agree in part, therefore, with Michael Lackey, who argues that Woolf's novels challenge academic philosophy. However, to read her work as "anti-philosophical," as he does, seems to miss the mark, because Woolf's engagement with Russell's ideas in fact involves her in the philosophical enterprise

and anticipates (as I will argue) various debates about language among analytic and pragmatic philosophers. See Michael Lackey, "Modernist Anti-Philosophicalism and Virginia Woolf's Critique of Philosophy," *Journal of Modern Literature* 29.4 (2006): 76–98. For a related critique of Lackey, see Timothy Mackin, "Private World, Public Minds: Woolf, Russell and Photographic Vision," *Journal of Modern Literature* 33.3 (2010): 112–130.

22 Banfield, *The Phantom Table*, 188, 187, 191, and Woolf, *TTL* 38.

23 For "mind-independence" see Banfield, 101. Banfield's work focuses, moreover, on Russell's *Theory of Knowledge* (1912–1914), and argues that "underlying Woolf's art was a thought, a philosophical project worthy of new attention – which is the theory of knowledge" (ix).

24 See Erich Auerbach, *Mimesis: The Representation of Reality in Western Literature*, trans. Willard R. Trask (Princeton: Princeton University Press, 1953). Timothy Mackin traces and expands upon this divide in Woolf criticism, 113.

25 See Bonnie Kime Scott, *In the Hollow of the Wave: Virginia Woolf and the Modernist Uses of Nature* (Charlottesville: University of Virginia Press, 2012), Louise Westling, "Virginia Woolf and the Flesh of the World," *New Literary History* 30.4 (1999): 855–875, and Derek Ryan, *Virginia Woolf and the Materiality of Theory* (Edinburgh: Edinburgh University Press, 2013). Christina Alt cautions that critics often "take current environmentalist assumptions and ecocritical theories as their starting point" (9), in their assumptions about Woolf and nature. Her approach, in contrast, reads Woolf within the context of Woolf's own time period's life sciences, an approach I mirror in my work with Woolf and philosophy. See Alt, *Virginia Woolf and the Study of Nature* (Cambridge, UK: Cambridge University Press, 2010).

26 Westling, 855.

27 Patricia Waugh, "'Did I not banish the soul?' Thinking Otherwise, Woolf-wise," *Contradictory Woolf: Selected Papers from the Twenty-First Annual International Conference on Virginia Woolf*, ed. Derek Ryan and Stella Bolaki (Clemson, SC: Clemson University Digital Press, 2012), 33.

28 Russell, "The Meaning of Meaning" (1926), *The Collected Papers of Bertrand Russell*, 9:138.

29 In fact, Wittgenstein called Russell's *The Conquest of Happiness* a "vomative." See Ray Monk, *The Duty of Genius* (New York: Penguin Books, 1991), 294.

30 Melba Cuddy-Keane, *Virginia Woolf, The Intellectual, and the Public Sphere* (Cambridge, UK: Cambridge University Press, 2003).

31 Russell, *A History of Western Philosophy* (New York: Simon & Schuster, 1945), 834.

32 Woolf wrote: "One does not like him . . . Yet he is brilliant of course . . . His adventures with his wives diminish his importance . . . Nevertheless, I should like the run of his headpiece," *DVW*, 2:295. Woolf's opinion of Russell was also affected by his relationship in 1911–1916 with Ottoline Morrell, with whom Woolf had a long ambivalent relationship until they finally became friends in the 1930s. See "A Modern Salon," rpt. in *Carlyle's House and Other*

Sketches, ed. David Bradshaw (London: Hesperus Press, 2003). For discussion of Woolf's relationship with Ottoline Morrell, see Hermione Lee, *Virginia Woolf* (London: Chatto & Windus, 1996), 273–277.

33 Woolf, Introduction to *Mrs. Dalloway* (New York: Modern Library, 1928), vi–viii.

34 Recent critical interest in Woolf's essay and essayistic style, which studies "the essay – defined by its indefiniteness, resistant to categorisation or containment, while both expressing and enacting its quest for freedom" (1), parallel my exploration of Woolf's vague style; see Judith Allen's *Virginia Woolf and the Politics of Language* (Edinburgh: Edinburgh University Press, 2010). See also Randi Saloman's *Virginia Woolf's Essayism* (Edinburgh: Edinburgh University Press, 2012).

35 Russell, "The Philosophy of Logical Atomism," *CPBR,* 8:161. It seems clear that Russell became interested in the problem of vagueness because of the American Pragmatists' writings on the subject. Russell also wrote the introduction to the selected works of Charles Peirce, calling Peirce, "beyond doubt ... one of the most original minds of the later nineteenth century, and certainly the greatest American thinker ever," Bertrand Russell, *Wisdom of the West* (Garden City, NY: Doubleday, 1959), 276.

36 See Russell, "Professors Dewey's *Essays in Experimental Logic*," *CPBR,* 8:132.

37 From "The Philosophy of Logical Atomism" (1918), in *Essays on Language, Mind and Matter, Collected Papers of Bertrand Russell*, 9 vols., ed. John G. Slater (London: Unwin Hyman), 9:xix–xx.

38 Russell, *V,* 61–68.

39 "There is no such entity *c* such that '*x* is golden and mountainous' is true when *x* is *c*, but not otherwise," clears up the evident confusion of a statement such as "The golden mountain does not exist," but the answer to the question, "What is it that does not exist?" (the golden mountain) implies some sort of existence. See for discussion, "Philosophy of Logical Analysis," *The History of Western Philosophy,* 831.

40 Mark Colyvan, "Russell on Metaphysical Vagueness," *Principia* 5.1–2 (2001): 91.

41 Russell, *The History of Western Philosophy,* 836.

42 This broadcast, the only known recording of Woolf's voice, is only preserved in part in the British Library National Sound Archive, and printed as "Craftsmanship," in *CE,* 2:245–251, hereafter cited as *C.*

43 Woolf to T. S. Eliot, [24 November 1929], *LVW,* 4:111.

44 *Radio Times* (1937), qtd. in S. N. Clarke, "Virginia Woolf's Broadcast and Her Recorded Voice," *The Virginia Woolf Bulletin*, 4 (2000): 17–8.

45 Quentin Bell, *Virginia Woolf, A Biography*, 2 vols. (London: Hogarth, 1972), 2:200.

46 Leila Brosnan, "'Words Fail Me': Virginia Woolf and the Wireless," *Virginia Woolf and the Arts: Selected Papers from the Sixth Annual Conference on Virginia Woolf*, eds. Diane F. Gillespie and Leslie K. Hankins (New York: Pace University Press, 1997), 138. See also Brosnan, *Reading Virginia Woolf's Essays and Journalism* (Edinburgh: Edinburgh University Press, 1997).

47 Brosnan, *Reading Virginia Woolf's Essays and Journalism*, 167.
48 Woolf, "Mr. Bennett and Mrs. Brown" (1924), *The Captain's Deathbed and Other Essays* (London: Harcourt Brace, 1950), 96.
49 See, for example, Makiko Minow-Pinkney, *Virginia Woolf and The Problem of the Subject* (Brighton, Sussex: Harvester Press, 1987), or Daniel Ferrer, *Virginia Woolf and the Madness of Language* (New York: Routledge, 1990).
50 Julia Kristeva, "Oscillation between Power and Denial," qtd. in Patricia Ondek Laurence, *The Reading of Silence: Virginia Woolf in the English Tradition* (Stanford: Stanford University Press, 1991), 26. Minow-Pinkney also, for example, outlines connections between Woolf's and Kristeva's theories of language.
51 Kate Flint, "Revising Jacob's Room: Virginia Woolf, Women and Language," *Review of English Studies* 42 (1991): 361–79.
52 Woolf to Margaret Llewelyn Davies, 23 January 1916, *LVW*, 2:78, 76. There is some ambiguity whether Woolf is referring to Carlyle, whom she is reading, or Russell's lectures. I believe she means that attending Russell's lectures in light of reading Carlyle's *Past and Present* emphasizes how silly Russell's lectures are.
53 Woolf to Margaret Lewis Davies, 23 January 1916, *LVW*, 2:76–77.
54 Woolf, "A Sketch of the Past," *MOB*, 115.
55 Woolf, "Romance and the Heart" (1923), *EVW*, 3:367.
56 Woolf, *Jacob's Room* (1922), ed. Sue Roe (London: Penguin Books, 1992), 98; hereafter cited as *JR;* Woolf, *The Voyage Out* (1915), (London: Penguin Books, 1992), 190.
57 Woolf, *The Voyage Out*, 97.
58 Woolf, "Mr. Bennett and Mrs. Brown," 115, 119.
59 Andrew Breeze argues that Woolf, like Hilaire Belloc, derived her word from "the anthology-piece *Animula vagula blandula*, composed by the Emperor Hadrian (76–138) as he lay dying," "Vagulous in Belloc and Virginia Woolf," *Notes and Queries* 58.1 (2011): 118.
60 Woolf, *MOB*, 64–5.
61 Katherine Mansfield, "A Ship Comes into the Harbour," *Athenaeum* (21 Nov. 1919): 1227. Woolf and Mansfield were both contributing (along with Leonard Woolf, Middleton-Murry, Eliot, and other writers that Woolf knew) to the *Athenaeum* at this point, so Mansfield's review was all the more biting. That may explain why the review so "irritated" Woolf, who detected "spite" in it. See *DVW*, 1:314.
62 Woolf to Roger Fry, 2 November 1919, *LVW*, 2:395.
63 Mansfield, "A Ship Comes into the Harbour," 1227, *ND*, 266.
64 Woolf, *ND*, 84.
65 William Shakespeare, *As You Like It* (4.1.106–8), *The Riverside Shakespeare*, ed. G. Blakemore Evans (Boston: Houghton Mifflin Company, 1974), 426.
66 For the connection between Woolf's aunt Lady Ritchie (the daughter of Thackeray) and Mrs. Hilberry (and the offense Woolf's portrayal caused) see Ronald McCail, "A Family Matter: *Night and Day* and Old Kensington," *The Review of English Studies, New Series* 38 (1987):23–39. Jane de Gay notes

that "Shakespeare becomes a touchstone for resisting patriarchal constructions" for both Richie and Woolf; see Jane de Gay, *Virginia Woolf's Novels and the Literary Past* (Edinburgh: Edinburgh University Press, 2006), 57.

67 Ann-Marie Priest, "Between Being and Nothingness: The 'Astonishing Precipice' of Virginia Woolf's *Night and Day*," *Journal of Modern Literature* 26.2 (2002–3): 66–80; 72.

68 Priest, 78.

69 Jocelyn Rodal contends that Woolf's portrayal of mathematics is not dismissive, arguing that Katharine's variables' "multiple contexts and applications" mirror, in a different version of expression, Woolf's tendency to create symbols that lack a specific referent. This may prove true until the resolution of the novel, where an "ancient fairytale" rather than "ugly" symbols soothe the young lovers. "Virginia Woolf on Mathematics: Signifying Opposition," *Contradictory Woolf: Selected Papers from the Twenty-First Annual International Conference on Virginia Woolf*, ed. Derek Ryan and Stella Bolaki (Clemson, SC: Clemson Digital Press, 2012), 202–208.

70 E. M. Forster called *Night and Day* "a deliberate exercise in classicism," *Abinger Harvest* (1936), (Penguin Books, 1974), 122; Woolf repeats his criticism in her diary: "N & D is a strictly formal & classical work; that being so one requires, or he requires, a far greater degree of lovability in the characters than in a book like V. O. which is vague and universal," *DVW,* 1:310.

71 This is the resounding final sentence of "On Not Knowing Greek," *CR*, 39.

72 See also Anne Fernald's useful reading of Woolf's relationship to the classics in *Virginia Woolf: Feminism and the Reader* (New York: Palgrave Macmillan, 2006).

73 Woolf to Lytton Strachey, 9 [10?] October 1922, qtd. in Robert Kiely, "*Jacob's Room* and *Roger Fry*: Two Studies in Still Life," *Modernism Reconsidered, Harvard English Studies* 11 (1983): 149.

74 One of her aunts, from whom she may have "caught" Romanticism, was her Great-Aunt Julia Margaret Cameron (1815–1879).

75 Woolf notes that "One must suppose, at least, that her emotions were not purely aesthetic, because, after [Mary] had gazed at the Ulysses for a minute or two, she began to think about Ralph Denham," *ND*, 65–66. Fanny, in *Jacob's Room,* similarly thinks of Jacob when she sees the Ulysses statue, and Jacob thinks of Sandra when he looks at the Erechtheum. Woolf foreshadows in *Night and Day* the pygmalianism (Havelock Ellis' term for erotic love of statues) that Bloom, Molly, and Stephen all experiences in *Ulysses,* and for Woolf it acts as a further example of how the Immortal Greek work is merely an illusion, the product of projected desire.

76 Margaret Comstock, "'The Current Answers Don't Do': The Comic Form of *Night and Day*," *Women's Studies* 4 (1977): 153–69.

77 In fact, as Jane Marcus points out, both girls protect their vocations. See Marcus, *Virginia Woolf and the Languages of Patriarchy* (Bloomington: Indiana University Press, 1987), 27.

78 James, *Harper's Weekly*, vol. ix, 1898, xvi–xvii; Woolf, "The Method of Henry James" (1918), rpt. in *EVW,* 2:346–349.

79 "We want to be rid of Realism," from Woolf, "The Tunnel" (1919), rpt. in *EVW*, 3:12.

80 Daniel Mark Fogel also notes the connection between James's quotation and Woolf's image in "Modern Fiction," although he does not connect it to the image in *Night and Day*. Fogel calls Woolf's change "an about-face for Woolf, a repudiation of what she had hailed in 1918 as 'the important side of James.'" Fogel, *Covert Relations: James Joyce, Virginia Woolf, and Henry James* (Charlottesville: University Press of Virginia, 1990), 139.

81 Woolf to Roger Fry, 27 May 1927, *LVW*, 3:385.

82 Woolf to Ethel Smyth, 16 October 1930, *LVW*, 4:231.

83 *JR*, 105.

84 *JR*, 60. The narrator of *Jacob's Room* states that she is a woman given that she has "ten years' seniority and a difference of sex" from Jacob Flanders, *JR*, 81.

85 Woolf, *Roger Fry: A Biography* (New York: Harcourt, Brace and Company, 1940), 290. Jacob's silence and his "curious indeterminacy" have perplexed critics since *Jacob's Room* was first published. See *Virginia Woolf: The Critical Heritage*, eds. Robin Majumdar and Allen McLurin (Routledge and Kegan Paul, 1975), 96; *Virginia Woolf: Critical Assessments*, ed. Eleanor McNees, Vol 3. (East Sussex: Helm Information, 1994), 3:182–3; Makiko Minnow-Pinkney, *Virginia Woolf and The Problem of the Subject*, 24–53.

86 Russell, "The Philosophy of Logical Atomism," 161.

87 Pamela Caughie takes a postmodern approach to *Jacob's Room*'s narrative strategy, arguing that "Woolf tests out various narrative perspectives" and we need to ask "new questions, ones that ask not whether or not the novel has a plot but what it does with plotting, not whether or not it has a central character but what it does with characterization" (70–71). These questions seem fundamental to reading the novel, although I believe that the interesting work begins when we ask what impact these narrative strategies have. See Caughie, *Virginia Woolf and Postmodernism: Literature in Quest & Question of Itself* (Urbana: University of Illinois Press, 1991).

88 Alex Zwerdling, "*Jacob's Room*: Woolf's Satiric Elegy," *Virginia Woolf and the Real World* (Berkeley: University of California Press, 1986), 62–83, 215, 333–335. Jed Esty argues that such a truncated *Bildungsroman* is characteristic of the modernist age. See *Unseasonable Youth* (Oxford, UK: Oxford University Press, 2012).

89 For discussion of the gaps in *Jacob's Room*, see Edward L. Bishop, "Mind the Gap: The Spaces in *Jacob's Room*," *Woolf Studies Annual* 10 (2004): 31–48, and for a tally of the extreme amount of minor characters in the novel (overall there are "172 unnamed and 25 named characters") see Bishop, "Introduction," *Jacob's Room*, ed. Edward L. Bishop (Oxford, UK: Blackwell Publishing, 2004), xxviii.

90 Michael Whitworth argues that "Woolf's questioning approach is in itself philosophical, and resembles the characteristic method of Moore and his generation of Cambridge philosophers," *Virginia Woolf* (Oxford, UK: Oxford University Press, 2005), 132.

91 Woolf's form here certainly shares much with two of her contemporaries, Eliot and Joyce; in fact it is during the composition of *JR* that her diary records the greatest competitive anxiety with them. In particular, chapter eight with its urban disjointed images often seems like a London version of *Ulysses'* "Wandering Rocks" episode. Woolf was conscious of this connection, wondering in her diary when she was writing if this was "being better done by Joyce?" and halting work altogether at one point when Eliot praised Joyce at dinner, see *DVW*,2:26, 69.

92 Woolf, did, in fact, censor her text by removing the most sexually explicit passages in the novel, those describing Mrs. Pascoe's relationship to her body and also Mrs. Flanders' open acknowledgment of her connection between Mr. Floyd and the gelded cat, "thinking how she had had him gelded & how she did not like red headed men." See Virginia Woolf's *Jacob's Room: The Holograph Draft*, Transcribed and Edited by Edward L. Bishop (New York: Pace University Press, 1998), 16, 56–57.

93 Woolf demonstrates the centrality of Jacob's actual room to her narrative plan by her note on the first page of the manuscript notebook: "Let us suppose that the Room will hold it together," Papers, Henry W. and Albert A. Berg Collection of English and American Literature, New York Public Library, Vol. 1, 1.

94 Sebastian Knowles, "Narrative, Death, and Desire: The Three Senses of Humor in *Jacob's Room*," *Woolf Studies Annual* 5 (1999): 106, the term "semiscent' is actually used by Zwerdling, however, to describe the narrator's switches in perspective, "*Jacob's Room*: Woolf's Satiric Elegy," 218.

95 *JR*, 61. Woolf explicitly connects "vibrating" to attraction in an angry letter to Vita Sackville-West, "Theres something that doesn't vibrate in you: It may be purposely – you don't let it: but I see it with other people, as well as with me: something reined – muted," notes *The Letters of Vita Sackville-West to Virginia Woolf*, eds. Louise DeSalvo and Mitchell A. Leaska (London: Hutchinson, 1984), 28. I think critics eschew the "effect of sex" on *JR* because of the known connection between Jacob and Thoby, but this means that the text's fixation on Jacob's multiple encounters with prostitutes, Clara, Florinda, etc., remains unsatisfactorily explained.

96 *JR*, *The Holograph Draft*, 149–151.

97 Woolf to Thoby Stevens, May 1903, *LVW*, 1:77, discussed in Lee, *Virginia Woolf*, 144–145.

98 Patricia Laurence, *The Reading of Silence, Virginia Woolf in the English Tradition* (Stanford, CA: Stanford University Press, 1991), 8.

99 Woolf wonders in *Moments of Being*, "What, I asked myself, when I read Herbert Fisher's [her cousin] autobiography the other day, would Herbert have been without Winchester, New College, and the Cabinet? What would have been his shape had he not been stamped and moulded by that great patriarchal machine?" (*MOB* 153).

100 Christine Froula, *Virginia Woolf and the Bloomsbury Avant-Garde* (New York: Columbia University Press, 2005), 69.

101 In fact, Woolf implies that it is just the existence of these "two sides" that leads to war; a point made more explicit in *Three Guineas*: "[T]he educational and professional structures of public life, which exclude women, are intrinsically hierarchical and therefore the basic causes of war," Cuddy-Keane, *Virginia Woolf, the Intellectual, and the Public Sphere,* 90.

102 Of course, pacifism, at least during the first war, was a cause that Russell and Woolf shared.

103 Woolf, "Introduction" to Julia Margaret Cameron, *Victorian Photographs of Famous Men & Fair Women*, ed. Tristram Powell (Boston: David R. Godine, 1973), 18. Woolf's relationship to photographs, especially in view of Russell's comment about a smudged photograph, is telling. Her Great-Aunt Julia Margaret Cameron (1815–1879) was the famed photographer whose method is "characterized by its unusual focus and the fact that she would not retouch any picture," Mark Hussey, *Virginia Woolf A to Z* (New York: Facts on File, 1995), 49. Woolf enjoys parodying these shadowy photographs – for example, in her satire *Freshwater*, a character modeled after her aunt exclaims "Take my lens, see that it is always slightly out of focus," *Freshwater: A Comedy*, ed. Lucio P. Ruotolo (San Diego: Harcourt Brace Jovanovich, 1985), 83. Many of Woolf's favorite photographs were these blurred images, which were some of the few artifacts from old Bloomsbury that made their way onto the walls in Bloomsbury and remained carefully preserved throughout the rest of Woolf's life. Woolf also enjoyed placing blurred photographs next to focused ones in her albums. For discussion of Woolf and photography see Diane F. Gillespie, "'Her Kodak Pointed at His Head': Virginia Woolf and Photography," *The Multiple Muses of Virginia Woolf*, ed. Gillespie (Columbia: University of Missouri Press, 1993), 113–147.

104 Woolf to Madge Vaughan, [June? 1906], *LVW,* 1:226–7.

105 It was not until quite far in the composition that Woolf changed the title, *DVW,* 3:257.

106 Beer, *The Common Ground,* 56.

107 "The Waves," Woolf wrote, was resolving itself "into a series of dramatic soliloquies," *DVW,* 3:312.

108 *DVW,* 3:285.

109 *TTL,* 38. For discussion of this crucial philosophical discussion in *To The Lighthouse*, see, for example, Whitworth, *Virginia Woolf,* 115–120, and Beer, *The Common Ground,* 29–47.

110 For "declarative discourse," see Beer, *The Common Ground,* 68.

111 Vanessa Bell to Virginia Woolf, 3 May 1927, *Selected Letters of Vanessa Bell*, ed. Regina Marler (London: Bloomsbury, 1994), 314. For the genesis of *The Waves*, see Michael Herbert and Susan Sellers, "Introduction," *W,* xxxix–c.

112 Woolf's similarity to Stein here is not totally unexpected because Woolf paralleled (with some chagrin) their linguistic experimentations. In a 1925 letter, for example, Woolf complains of "lying crushed under an immense manuscript of Gertrude Stein's" and continues, "For my own part I wish we could skip a generation – skip Edith and Gertrude and Tom and Joyce and

Virginia and come out in the open again, when everything has been restarted, and runs full tilt, instead of trickling and teasing in this irritating way," Woolf to Roger Fry, 16 September 1925, *LVW*, 3:209.

113 See Edward L. Bishop, *A Virginia Woolf Chronology* (London: Macmillan, 1989), 102–110.

114 "The Narrow Bridge of Art" (1927), *CE*, 2:218–229.

115 *DVW*, 3:34.

116 Woolf, qtd. in J. W. Graham, "Point of View in *The Waves*: Some Services of the Style," *University of Toronto Quarterly* 39 (1970): 193–211, and *DVW*, 4:63.

117 Jane Marcus, "Britannia Rules *The Waves*," *Decolonizing Tradition: New Views of Twentieth-Century 'British' Literary Canons*, ed. Karen Lawrence (Urbana: University of Illinois Press, 1992), 136–162.

118 J. W. Graham, "Point of View in *The Waves*: Some Services of the Style," 196.

119 Woolf to G. L. Dickinson, 27 October 1931, *LVW*, 4:397.

120 Woolf, "A Sketch of the Past," *MOB*, 72.

121 My reading of Woolf's vague philosophy therefore dovetails nicely with Froula's reading of *The Waves* through "the lens of physics." She argues that "The discoveries of the new physics – the wave/particle paradox, the uncertainty principle, the dissolution of subject/object duality, the phenomenon of entities mutually interacting at a distance without apparent physical mediation, governed by probability waves – contradict the common sense not just of Newtonian physics but even of Einstein's relativistic universe," *Virginia Woolf and the Bloomsbury Avant-Garde*, 204.

122 Whitworth, *Virginia Woolf*, 127.

123 Rosenbaum, "The Philosophical Realism of Virginia Woolf," 325.

Chapter 3

1 Ludwig Wittgenstein, *Philosophical Investigations*, trans. G. E. M. Anscombe (Oxford, UK: Blackwell, 1953), §109, hereafter cited as *PI*.

2 James Joyce, *Finnegans Wake* (1939), ed. Seamus Deane (London: Penguin, 1992), 119:4–6, hereafter cited as *FW*.

3 Joyce, "The Study of Languages" (1899), rpt. in *James Joyce: Occasional, Critical, and Political Writing*, ed. Kevin Barry (Oxford, UK: Oxford University Press, 2000), 12–16.

4 Bertrand Russell, Introduction, *Tractatus Logico-Philosophicus*, trans. C. K. Ogden (London: Routledge & Kegan Paul, 1922), 8, hereafter cited as *T*.

5 Ironically, on the manuscript, Joyce's arguments in favor of language's "precision" and "regulations" are further undermined by his examiner's marginal criticism, reprimanding his "very loose structure." MS rpt. in *James Joyce Archive*, ed. Michael Groden, vol. 2 (New York: Garland, 1978), 35.

6 Anthony Burgess, *ReJoyce* (New York: Norton & Co., 1968), 50.

7 Joyce to Harriet Shaw Weaver, 22 October 1925, *Selected Letters of James Joyce*, 310.

8 See James Conant, "The Method of the *Tractatus*," *From Frege to Wittgenstein: Perspectives on Analytic Philosophy*, ed. Erich H. Reck (Oxford, UK: Oxford University Press, 2002), 374–462.
9 Russell, Introduction, *T*, 8.
10 For discussion see Cora Diamond, "Ethics, Imagination, and the Method of Wittgenstein's *Tractatus*," *The New Wittgenstein*, eds. Alice Crary and Rupert Read (London: Routledge, 2000), 149–173, and James Conant, "Throwing Away the Top of the Ladder," *The Yale Review* 79 (1990): 328–364. Michael LeMahieu argues that Russell's way of reading the *Tractatus*—it "attempts to rid ordinary language of nonsense"—made the *Tractatus* something of a "sacred text" for the logical positivists in the Vienna Circle. See "Nonsense Modernism: The Limits of Modernity and the Feelings of Philosophy in Wittgenstein's *Tractatus*," *Bad Modernisms* 68–93. For examples and analysis of the resolute approach see Michael LeMahieu, "Nonsense Modernism"; Karen Zumhagen-Yekplé, "The Everyday's Fabulous Beyond: Nonsense, Parable, and the Ethics of the Literary in Kafka and Wittgenstein," *Comparative Literature*, 64:4 (2012), 429–445; and Ben Ware, "Ethics and the Literary in Wittgenstein's *Tractatus Logico-Philosophicus*, *Journal of the History of Ideas* 72:4 (2011), 596–611. Alfred Nordmann argues the resolute reading limits Wittgenstein's provocation too strictly to Frege and Russell. See *Wittgenstein's Tractatus: An Introduction* (Cambridge, UK: Cambridge University Press, 2005), 12–13.
11 *PI*, Preface (no page number) and *PI* §1:23.
12 Ford Madox Ford, Letter to the Editor, *Saturday Review of Literature* (3 June 1939), rpt. in *The Ford Madox Ford Reader*, ed. Sondra J. Stang (New York: Ecco Press, 1986), 290.
13 Joyce, *FW*, 3:18. For further examination of aesthetics and Wittgenstein's "Picture theory," see S. P. Rosenbaum, "Wittgenstein in Bloomsbury," *The British Tradition in Twentieth-Century Philosophy*, 68.
14 For the nominalist approach to Wittgenstein's *Tractatus* see Andrew Newman, *The Correspondence Theory of Truth: An Essay on the Metaphysics of Predication* (Cambridge, UK: Cambridge University Press, 2002). Of course, as with all things Tractarian, there is a school that vehemently disagrees with this reading. See Newman, 62–3.
15 Joyce to Harriet Shaw Weaver, 16 October 1926, *Letters of James Joyce*, 3 vols., vol. 1, ed. Stuart Gilbert, vols. 2 and 3, ed. Richard Ellmann (New York: Viking, 1957, 1966), 3:144.
16 Joyce, "A Portrait of the Artist" (1904), rpt. in *Joyce: Poems and Shorter Writings*, eds. Richard Ellmann, A. Walton Litz, and John Whittier Ferguson (London: Faber and Faber, 1991), 218.
17 North, *Reading 1922*, 37.
18 Marjorie Perloff, *Wittgenstein's Ladder: Poetic Language and the Strangeness of the Ordinary* (Chicago: The Chicago University Press, 1996), 76.
19 North, *Reading 1922*, 63–64.

20 For discussion of Wittgenstein and philosophy as therapy see *The Literary Wittgenstein*, ed. John Gibson and Wolfgang Huemer (London: Routledge, 2004), 1–2, 75–91.
21 For discussion of why *Finnegans Wake* is often the beloved text of philosophers, see Reed Way Dasenbrock, "Philosophy after Joyce: Derrida and Davidson," *Philosophy and Literature* 26:2 (2002): 343.
22 Joyce, qtd. in Richard Ellmann, *James Joyce*, rev. edition (Oxford, UK: Oxford University Press, 1982), 546. Hereafter cited as *JJ*.
23 Joyce, "The Study of Languages," 15.
24 Wittgenstein, "A Lecture on Ethics" (1929/30), rpt. in *The Philosophical Review* 74.1 (1965): 12.
25 Samuel Beckett, "Dante . . . Bruno. Vico.. Joyce," *Our Exagmination Round His Factification For Incamination of Work in Progress* (Paris: Shakespeare & Co, 1929), 15.
26 Wittgenstein, "A Lecture on Ethics," 12.
27 North, *Reading 1922*, 60.
28 J. W. Scott, "Ogden, Charles Kay (1889–1957)," *Oxford Dictionary of National Biography*, 2004, Oxford University Press, 12 September 2012. http://www.oxford.dnb.com/view/article/35293.
29 Wittgenstein, *Culture and Value*, ed. G. H. von Wright, in collaboration with Heikki Nyman, trans. Peter Winch (Chicago: University of Chicago Press, 1980), 52e.
30 *U*, 273.
31 For a strong overview of Joyce and classical philosophy see Fran O'Rourke, "Philosophy," *James Joyce in Context*, ed. John McCourt (Cambridge, UK: Cambridge University Press, 2009), 320–331, and see also William T. Noon, *Joyce and Aquinas* (New Haven, CT: Yale University Press, 1957). For poststructuralism see, for example, Derek Attridge and Daniel Ferrer, eds., *Post-Structuralist Joyce: Essays from the French* (Cambridge, UK: Cambridge University Press, 1984), Colin MacCabe, *James Joyce and the Revolution of the Word* (1978), (London: Palgrave, 2003), and Margot Norris, *The Decentered Universe of 'Finnegans Wake': A Structuralist Analysis* (Baltmore: Johns Hopkins University Press, 1976). Julia Kristeva, Hélène Cixous, Jacques Lacan and Jacques Derrida all acknowledge Joyce's influence: "therefore current developments linking feminism and postructuralism may be considered partly as the blooming of seeds Joyce planted," Sheldon Brivic, *Joyce's Waking Women* (Madison: The University of Wisconsin Press, 1995), 6–7. Ihab Hassan notes that "all good structuralists go to *Finnegans Wake* on their way to heaven," to which Dettmar adds all "poststructuralists"; see Ihab Hassan, *The Postmodern Turn: Essays in Postmodern Theory and Culture* (Columbus: The Ohio State University Press, 1987), 107, and Dettmar, *The Illicit Joyce of Postmodernism* (Madison: The University of Wisconsin Press, 1996), 209. For an effort to distinguish the legacy of Wittgenstein from deconstruction, see Martin Stone, "Wittgenstein on Deconstruction," *The New Wittgenstein*, 83–117.

32 Jean-Michel Rabaté, "Philosophy," *A Companion to Modernist Literature and Culture*, ed. David Bradshaw and Kevin J. H. Dettmar (West Sussex: Wiley-Blackwell, 2002), 9.

33 Laurent Milesi, "Joyce, Language, and Languages," *Palgrave Advances in James Joyce Studies*, ed. Jean-Michel Rabaté (Basingstoke, UK: Palgrave MacMillan, 2004), 148. For the debate about Joyce's familiarity with Saussure, see Kristen L. Olson, "The Plurabilities of 'Parole': Giordano Bruno and the Cyclical Trope of Language in *Finnegans Wake*," *James Joyce Quarterly* 42/43:1/4 (2004–2006): 255.

34 Derrida, "Ulysses Gramophone: Hear Say Yes in Joyce" (1984), qtd. in Laurent Milesi, "Introduction: Language(s) with a Difference," *James Joyce and the Difference of Language*, ed. Milesi (Cambridge, UK: Cambridge University Press, 2003), 8.

35 For discussion of Saussure's meaning of a language game see Roy Harris, *Language, Saussure and Wittgenstein: How to Play Games with Words* (London: Routledge, 1990).

36 Benoit Tadié, "'Cypherjugglers going the highroads': Joyce and Contemporary Linguistic Theories," *James Joyce and the Difference of Language*, 50.

37 See North, *Reading 1922*, 32.

38 Perhaps the *Wake*'s "withumpronounceable" (*FW* 479:09) could refer to Wittgenstein, or the "parrotbook of Datas traduced into jingle janglage" by "a coward's castle pulpiticianer and apostle walker" could refer to the translation of the *Tractatus* written by Wittgenstein, a Cambridge Apostle. For an imagined meeting of Wittgenstein and Bloom, see Terry Eagleton, *Saints and Scholars* (London: Verso, 1987).

39 Wittgenstein did, however, enjoy some modernist literature, for example, Woolf's *Mrs. Dalloway*.

40 Joyce to Sylvia Beach [September? 1927], *James Joyce's Letters to Sylvia Beach*, eds. Melissa Banta and Oscar A. Silverman (Bloomington: Indiana University Press, 1987), 129; Joyce to Harriet Shaw Weaver, 27 May 1929, *Letters of James Joyce*, 1:279–80; Christopher Butler, "Joyce the Modernist," *Cambridge Companion to James Joyce*, ed. Derek Attridge (Cambridge, UK: Cambridge University Press, 2004), 75.

41 Joyce, *FW*, 267:1–3. See also Jean-Michel Rabaté, "Joyce and Jolas: Late Modernism and Early Babelism," *Journal of Modern Literature* 22.2 (1998–9): 245–252.

42 The existing scholarship is composed of three main items: David A. White, "The Labyrinth of Language: Joyce & Wittgenstein," *James Joyce Quarterly* 12 (1975): 294–304, Thomas C. Singer, "Riddles, Silence, and Wonder: Joyce and Wittgenstein Encountering the Limits of Language," *ELH* 57.2 (1990): 459–484, and Brett Bourbon, *Finding a Replacement for the Soul: Mind and Meaning in Literature and Philosophy* (Cambridge, UK: Harvard University Press, 2004). White's useful introduction notes many similarities between the logomania of Joyce and Wittgenstein; Singer's account connects Joyce and Wittgenstein in order to argue that Hans Gabler should not have reintroduced

"love" as the "word known to all men" in his edition. Bourbon investigates how "we are constituted by language," and asks "Could one's humanity, in some sense yet to be determined, rest on how one writes or understands the relation between first person expressions of meaning and third person scientific descriptions of human beings and the world?" (6).

43 Michael Bell, "The Metaphysics of Modernism," *The Cambridge Companion to Modernism*, ed. Michael Levenson (Cambridge, UK: Cambridge University Press, 1999), 19.

44 Wittgenstein, *Culture and Value*, 58e; Beckett, "Dante ... Bruno. Vico.. Joyce," 14.

45 For discussion see Perloff, *Wittgenstein's Ladder*, 42–43.

46 Wittgenstein, *Culture and Value*, 24e; Terry Eagleton, "Mystic Mechanic," *The Times Literary Supplement* (29 April 2005), 10.

47 Joyce, "A Portrait of the Artist," (1904), 215–216.

48 Joyce, *Stephen Hero*, ed. Theodore Spencer (New York: New Directions, 1944), 96, hereafter *SH*; *P*, 229–32; *U*, 178–9.

49 Stanislaus Joyce, qtd. in Jacques Aubert, *The Aesthetics of James Joyce* (Baltimore: The Johns Hopkins University Press, 1992), 4.

50 Joyce, postcard, April 16, 1927, Gen MS 112, Box 1, Folder 27, Beinecke Rare Book and Manuscript Library, Yale University; Ezra Pound to A. Llewelyn Roberts, 3 August 1915, *Letters of James Joyce*, 2:359.

51 Joyce, letter to Harriet Shaw Weaver, May 21, 1926, Gen MS 112, Box 1, Folder 27, Beinecke Rare Book and Manuscript Library, Yale University.

52 Christopher Butler, "Joyce the Modernist," 73.

53 Wyndham Lewis, *Time and Western Man* (London: Chatto and Windus, 1927), 107. For an interesting summary of the long-standing critique of Joyce as merely a stylist see Derek Attridge, "Judging Joyce," *Modernism/modernity* 6.3 (1999): 15–32.

54 The "therapeutic" reading of Wittgenstein is very popular in more recent collections such as *The New Wittgenstein*.

55 Arthur Power, *Conversations with James Joyce*, ed. Clive Hart (London: Millington, 1974), 98.

56 Power, *Conversations with James Joyce*, 98.

57 See also Aubert, *The Aesthetics of James Joyce*. Kevin Dettmar questions the success of Joyce's distancing: "There are signs ... Joyce was aware of Stephen's limitations and tried to some extent to distance himself from them; but Joyce's irony was too little, too late," *The Illicit Joyce of Postmodernism: Reading Against the Grain*, 10–11.

58 Frank Budgen, *James Joyce and the Making of Ulysses* (Bloomington: Indiana University Press, 1960), 67–8. See also this preoccupation in *Letters of James Joyce*, 1:135, 175.

59 Ezra Pound, "Dubliners and Mr. James Joyce," *The Egoist* 1.14 (July 1914): 267.

60 Hugh Kenner, *Joyce's Voices* (London: Faber and Faber, 1978), 18. These narrative theories abound: For example, Bernard Benstock, "The Benstock Principle," *The Seventh of Joyce* (Bloomington: Indiana University Press, 1982),

18, or "the Arranger" concept in David Hayman, *Ulysses: The Mechanics of Meaning* (Madison: University of Wisconsin Press, 1982), or for discussion see Christine van Boheemen, *The Novel as Family Romance: Language, Gender, and Authority from Fielding to Joyce* (Ithaca: Cornell University Press, 1987), 156–157. I believe the "The Uncle Charles Principle" suffices and can be extrapolated for most examples.

61 David Lodge, *The Modes of Modern Writing: Metaphor, Metonymy, and the Typology of Modern Literature* (London: Arnold, 1977), 130.

62 Joyce to Harriet Shaw Weaver, 24 June 1921, *Letters of James Joyce*, 1:167.

63 Joyce, "Oscar Wilde: The Poet of 'Salomé'" (1909), rpt. in *The Critical Writings of James Joyce*, eds. Ellsworth Mason and Richard Ellmann (New York: The Viking Press, 1959), 202.

64 Pound, "The New Sculpture," *The Egoist* 1.4 (Feb. 1914): 67–68.

65 See *JJ*, 349–350.

66 For discussion of Wittgenstein's turn away from his early "transcendental idealism" of Schopenhauer "under the influence of Frege's conceptual realism," see Hans-Johann Glock, "The Development of Wittgenstein's Philosophy," *Wittgenstein: A Critical Reader*, ed. Glock (Oxford, UK: Blackwell Publishers, 2001), 1–3.

67 Wittgenstein, *Culture and Value*, 15e.

68 Wittgenstein, *On Certainty*, eds. G. E. M. Anscombe and G. H. von Wright, trans. Denis Paul and G. E. M. Anscombe (New York: Macmillan, 1958), 422.

69 For discussion see Russell B. Goodman, "Wittgenstein and Pragmatism," *Parallax* 4.4 (1998): 91–105, and Hilary Putnam, "Was Wittgenstein a Pragmatist?" *Pragmatism: An Open Question* (Oxford, UK: Blackwell, 1995), 27–56.

70 Wittgenstein to Russell, June 22, 1912, *Ludwig Wittgenstein: Letters to Russell, Keynes, and Moore*, ed. G. H. von Wright (Oxford: Basil Blackwell, 1974), 10.

71 Joyce, *The Critical Writings*, 135.

72 F. C. S. Schiller, *Humanism: Philosophical Essays* (1903) (London: Macmillan, 1912), 15.

73 Stanislaus alleged that Joyce's "interest in Pragmatism was slight, hardly more than a certain curiosity regarding a school of philosophy ... which, he held, avoided philosophical difficulties by sidestepping nimbly," *The Critical Writings*, 135–136.

74 *U*, 49.

75 Wittgenstein to Russell, 19 August 1919, *Ludwig Wittgenstein: Letters to Russell, Keynes, and Moore*, 71.

76 It is not that Russell necessarily misunderstood Wittgenstein's "main point" but instead found it spurious, calling it "a curious kind of logical mysticism," Bertrand Russell, *My Philosophical Development* (New York: Simon and Schuster, 1959), 114. For discussion of how Russell misrepresented the *Tractatus*, see Teresa M. Iglesias, "Russell on Vagueness and Wittgenstein's *Tractatus*," in *Wittgenstein and His Impact on Contemporary Thought*, eds. Elisabeth Leinfellner, et al. (Vienna: Hölder-Pichler-Tempsky, 1978), 46–49.

77 Andrew Thacker, "A Language of Concrete Things: Hulme, Imagism and Modernist Theories of Language," *T. E. Hulme and the Question of Modernism*, eds. Edward P. Comentale and Andrzej Gasiorek (Burlington: Ashgate, 2006), 47.
78 Quoted and further discussed in Thacker, 47.
79 Wittgenstein, *Philosophical Grammar*, ed. Rush Rhees, trans. Anthony Kenny (Oxford: Basil Blackwell, 1974), 236–240.
80 Wittgenstein, *Philosophical Grammar*, 236, 240.
81 Wittgenstein, *Philosophical Grammar*, 240.
82 David Michael Wolach, "Wittgenstein and the Sorites Paradox," *Sorites* 19 (2007): 58–60.
83 Wittgenstein, *Culture and Value*, 7e.
84 Singer, "Riddles, Silence, and Wonder," 469.
85 Singer, "Riddles, Silence, and Wonder," 469.
86 Joyce to Nora Barnacle, [About 1 September 1904], *Letters of James Joyce*, 2:50.
87 Marilyn French, "Joyce and Language," *James Joyce Quarterly* 19 (1982): 239–255. For discussion of the ironic recursive format of Stephen's diary see Michael Levenson, "Stephen's Diary in Joyce's *Portrait* – The Shape of Life," *ELH* 52.4 (1985): 1017–1035.
88 Typescript of Reader's Report, Gen MS 112, Box 2, Folder 49, Beinecke Rare Book and Manuscript Library, Yale University. The report continues: "And at the end of the book there is a complete falling to bits; the pieces of writing and the thoughts are all in pieces and they fall like damp, ineffective rockets."
89 For discussion of the novel's concluding "irony" – "while Stephen strikes heroic poses, his language plays a comedy" – see Levenson, "Stephen's Diary in Joyce's *Portrait* – The Shape of Life," 1028.
90 *U*, 621.
91 Wittgenstein, "A Lecture on Ethics," 7.
92 Harry Levin, *James Joyce: A Critical Introduction* (New York: New Directions, 1960), 207, and T. S. Eliot, "Ulysses, Order and Myth" (1923), rpt. in *SPTSE*, 175.
93 See "Fuzzy Studies: A Symposium on the Consequence of Blur," Jeffrey M. Perl, Natalie Zemon Davis, and Barry Allen, *Common Knowledge* 18.3 (2012): 420.
94 Dinda L. Gorlée, *Semiotics and the Problem of Translation: With Special Reference to the Semiotics of Charles S. Peirce* (Amsterdam: Rodopi, 1994), 98.
95 Karen Lawrence, *The Odyssey of Style in Ulysses* (Princeton, NJ: Princeton University Press, 1981), 11.
96 Joyce, too, was often unsure what to call *Ulysses*, and interchanged the terms, "epic," "encyclopædia," "mistresspiece," while Ezra Pound called it the "supernovel." For discussion see Jeri Johnson, "Introduction," *U*, xiii.
97 Holbrook Jackson, "*Ulysses* à la Joyce," in *James Joyce: The Critical Heritage*, ed. Robert H. Deming, 2 vols. (London: Routledge & Kegan Paul, 1970), 1:198–200. For further discussion of the ways that Joyce and Wittgenstein both need to risk what Stanley Cavell calls "fraudulence" see Michael Fischer, "Wittgenstein as a Modernist Philosopher," *Philosophy and Literature* 17.2 (1993): 281–282.

98 *PI* II:190e.

99 Eliot, "Lettres d'Angleterre: Le Style dans la prose anglaise contemporaine," in *La Nouvelle Revue Française* 19 (July–Dec. 1922): 751–756.

100 Colin MacCabe, *James Joyce and the Revolution of the Word*, 4–5. Hugh Kenner quotes Joyce's promoting the reader's role: "'Really it is not I who am writing this crazy book,' said Joyce of *Finnegans Wake*, 'It is you, and you, and you, and that man over there, and that girl at the next table,'" *The Pound Era* (Berkeley: University of California Press, 1971), 126.

101 See also, Marilyn French, *The Book as World: James Joyce's Ulysses* (Cambridge, MA: Harvard University Press, 1976).

102 Ben Ware argues that Wittgenstein's move to pull away the ladder "also strikes an emotional blow – presenting an elaborate picture of the reader's own philosophical desires before eventually turning them in on themselves." Joyce's merging of his characters and rejection of earlier styles works this same way. See Ware, "Ethics and the Literary in the *Tractatus Logico-Philosophicus*," 605.

103 Joyce, *U*, 193. The "greyedauburn" connection was suggested in a lecture by Ronald Bush, Oxford University, Oxford, UK, 1998.

104 Christopher Butler, *Early Modernism: Literature, Music, and Painting in Europe, 1900–1916* (Oxford: Clarendon Press, 1994), 100–101.

105 Van Boheemen, *The Novel as Family Romance*, 15 and 162.

106 Joyce to Carlo Linati, 21 September 1920, *Selected Letters of James Joyce*, 271.

107 Joyce, *Stephen Hero*, 77, and *U*, 17.

108 Aquinas, *Summa Contra Gentiles* (1259–1264) rpt. in *St. Thomas Aquinas on Politics and Ethics*, ed. and trans. Paul E. Sigmund (New York: Norton Critical Edition, 1988), 3.

109 Cavell's notions of "metaphysical finitude" and "acknowledgment" are relevant here. See *Must We Mean What We Say?*, 262–263 and *The Claim of Reason*, 389.

110 Joyce to Nora Barnacle, 29 August 1904, *Letters of James Joyce*, 2:48.

111 Wittgenstein, *Culture and Value*, 43e.

112 Joyce, qtd. in Frank Budgen, "James Joyce," *James Joyce: Two Decades of Criticism*, ed. Seon Givens (New York: Vanguard Press, 1963), 24.

113 Wittgenstein, *Culture and Value*, 56e.

114 See also James H. Maddox, Jr., *Joyce's Ulysses and the Assault upon Character* (New Brunswick, NJ: Rutgers University Press, 1943), 1–2.

115 *The Oxford English Dictionary*, 2nd edition, eds. J. A. Simpson and E. S. C Weiner, vol. 2 (Oxford, UK: Clarendon Press, 1989), 264–265.

116 Beckett, "Dante . . . Bruno. Vico. Joyce," 4.

117 Vicki Mahaffey, *Reauthorizing Joyce* (Cambridge, UK: Cambridge University Press, 1988), 10, and *P*, 180.

118 See Jacques Derrida, *Of Grammatology*, trans. Gayatri Chakravorty Spivak (Baltimore: Johns Hopkins University Press, 1976).

119 Don Gifford with Robert J. Seidman, *Ulysses Annotated* (Berkeley, University of California Press, 1988), 19.

120 Joyce to Harriet Shaw Weaver, 7 October 1921, *Letters of James Joyce*, 1:172.

121 Similar to "Penelope," the *Wake* can be seen as a predecessor to *écriture féminine*, as its language works as Hélène Cixous' "anti-logos" weapon. For discussion of *écriture feminine*, see *The Hélène Cixous Reader*, ed. Susan Sellers (New York: Routledge, 1994), xxix. "What would happen to logocentrism, to the great philosophical systems, to the order of the world in general if the rock upon which they founded this church should crumble?" asks Cixous, 40.

122 Wittgenstein, "A Lecture on Ethics," 3.

123 Wittgenstein, "A Lecture on Ethics," 8, 12.

124 Woolf's nephew, Julian Bell, wrote a satirical poem about Wittgenstein, a lecturer when Bell was at Cambridge, which highlights this tendency: "For he talks nonsense, numerous statements makes, / Forever his vow of silence breaks: / Ethics, aesthetics, talks of day and night, / And calls things good or bad, and wrong or right," qtd. in Monk, *Ludwig Wittgenstein: The Duty of Genius*, 257.

125 Wittgenstein, "A Lecture on Ethics," 11–12.

126 For Wittgenstein's complicated relationship to his Catholic and Jewish inheritance, see Monk, *Ludwig Wittgenstein: The Duty of Genius*, 579–580 and 313–317.

127 Wittgenstein, *Culture and Value*, 52e.

128 Ogden's translation of *The Tractatus*, his collaboration with I. A. Richards on *The Meaning of Meaning*, and his work on Jeremy Bentham's *Panopticism and Theory of Fictions* all contributed to the formation of Basic English. See Damon Franke, *Modernist Heresies: British Literary History, 1883–1924* (Columbus: The Ohio State University Press, 2008), 198–200, for an examination of Bentham's influence on Basic. Although Wittgenstein was not kind about Ogden's later works, such as *The Meaning of Meaning*, he preferred Ogden's carefully edited and published English version of the *Tractatus* to that published in German the year before. I. A. Richards claimed that "Neither [Ogden] nor I could much esteem what – obscurely – came through [the *Tractatus*'] pontifical pronouncements"; however, the copious editorial correspondence between Ogden and Wittgenstein undermines Richards's later assessment. See *C. K. Ogden, A Collective Memoir*, eds. P. Sargant Florence and J.R. L. Anderson (London: Elek Pemberton, 1977), 102, and Monk, *Ludwig Wittgenstein: The Duty of Genius*, 206–207.

129 North, *Reading 1922*, 58–64.

130 I.A. Richards, *Basic English and Its Uses* (New York: W. W. Norton & Co., 1943), 28, hereafter cited as *Basic*.

131 Ogden, "Preface" to *Tales Told of Shem and Shaun: The Fragments from Work in Progress* (Paris: The Black Sun Press, 1929), ix, hereafter cited as *Tales*.

132 I discuss this contentious history and questions of translation in "Justice for the 'Illstarred Punster': Samuel Beckett and Alfred Péron's Revisions of 'Anna Lyvia Pluratself," *James Joyce Quarterly*, 41.3 (2004): 469–487.

133 Jesse Schotter, "Verbivocovisuals: James Joyce and the Problem of Babel," *James Joyce Quarterly* 48:1 (2010): 89.

134 Winston Churchill to "The President of the United States of America," 20 April 1944, FDR Presidential Library and Museum Papers. Marist College. 12 Sep. 2012, <http://www.docs.fdrlibrary.marist.edu/psf/box37/t335k04.html>
135 Ogden, *Debabelization: With a Survey of Contemporary Opinion on the Problem of a Universal Language* (London: Kegan Paul, Trench, Trubner & Co, 1931), 12.
136 Tim Conley, "Language and Languages," *James Joyce in Context*, 317.
137 Ogden, Introduction to "James Joyce's 'Anna Livia Plurabelle,' in Basic English" (1932), rpt. in *In Transition: A Paris Anthology*, ed. Noel Riley Fitch (London: Secher & Warburg, 1990), 135.
138 Joyce to Harriet Shaw Weaver, 7 March 1924, *Letters of James Joyce*, 1:213.
139 Joyce to Harriet Shaw Weaver, 1 February 1927, *Selected Letters of James Joyce*, 318–319.
140 Ogden, trans., "James Joyce's 'Anna Livia Plurabelle,' in Basic English," 139, hereafter cited as "Basic ALP."
141 Ogden, Introduction to "James Joyce's 'Anna Livia Plurabelle,' in Basic English," 135.
142 See Franke, *Modernist Heresies*, 204–205, and John Bishop, *Joyce's Book of the Dark: 'Finnegans Wake'* (Madison: University of Wisconsin Press, 1986).
143 Beckett, "Dante . . . Bruno. Vico. Joyce," 14.
144 Jean-Michel Rabaté, *James Joyce and the Politics of Egoism* (Cambridge, UK: Cambridge University Press, 2001), 149, and Susan Shaw Sailer, "Universalizing Languages: *Finnegans Wake* Meets Basic English," *James Joyce Quarterly* 36.4 (1999): 866.
145 Sailer, 864.
146 Rosa Maria Bollettieri Bosinelli also highlights this lack of irony, concluding: "il brano non evoca nessuna emozione" (this passage fails to evoke emotion), in *Anna Livia Plurabelle di James Joyce*, ed. Bosinelli (Torino: Giulio Einaudi, 1996), 66.
147 Joyce, *Anna Livia Plurabelle* (1931), trans. S. Beckett, I. Goll, E. Jolas, P. Léon, A. Monnier, A. Péron, P. Soupault, J. Joyce, rpt. in Bosinelli, 29.
148 W. V. Costanzo, "The French Version of *Finnegans Wake*: Translation, Adaptation, Recreation," *James Joyce Quarterly* 9.2 (1972): 235.
149 Joyce to Harriet Shaw Weaver, 20 May 1927, *Letters of James Joyce*, 1:253–54.
150 Joyce to C. K. Ogden, Summer 1928, MS, Henry W. and Albert A. Berg Collection of English and American Literature, New York Public Library. Aaron Jaffe also notes that along with Joyce, I. A. Richards, G. B. Shaw, T. S. Eliot, Ezra Pound, George Orwell, and many others admired Basic. See Jaffe, "Adjectives and the Work of Modernism in an Age of Celebrity," *The Yale Journal of Criticism* 16.1 (2003): 6–7.
151 Ogden, "Anna Livia Plurabelle," (1931), qtd. in Franke, 203.
152 Stanley Stewart, "Was Wittgenstein a Closet Literary Critic?" *New Literary History* 34.1 (2003): 48; Ogden, Introduction to "James Joyce's 'Anna Livia Plurabelle,' in Basic English," 135.

153 Ogden, *Debabelization*, 167 and Winston Churchill to "The President of the United States of America," 20 April 1944.
154 H. G. Wells, *The Shape of Things to Come* (London: Penguin Books, 2005), 431–432.
155 Norman Pritchard, "Basic English Today. A Postscript," *C. K. Ogden: A Collective Memoir*, eds. P. Sargent Florence and J. R. L. Anderson (London: Elek Pemberton, 1977), 174–175.
156 See Jesse Schotter for further discussion, 93.
157 Derrida, "Two words for Joyce," *Post-Structuralist Joyce: Essays From the French*, eds. Derek Attridge and Daniel Ferrer (Cambridge, UK: Cambridge University Press, 1984), 145–159, and Umberto Eco, Introduction to Bosinelli, *Anna Livia Plurabelle di James Joyce*, xi.
158 Wittgenstein, qtd. in Gorlée, *Semiotics and the Problem of Translation: With Special Reference to the Semiotics of Charles S. Peirce*, 90. See Gorlée for further discussion of Wittgenstein's change of opinion over the question of translation and how his later view mirrors certain elements of Peirce's semiotics. North discusses the way that the *Tractatus* itself in its original German/ English translation version demonstrates the impossibility of a perfect symbolism. See also North, 31–64.
159 Wittgenstein, qtd. in Gorlée, 110.
160 Robert B. Pippin, *Modernism as a Philosophical Problem*, 2nd Edition (Oxford, UK: Blackwell, 1999).

Chapter 4

1 Eliot, *Four Quartets*, 17; "The Perfect Critic" (1920), rpt. in *SPTSE*, 51.
2 Eliot to his mother, Charlotte C. Eliot, March 29, 1919, *The Letters of T. S. Eliot*, 3 vols., vols. 1 and 2, ed. Valerie Eliot and Hugh Haughton, vol. 3, ed. Valerie Eliot and John Haffenden (London: Faber and Faber, 2009, 2012), 1:331 (emphasis Eliot's). Hereafter *LOTSE*.
3 Michael Levenson, *A Genealogy of Modernism*, 167; René Wellek, *A History of Modern Criticism: 1750–1950*, vol. 5 (New Haven: Yale University Press, 1986), 176; Delmore Schwarz, "T. S. Eliot as the International Hero," *The Waste Land*, ed. Michael North (New York: Norton Critical Editions, 2000), 34. Cynthia Ozick's declaration in *The New Yorker* that "we do know for certain that we no longer live in the literary shadow of T. S. Eliot," smacks of wishful thinking (see "T.S. Eliot at 101," *The New Yorker*, 20 Nov. 1989: 119–154), as *Modernism/modernity*'s "Eliot in the 21st Century" Special Issue (September 2004); works examining Eliot's impact on postcolonial literatures, such as Charles Pollard, *New World Modernisms: T. S. Eliot, Derek Walcott, and Kamau Brathwaite* (Charlottesville: University of Virginia Press, 2004); the continued heated debate about Eliot and anti-Semitism (post Anthony Julius's *T. S. Eliot, Anti-Semitism, and Literary Form* (Cambridge, UK: Cambridge University Press, 1995); and Marjorie Perloff's reappraisal of

"Avant-Garde Eliot" in *21st-Century Modernism* (London: Blackwell, 2002), all demonstrate. See also the continued centrality of Eliot in new works in modernist studies including Sarah Cole, *At the Violet Hour: Modernism and Violence in England and Ireland* (Oxford, UK: Oxford University Press, 2012) and Andrew Goldstone, *Fictions of Autonomy: Modernism from Wilde to de Man* (Oxford, UK: Oxford University Press, 2013).

4 This book went to press just as the first two volumes of *The Complete Prose of T. S. Eliot* became available, which will prove a major asset to Eliot scholars. The collected letters, however, remain frustratingly incomplete, particularly due to the lack of correspondence with Emily Hale, which remains closed at Princeton until 2020. See Paul Batchelor, 17 October 2012, <http://www.guardian.co.uk/books/2012/jul/13/ts-eliot-letters-volume-3-review>.

5 For example, see Ron Bush, *T. S. Eliot: The Modernist in History* (Cambridge, UK: Cambridge University Press, 1991), 195.

6 Barry Cullen, "The Impersonal Objective: Leavis, the Literary Subject, and Cambridge Thought," *F. R. Leavis: Essays and Documents*, ed. Ian MacKillop and Richard Storer (Sheffield, UK: Sheffield Academic Press, 1995), 151.

7 For the "return to empiricism," see Heather Love, "Close but Not Deep: Literary Ethics and the Descriptive Turn," *New Literary History* 41:2 (Spring 2010): 382. While Love praises projects such as Sharon Marcus's and Stephen Best's "surface reading" and Franco Moretti's "distant reading" for "decentering the human" in humanism and for providing, to take her example, a sociological and ethical reading of *Beloved* that "depth hermeneutics" would miss, she also emphasizes what these empirical readings would lose. See also Best and Marcus, "Surface Reading: An Introduction," *Representations* 108:1 (2009): 1–21, and Franco Moretti, *Distant Reading* (London: Verso, 2013).

8 Eliot to Norbert Wiener, 6 January 1915, *LOTSE*, 1:87.

9 Harold Bloom, *The Anxiety of Influence* (New York: Oxford University Press, 1997).

10 For discussion of Eliot's own part in fostering his unpleasant reputation see David E. Chinitz, *T. S. Eliot and the Cultural Divide* (Chicago: University of Chicago Press, 2003) and Matthew Hart, "Visible Poet: T. S. Eliot and Modernist Studies," *American Literary History* 19:1 (2007): 174–189.

11 Cullen, "The Impersonal Objective: Leavis, the Literary Subject, and Cambridge Thought," 151.

12 Eliot, *The Varieties of Metaphysical Poetry* (London: Faber and Faber, 1993), 60.

13 Eliot, *Four Quartets*, 44.

14 Hugh Kenner, "Eliot and the Voices of History," *T. S. Eliot: Man and Poet*, ed. Laura Cowan, vol. 1 (Orono, ME: The National Poetry Foundation, Inc., 1990), 71.

15 Kenner, "Eliot and the Voices of History," 71.

16 Preface to *For Lancelot Andrewes* (1928), rpt. in *SPTSE*, 18–9.

17 Eliot, *To Criticize the Critic* (London: Faber and Faber, 1965), 16.

18 Eliot, Preface to *The Sacred Wood* (London: Methuen & Co, 1928), vii. Bernard Bergonzi diagnoses this doubleness less kindly: "[M]uch of Eliot's

prose," he argues, "can convey an effect of extreme evasiveness despite its polemical sharpness of tone," *T. S. Eliot* (New York: Macmillan, 1972), 26.

19 The idea of Eliot's dual personae as an experimental poet and conservative critic is now an Eliotic truism. See, for example, James Olney, "Where is the real T. S. Eliot or, The Life of the Poet," in *The Cambridge Companion to T. S. Eliot*, ed. A. David Moody (Cambridge, UK: Cambridge University Press, 1994) and, for his doubleness in relation to gender, see *Gender, Desire, and Sexuality in T. S. Eliot*, eds. Cassandra Laity and Nancy K. Gish (Cambridge, UK: Cambridge University Press, 2004).

20 Eliot, *Knowledge and Experience in the Philosophy of F. H. Bradley* (New York: Farrar, Straus and Company, 1964), hereafter cited as *KE*.

21 Jeffrey Perl, *Skepticism and Modern Enmity: Before and After Eliot* (Baltimore: Johns Hopkins Press, 1989), 45.

22 For Eliot as Bradleyian see Ann Bolgan, "The Philosophy of F. H. Bradley and the Mind and Art of T. S. Eliot: An Introduction," *English Literature and British Philosophy*, ed. S. P. Rosenbaum (Chicago: Chicago University Press, 1971), 251–277; Lewis Freed, *The Critic as Philosopher* (LaSalle, IN: Purdue University Press, 1979) and Michael Levenson, *A Genealogy of Modernism*, 187.

23 Eliot to Norbert Weiner, 6 January 1915, *LOTSE*, 1:81. The most comprehensive reading of Eliot and philosophy is Donald J. Childs, *From Philosophy to Poetry: T. S. Eliot's Study of Knowledge and Experience* (New York: Palgrave, 2001). For Eliot's skepticism/pragmatism see Childs, *From Philosophy to Poetry*; Walter Benn Michaels, "Philosophy in Kinkanja: Eliot's Pragmatism" *Glyph 8*, ed. W. B. Michaels (Baltimore: Johns Hopkins University Press, 1981), 170–202; M. A. R. Habib, *The Early T. S. Eliot and Western Philosophy* (Cambridge, UK: Cambridge University Press, 1999); and Gregory Brazeal, "The Alleged Pragmatism of T. S. Eliot," *Philosophy and Literature* (2006), 30:263. For the fruits of Eliot's self-proclaimed "temporary conversion to Bergsonism" (in "A Sermon Preached in Magdalene College Chapel" (1948), rpt. in *Inventions of the March Hare*, ed. Christopher Ricks (London: Faber and Faber, 1996), 411), see Donald Childs, "T. S. Eliot's Rhapsody of Matter and Memory," *American Literature* 63 (1991): 474–488. Jeffrey Perl incorporates Eliot's late social criticism to suggest that Eliot's abandonment of philosophy and his reversals of opinion "prefigure the movement, some decades later, of philosophers like Richard Rorty out of mainstream philosophy." See Perl, "The Language of Theory and the Language of Poetry," *T. S. Eliot*, ed. Harriet Davidson (London: Longman, 1999), 63. Eliot's assertion that he is a "thoroughgoing pragmatist – but so thoroughgoing that I am sure there is nothing for it but to assume that there are fixed meanings, and that Truth is always the same," certainly recalls William James's pragmatic statement that his first act of free will was to believe in free will. Eliot to John Middleton Murry, 8 February 1927, *LOTSE*, 3:415.

24 Eliot to Norbert Wiener, 6 January 1915, *LOTSE*, 1:87.

25 Richard Shusterman, "Eliot and Logical Atomism," *ELH* 49.1 (1982): 165.

26 In his dissertation, for example, Eliot questions "the curious dualism of Mr. Russell," which fails to account for "a world which is always partially in

time, but never wholly in time, with respect to any of its elements" (*KE* 101). For Eliot, Russell's conviction about a solid, external world leads to contradictions: "While the real world of epistemology is hard and fast, its *whatness* and its *thatness* inseparably germinated, the real world of practice is essentially vague, unprecise, swarming with what are, from a metaphysical point of view, insoluble contradictions" (*KE* 136). Russell's failure to see the difference between the precise world of epistemology and the vague world of practice means that he refuses to see that "the present King of France," for example, may not name a person but may be a useful term for "real objects in imaginary spheres" (*KE* 135). Russell's devotion to a "ready made" world, rather than to what Eliot calls a "constructed, or constructing itself" world, means he believes science and math can answer questions that Eliot believes must be left to the philosopher (*KE* 136). Eliot levels this criticism at both Russell and I. A. Richards as scientists in 1927, when he questions their tendency "to ask a supra-scientific question, and to give merely a scientific answer," "Literature, Science, and Dogma," *The Dial* 82:3 (March 1927): 241.

27 Eliot himself comments on his own tendency to push a scientific approach to literary criticism in his youth, which he tempers with a push to a more "enjoyment"-oriented criticism in a later, more academic period of literary scholarship. See "The Frontiers of Criticism," *On Poetry and Poets* (London: Faber and Faber, 1957), 117–118, hereafter *OPP*.

28 "Hamlet and His Problems" (1919), "Tradition and the Individual Talent" (1919), "The Metaphysical Poets" (1921), "The Perfect Critic" (1920), rpt. in *SPTSE*, 45–49, 37–44, 59–67, 50–58.

29 T. S. Eliot, "A Commentary," *Criterion* (April 1924), 231.

30 Eric Svarny, *"The MEN of 1914": T. S. Eliot and Early Modernism* (Milton Keynes: Open University Press, 1988), 19. For the influence of Hulme on Imagism, see Robert Ferguson, *The Short Sharp Life of T. E. Hulme* (London: Allen Lane, 2002), 63–69. Also for discussion of the ambivalent attitude of Eliot toward sentiment and sentimentality see Anthony Cuda, *The Passions of Modernism: Eliot, Yeast, Woolf, and Mann* (Columbia, SC: University of South Carolina Press, 2010).

31 T. E. Hulme, "Lecture on Modern Poetry" (1908), rpt. in *Selected Writings*, ed. Patrick McGuiness (Manchester: Carcanet, 1998), 63–65.

32 Eliot, *The Use of Poetry and The Use of Criticism* (Cambridge, MA: Harvard University Press, 1933), 149.

33 Hulme, "Romanticism and Classicism" (1911), rpt. in *Selected Writings*, 74–76. See also Frank Kermode for his argument that Hulme "disastrously misrepresents Romantic philosophy," *Romantic Image* (New York: Vintage Books, 1964), 125.

34 Svarny, "*The MEN of 1914,*" 20, and Eliot, *SPTSE*, 70.

35 Hulme, *Speculations: Essays on Humanism and Philosophy of Art*, ed. Herbert Read (London: Routledge and Kegan Paul, 1924), 41–42. For a longer discussion of the changes in Hulme's philosophy see Ferguson, *The Short Sharp Life of T. E. Hulme* and Levenson, *A Genealogy of Modernism*, 80–102.

36 Lyndall Gordon, *Eliot's Early Years* (Oxford, UK: Oxford University Press, 1977), 49.
37 Eliot, "The Relationship between Politics and Metaphysics," unpublished, 1913/4. The T. S. Eliot Collection, Houghton Library, Harvard University.
38 Ronald Schuchard examines Russell's private papers to demonstrate that at some point Eliot most likely discovered the four-year affair between his wife and Russell that began shortly after the Eliots were married. He also argues that Russell's and Vivienne's betrayal in fact partially explains the unhappiness and sexual repulsion characterizing Eliot's early quatrain poems. See Schuchard, *Eliot's Dark Angel* (Oxford, UK: Oxford University Press, 1999), 91. For further discussion of Russell's tempestuous personal life and his gradual loss of contact with many of his earlier intimate friends, including D. H. Lawrence and Wittgenstein, see Ray Monk, *Bertrand Russell: The Ghost of Madness 1921–1970* (New York: The Free Press, 2000).
39 Russell to Charlotte C. Eliot, 3 October 1915, *LOTSE*, 1:129–30; Russell to Charlotte C. Eliot, 3 December 1915, *LOTSE*, 1:134.
40 Russell to Ottoline Morell, 10 November 1915, qtd. in *The Autobiography of Bertrand Russell*, 2:64. Eliot also apparently wrote an article (now lost) on Russell's *Principles of Social Reconstruction*, which he sent to Russell in 1917, but later admitted to Russell he had decided not to publish, on the grounds that "I have no desire to do either your point of view or my own an injustice," Eliot to Russell, 13 March 1917, *LOTSE*, 1:179.
41 Eliot to Eleanor Hinkley, 21 March 1915, *LOTSE*, 1:100; Robert Sencourt, *T. S. Eliot: A Memoir*, ed. Donald Adamson (New York: Dodd, Mead and Company, 1971), 49. Eliot wrote to Russell upon Russell's winning an award, "It is a fitting though belated tribute to the author of *The Philosophy of Leibnitz*, the *Principia* and the other works on which I fed thirty-five years ago," Eliot to Russell, 10 June 1949, *The Autobiography of Bertrand Russell*, 3:57–58.
42 Eliot, "Style and Thought," *The Nation* (23 March 1918): 770.
43 Eliot, "Style and Thought," *The Nation* (23 March 1918): 770.
44 Eliot, "Commentary," *Criterion* 6 (1927): 291.
45 Eliot, "Reflections on Contemporary Poetry," *The Egoist* 4.8 (September 1917): 118–119.
46 Eliot, *The Sacred Wood*, xvi.
47 Shusterman expands upon the similarities between Eliot and Russell arguing that "Eliot's emphasis on analysis, logic, clarity, precision, sensation, the scientific, and the factual can readily be explained as influenced by aspects of Russell's philosophy," Shusterman, *T. S. Eliot and the Philosophy of Criticism*, 29. My reading of the origins of Eliot's hatred of vagueness largely dovetails with Shusterman, although I do think he underestimates Eliot's early (as early as 1913) and consistent derision toward Russell's realism.
48 Russell, "The Philosophy of Logical Atomism," qtd. in Shusterman, "Eliot and Logical Atomism," 168.

49 See, for example, "Tradition and the Individual Talent," (1917), SE 13–22; "Swinburne as Poet" (1920), *SE* 323–327. Eliot also consistently places phrases in scare quotes, which he then proceeds to analyze or pin down.

50 Eliot, "The Love Song of J. Alfred Prufrock," in *The Complete Poems and Plays of T. S. Eliot* (London: Faber and Faber, 1969), 14, hereafter *CPP.*

51 Timothy Materer, "T. S. Eliot's Critical Program," *The Cambridge Companion to T. S. Eliot*, 49.

52 Eliot, *SPTSE*, 40. J. W. N. Sullivan, the *Athenaeum*'s assistant editor and science writer, also influenced the scientific motifs in Eliot's essays during his *Sacred Wood* period; see Michael Whitworth, "Pièces d'identité: T. S. Eliot, J. W. N. Sullivan and Poetic Impersonality," 149–170. Russell was simultaneously submitting articles on scientific topics (signed by X) such as "Einstein's Theory of Gravitation."

53 Critics have traced a myriad of philosophical influences on Eliot's term the "objective correlative" included (but not limited to) Bradley, Meinong, Russell, Moore, Husserl, Hegel, Nietzsche, and Santayana. Nonphilosophical influences tend to include Pater, Emerson, and the Boston artist Washington Allston.

54 Shusterman similarly notes that "Eliot seems to echo many of the motifs of Russell's theory of language," but fails to elaborate upon these similarities. See Shusterman, "Eliot and Logical Atomism," 172.

55 Eliot, "The Social Function of Poetry" (1945), *OPP*, 23.

56 Eliot's "Can 'Education' Be Defined?" was originally a part of a lecture series delivered at the University of Chicago in November 1950. It is printed in *To Criticize the Critic*, 61–76.

57 Eliot, *To Criticize the Critic*, 67. Stanley Cavell, emphasizing Austin's "obsession with the *use* of expressions" notes: "Wittgenstein's motive (and this much is shared by Austin) is to put the human animal back into language and therewith back into philosophy," *The Claim of Reason: Wittgenstein, Skepticism, Morality, and Tragedy* (Oxford, UK: Oxford University Press, 1979), 206–207.

58 Eliot, *To Criticize the Critic*, 65–66.

59 Perl, "The Language of Theory and the Language of Poetry," 68.

60 Eliot, "A Commentary," *The Criterion* 2:7 (April 1924): 233.

61 Eliot, introduction to Josef Pieper's *Leisure, the Basis of Culture* (1952), in James E. Miller Jr., *T. S. Eliot: The Making of an American Poet* (University Park, PA: The Pennsylvania State University Press, 2005), 167–168.

62 For the way the Vienna Circle evolved from Frege and Russell, see Michael Beaney, *The Analytic Turn*, ed. Beaney (New York: Routledge, 2007), 5–6.

63 Russell, *The Autobiography of Bertrand Russell*, 2:9.

64 Hence Eliot's important relationship to what Louis Menand calls "university-based literary criticism." See Menand, "T. S. Eliot and Modernity," *The New England Quarterly* 69.4 (1996): 579, and Gail McDonald, *Learning to Be Modern: Pound, Eliot and the American University* (Oxford, UK: Clarendon Press, 1993).

65 Eugene Jolas, "Proclamation" (1929), rpt. *In Transition*, 19; Eysteinsson, *The Concept of Modernism*, 9.
66 Levenson, *A Genealogy of Modernism*, 218–219.
67 Eliot, "The Perfect Critic," *SPTSE*, 54.
68 Samuel Beckett, *Endgame, The Theatrical Notebooks of Samuel Beckett*, ed. S. E. Gontarski, vol. 2, (New York: Grove Press, 1992), 3.
69 Gerald Graff sketches a more thorough investigation into the "series of conflicts" that describes literary studies in *Professing Literature: An Institutional History* (Chicago: University of Chicago Press, 1987), 14.
70 An objection could be leveled that New Criticism saw itself as opposed to science and, in fact, working to preserve a realm for literature in a scientific world; nonetheless; it created a pseudo-scientific sounding approach to legitimize literary studies as an academic discipline. Ransom's argument is exemplary: "Criticism must become more scientific, or precise and systematic," although, "It will never be a very precise science," "Criticism, Inc.," *Selected Essays of John Crowe Ransom*, ed. Thomas Daniel Young and John Hindle (Baton Rouge: Louisiana State University Press, 1984), 94.
71 Jeffrey Perl, "Introduction: 'Abominable Clearness,'" *Common Knowledge* 17:3 (2011), 441–442, hereafter *CK*.
72 Wai Chee Dimock, "Weak Theory: Henry James, Colm Tóibín, and W. B. Yeats," *Critical Inquiry* 34:4 (Summer 2013), 733–734; Eve Kosofsky Sedgwick, *Novel Gazing: Queer Readings in Fiction* (Durham, NC: Duke University Press, 1977), Silvan S. Tomkins, *Affect Imagery Consciousness* (New York: Spring Publishing, 1963).
73 Richard Rorty caricatures many "deconstructive" readings as saying: "Find something that can be made to look self-contradictory, claim that that contradiction is the central message of the text, and ring some changes on it," and that the school of Paul de Man, in particular, reads "texts as testifying to 'the presence of a nothingness,'" Rorty, "Remarks on Deconstruction and Pragmatism," *Deconstruction and Pragmatism*, ed. Chantal Mouffe (London: Routledge, 1996), 15.
74 Poirier, *Poetry and Pragmatism*, 136.
75 He draws a link between Russell and the grouping of Ogden, Richards, and Empson. Unpublished Lecture Notes to "The Contemporary Novel" (1933). T. S. Eliot Papers. Houghton Library, Harvard University, hereafter *LCN*.
76 Ackroyd, *T.S. Eliot* (London: Penguin Books, 1993), 107.
77 Eliot, "*Ulysses*, Order and Myth," *SPTSE*, 178; Eliot, "The Hawthorne Aspect" (1918), rpt. in *The Question of Henry James*, ed. F. W. Dupee (New York: Octagon Books, 1973), 117; Eliot *LCN*; Eliot, "London Letter," *Dial* 71.2 (1921): 215.
78 Joyce to Harriet Shaw Weaver, 19 November 1923, *Selected Letters of James Joyce*, 297.
79 For Joyce's reaction to the negative review, see *JJ*, 607 and *SPTSE*, 177.
80 T. S. Eliot, "Introduction," *Introducing James Joyce: Selection of Joyce's Prose* (London: Faber and Faber, 1942), 5.

81 Eliot, "Introduction," *Introducing James Joyce*, 7.
82 Seamus Deane, "Introduction," *FW*, ix.
83 Eliot, "The Approach to James Joyce," *The Listener* (14 October 1943), 446–7.
84 Eliot, "The Approach to James Joyce," 447.
85 Eliot, "The Approach to James Joyce," 447.
86 Eliot, "A Prediction in Regard to Three English Authors" (1924), rpt. in part as "A Prediction," *Henry James: A Collection of Critical Essays*, ed. Leon Edel (Englewood Cliffs, NJ: Prentice Hall, 1963), 55.
87 Eliot, "In Memory of Henry James" (1918), rpt. in Dupee, *The Question of Henry James*, 110.
88 Eliot, "In Memory," 110.
89 Eliot, "The Hawthorne Aspect," 116; "In Memory," 108.
90 Eliot, "A Prediction," 56.
91 See also Denis Donoghue, *Words Alone* (New Haven, CT: Yale University Press, 2000), 29, 106; Adam Parkes, "Collaborations: Henry James and the Poet-Critics," *Henry James Review* 23 (2002): 282–293; Alan Holder, "T. S. Eliot on Henry James," *PMLA* 79.4 (1964): 490–497.
92 Eliot, "Portrait of a Lady" (1915) *CPP*, 18.
93 Eliot to Woolf, 1 May 1924, *LOTSE*, 2: 388, qtd. in Lee, *Virginia Woolf*, 445.
94 Eliot to his father, Henry Ware Eliot, 31 October 1917, *LOTSE*, 1:228.
95 Eliot, "London Letter," *Dial* 71.2 (1921), 215.
96 Michael Edward Kaufman, "Virginia Woolf, *TLS* Reviews and Eliotic Modernism," *Virginia Woolf and the Essay*, eds. Beth Carole Rosenberg and Jeanne Dubino (New York: St. Martin's Press, 1997), 144.
97 Feiron Morris (Vivienne Eliot) (1925), rpt. in *Virginia Woolf, The Critical Heritage*, eds. Robin Majumdar and Allen McLaurin (London: Routledge & Kegan Paul, 1975), 134, 135, 136–137.
98 For further discussion of the relationship between Eliot and Woolf, see Gabrielle McIntire, *Modernism, Memory, and Desire: T. S. Eliot and Virginia Woolf* (Cambridge, UK: Cambridge University Press, 2008).
99 Eliot to Virginia Woolf, 22 May 1924, *LOTSE*, 2:430. For discussion of unpublished letters between Eliot and Woolf, see Lee, *Virginia Woolf*, 445–453.
100 Woolf, "Character in Fiction" (1924), *EVW*, 3:515–516.
101 Eliot to Virginia Woolf, 22 May 1924, *LOTSE*, 2:430.
102 Woolf, "*The Golden Bowl* Reading notes," rpt. in *EVW*, 1:386, "Mr Howells on Form" (1918), rpt. in *EVW*, 2:325.
103 Eliot, "Le Roman Anglais Contemporain" (1927), rpt. in *Virginia Woolf: The Critical Heritage*, 191–192. Eliot emphasizes that Woolf's writing has "in a sense, a construction, though it may not be a structure," 192. Even in the obituary Eliot wrote for Woolf he emphasizes her qualities "form a whole which is more than the sum of the parts," and "[w]ith the death of Virginia Woolf, a whole pattern of culture is broken," (1941) rpt. in *The Critical Heritage*, 431.
104 René Wellek, "The New Criticism: Pro and Contra," *Critical Inquiry* 4.4 (1978): 613; Richard Calhoun, "A Study of the New Criticism," *Ideas: The Student Journal of Philosophy* 4.1 (1995): 19.

105 For discussions of significant disagreements among the so-called New Critics, see Wellek, "The New Criticism," 611–624, Douglas Mao, "The New Critic and the Text-Object," *ELH* 63.1 (1996): 227–252, and Gail McDonald, "Eliot and the New Critics," *A Companion to T. S. Eliot*, ed. David E. Chinitz (West Sussex: Wiley-Blackwell, 2009), 411–422.
106 John Crowe Ransom, *The New Criticism* (Norfolk, CT: New Directions, 1941), 140.
107 Eliot, "The Frontiers of Criticism," *OPP*, 113. Doug Mao qualifies "the charge of antihistoricism leveled against New Critical Poetics," see Mao, "The New Critic and the Text-Object," 234.
108 I. A. Richards, *Practical Criticism: A Study of Literary Judgment* (London: K. Paul, Trench and Trubner, 1929), 10. For more on the relationship between Eliot and Richards and their mutual explanation of literary allusions as a kind of obscure powerful association, see Ron Bush, "'intensity by association': T. S. Eliot's Passionate Allusions," *Modernism/modernity* 20:4 (2013): 709–727.
109 Wellek, "The New Criticism," 618.
110 Menand, "T. S. Eliot and Modernity," 558.
111 Michael Edward Kaufman, "T. S. Eliot's New Critical Footnotes to Modernism," *Rereading the New*, ed. Kevin J. H. Dettmar (Ann Arbor: The University of Michigan Press, 1992), 81.
112 T. S. Eliot, "Prose and Verse," *The Chapbook* 22 (April 1921), 9.
113 William Empson, "Virginia Woolf" (1931), rpt. in *Virginia Woolf: The Critical Heritage*, 304–308.
114 Blackmur becomes gradually less pleased with James's formal attributes. See Parkes, "Collaborations," 288, and Blackmur, *The Lion and the Honeycomb* (New York: Harcourt, 1955). For Joyce discussion see Jeri Johnson, "Introduction," *U*, xviii, and A. Walton Litz, "Pound and Eliot on *Ulysses*: the Critical Tradition," *Ulysses: Fifty Years*, ed. Thomas F. Staley (Bloomington: Indiana University Press, 1972), 5–18.
115 Paul Fry argues vehemently against Empson as a New Critic, or "as a barmy uncle of the American New Critics." His need, however, to argue for "Empson's lack of interest in ontological objects, verbal icons, well-wrought urns, and the like" demonstrates the fact that Empson still continues to be identified with the New Criticism. Fry, *William Empson: Prophet Against Sacrifice* (New York: Routledge, 1991), 5, 14.
116 William Empson, *Argufying*, ed. John Haffenden (Iowa City: University of Iowa Press, 1987), 230.
117 William Empson, *Seven Types of Ambiguity* (1930) (New York: New Directions, 1947), 236, 7, hereafter *E*.
118 Review, *New Republic* 66 (11 March 1931); Review, *TLS* (December 1930), 1082.
119 Paul de Man, *Blindness and Insight: Essays in the Rhetoric of Contemporary Criticism* (Minneapolis: University of Minnesota Press, 1983), 241.
120 Shuli Barzilai and Morton Bloomfield, "New Criticism and Deconstructive Criticism, or What's New?," 154.

121 Kenneth Asher, *T. S. Eliot and Ideology* (Cambridge, UK: Cambridge University Press, 1995), 1.

122 I do not have the space here to do justice to the relationship between later Saussure and Wittgenstein or to compare the approaches of poststructural and Ordinary Language Philosophy. For a useful starting point of terminological, methodological, and philosophical differences, see Toril Moi, "'They practice their trades in different worlds': Concepts in Poststructural and Ordinary Language Philosophy," *New Literary History* 40:4 (2009): 801–824.

123 See for example, Terry Eagleton, *After Theory* (New York: Basic Books, 2003).

124 Rorty, *Objectivity, Relativism, and Truth: Philosophical Papers*, Vol. 1 (Cambridge, UK: Cambridge University Press, 1991), 44, qtd. in Perl, 443.

125 van Deemter, *Not Exactly*, 190. For more on fuzzy logic, see van Deemter, 187–218.

A full bibliography is available on my website: meganquigley.com

Index

Note: While most writers appear in subheadings by surname only, Henry James and William James appear thus in order to differentiate the two. Works by individual authors appear at the end of the author's main entry, but novels discussed at length have their own main index entry. This index was created with the help of Meg Davies (Fellow of the Society of Indexers).

Lightning Source UK Ltd.
Milton Keynes UK
UKHW010423290520
364011UK00012B/202

9 781107 089594